BEST BIRDWATCHING
NORTH WALES

by

Alan Davies and Owen Roberts

BUCKINGHAM PRESS LTD

in association with

SWAROVSKI
OPTIK

Published in 2007 by:
Buckingham Press Ltd, 55 Thorpe Park Road, Peterborough
Cambridgeshire PE3 6LJ, United Kingdom
Tel/fax: 01733 561 739
e-mail: buck.press@btinternet.com

© Buckingham Press Ltd 2007

ISBN 978-0-955033-94-0
ISSN 0144-364 X

Editor: David Cromack
Design and maps: Hilary Cromack
Publisher: Hilary Cromack

About the authors:
Welshman **Alan Davies** is a partner in Birdline Wales and since 2000 he has been the Site Manager of the RSPB Conwy nature reserve – in both roles he has sought to share his passion for birds with others.
Owen Roberts, who was born in Manchester, spent eight years working in Wales before retiring to Pembrokeshire, where he co-authored *Birding In Pembrokeshire*.

Cover illustration:
Against a scenic Snowdonia backdrop, artist **Steve Cale** has incorporated images of some key bird species of North Wales – Ring Ouzel, Black Grouse, Hen Harrier and Red Kite. Steve, one of Britain's most popular bird artists, welcomes commissions and can be contacted on 01328 829 589.

Black and white illustrations:
Kevin Thomas Jones is a promising young wildlife artist currently completing his degree in illustration at Blackpool and The Fylde College. He can be contacted via Buckingham Press.

Printed and bound in Great Britain by:
Cambridge University Press, Cambridge UK.

Buckingham Press Ltd is registered in England and Wales, no 533739.
Registered office: 55 Thorpe Park Road, Peterborough PE3 6LJ.

CONTENTS

CONTENTS

FROM the wader haunts of the Inner Dee estuary to the rugged coastal cliffs of Anglesey, from the peace and tranquillity of oak woodlands in spring to the grandeur of the Snowdonian landscape, North Wales has so much to offer the visiting birdwatcher and within the pages of this impressive guide you will be led gently to all the best places.

It is hard to think of anyone more qualified to extol the delights of North Wales and its birds than Alan Davies – his involvement with Birdline Wales has meant birders throughout the UK are able to obtain up-to-the-minute news of all the latest rarities and for the past six years he has been part of the RSPB team turning the Conwy nature reserve into a 'must visit' destination.

Throughout the rigours of gathering information, checking facts and visiting sites, he has been ably supported by an equally keen birding enthusiast, Owen Roberts, and now you can enjoy the benefits of their labour.

Here at Swarovski Optik, we are delighted to once again lend our support to Buckingham Press as they extend their deservedly popular *Best Birdwatching Sites* series of guide books. The two companies have a shared commitment to creating products that are innovative and which bring genuine benefits to the birdwatching community. I am sure that as you explore the sites of North Wales, you'll agree *Best Birdwatching Sites In North Wales* is another winner.

John Brinkley
Managing Director, Swarovski Optik

DEDICATION

The authors wish to dedicate this book to the birders of North Wales, both past and present. In particular, we must mention our good friend Ken Croft, whose patience and commitment has led to the discovery of so many good birds on Anglesey, and to the memory of his mother, Betty, for so long his field companion when many of his finds were made.

INTRODUCTION

THOUGH OUR involvement with birding in North Wales has developed along very different routes, together we have enjoyed many special birding days in this wonderful part of the country.

Highlights have to be setting the then Welsh day-list record of 133 species in the old county of Gwynedd in 1997, and the glorious failure to beat that record the following year. I say glorious because we failed mainly as a result of finding two Bonaparte's Gulls at Beddmanarch Bay during the afternoon of the attempt! As you might imagine, the resultant furore preventing much further listing during what remained of the day, though we did find a drake Ring-necked Duck at nearby Holyhead Harbour a couple of hours later.

Also notable was the finding of two Wilson's Phalaropes (the first UK multiple sighting) on a tiny pool in 1991 on what was to become the RSPB's Conwy Reserve. I also remember mad dashes to Dinas Dinlle for Sharp-tailed Sandpiper, Holyhead for Killdeer, Cemlyn Bay for Bridled Tern, and for many more good birds over the years. Of course there were many disappointments and birdless days – the nature of our hobby – but always there was the beauty of the North Wales countryside and coast to temper these.

Alan was born near, and went to school in, Conwy, and other than for brief periods of contract work with the RSPB and the National Trust in his late teens (watching over Golden Eagles in the Lake District and Little Terns at Blakeney Point) has lived there, or nearby, for the 25 years since.

During this time his appetite for birding in North Wales has been voracious. Since its inception in 1989 he has been a partner in Birdline Wales, putting him in pole position to keep abreast of all that has happened in Welsh birding over the years. Six years ago he landed his dream job as Site Manager of the RSPB'S Conwy Reserve and has been able to enthuse the many visitors with his knowledge and love of birds in North Wales.

I, on the other hand, enjoyed only a relatively brief sojourn in North Wales, for eight years from 1988. Born near Manchester, my early birding years were spent tramping the Pennine moors, usually seeing very little. Work took me to Merseyside in the late 1970s and Fylde in the early 1980s, where I saw more birds than Manchester, but it was another work-related move to North Wales in 1988 that really saw my north-west list take off.

I met Alan at the site of the first Pallas's Warbler to grace mainland North Wales (the Great Orme in autumn 1988) and eventually we became good friends, enabling me to gain a knowledge of the area and its birds far greater than would have been possible otherwise in my nine year stay.

On leaving North Wales I retired to Pembrokeshire, where I lived for six years before moving, yet again, to my native North-West England. After my time in Pembrokeshire I co-wrote *Birding in Pembrokeshire* (2004), and therein lies my involvement with this book.

Confident with the success of the Pembrokeshire book, a third of which was a site guide to

INTRODUCTION

the county, I persuaded Alan that the lack of a site guide to North Wales was a gap that needed filling. He agreed, and to our delight, so did Hilary and David Cromack at Buckingham Press, who kindly agreed to publish our efforts in this, their *Best Birdwatching Sites* series.

Owen Roberts

ACKNOWLEDGEMENTS

The authors would like to express their thanks to all those who go birding in North Wales, for it is their efforts over the years that have provided the material to make this book possible. However, we are especially grateful to Ken Croft, whose in-depth knowledge of Anglesey and its birds was made freely available to us, contributing hugely to many of the sites on the island. We must also give particular mention to the following, as each made major contributions to individual sites: Simon Hugheston-Roberts, the Caernarfon area; Steve Culley, Angelsey; Marc Berw-Hughes, the Llandudno area; Steve Stansfield, Bardsey; Paul Kenyon, Newcwys Mountain; and Norman Hallas and Kevin Smith, who compiled much of the Wrexham text. Our thanks go to the Deeside Naturalists Society for permission to include material for Connah's Quay Nature Reserve from its website. We also wish to thank Steve Cale for his splendid front cover illustration and Kevin Thomas Jones for the black and white illustrations that so enhance the text. To anyone we have omitted, we apologise. For any errors or omissions, we take sole responsibility.

Our last words are for our partners, Glynis Roberts, who prepared the maps and Ruth Miller, who typed much of the text. We are grateful to you both, not only for your direct contributions to the book, but also for your unfailing support during the project.

HAVE YOUR SAY

EXPERIENCE gained over many years has gone into the content of this book, but inevitably, you will have favourite places of your own that we have not mentioned.

I would be delighted to hear from readers willing to share information on places they think deserve a place in subsequent editions of this book and to receive updates on site changes and new access details, together with your suggestions and corrections.

Feel free to write to Owen Roberts, c/o Buckingham Press Ltd, 55 Thorpe Park Road, Longthorpe, Peterborough PE3 6LJ or email me at admin@buckinghampress.com

The publishers' goal is to bring out new editions on a regular basis so that information can be kept as up-to-date as possible.

WHY THIS SITE GUIDE?

THERE ARE SEVERAL guides to North Wales wildlife sites available for you to buy, so why choose this one? We shall explain the benefits we've tried to incorporate into this particular guide book.

When we visit a bird site, particularly one we haven't visited before, we want to know:

1. Exactly what are we likely to see at the time of year we are visiting
2. The likelihood of seeing the birds listed in the site guide.

For instance, how many times have you been to a reserve in Winter and seen Merlin on the sightings board? Lots. And how many Merlins have you seen? Not many, we'll bet! In this guide, you will find Merlin listed for many reserves, but you will also be given an idea of how likely you are to see one. This is expressed by a percentage score after the name of each target bird for each site.

The fact that Merlins zip through a reserve once a day in winter doesn't mean you will see one, and this guide makes that obvious. In this way, visiting birdwatchers will not let their hopes rise too high, but will know which birds are most likely to be encountered.

All **sites are listed in alphabetical order,** so no more struggling to find site 3.14, or reading through reams of text to find the site you want. Sites are also cross-referenced on pages for **Disabled Access, Partly Disabled Access,** and **Public Transport Access.** This feature makes it easy to look up which sites are accessible for you. You then simply turn to the site guide page for more details.

Another bugbear is that many site guides hide the most important information in masses of text. **This guide displays the most relevant facts prominently** (when to visit, grid reference of parking area, target species, likelihood of seeing your targets). More detailed background information is given in the adjoining text, but the important stuff is up front.

Another important feature of this book is that it is up-to-date. Every site has been visited in 2006 or 2007 and any changes to previous visits noted. Of course, things may have changed since we last visited, and some sites we frequented in 2006 altered from one visit to the next, which was quite frustrating at times. The birding scene in North Wales is, quite literally, changing day by day. **This makes the Contacts section for each site an essential feature,** enabling visitors to check details of opening times, entrance fee, etc. before their trip.

Complete beginners will find that the **Calendar section details the seasonal comings and goings of birds in North Wales,** plus a list of birdwatching sites recommended according to the season. More experienced birders may wish to visit somewhere they have heard about but not yet visited. In either case, the reader can easily locate the relevant page, as sites are arranged in alphabetical order.

The layout for each site is designed to help you make the most of your visit. As stated above, important information (e.g. parking) is easy to find but this guide comes into its own as

the background text takes you on the walk itself. The best areas for certain target species are described, as are tips on fieldcraft, enabling the birdwatcher to make the most of their visit.

In a nutshell, this book is designed to enable any birdwatcher visiting North Wales to confidently plan a day, weekend, or longer holiday, seeing exactly what they want to see, when they want to see it (within reason!), no matter how experienced or inexperienced they may be.

Finally, every effort has been made to check, check and check again the details for each site. If you find that this guide is incorrect in any way, please let us know so that we can amend the details in future editions. Also, we would be extremely happy to hear from you if you have enjoyed a day out at one of the sites mentioned: it would make all our hard work worthwhile!

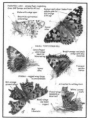

THE BIRDWATCHER'S CODE OF CONDUCT

Around three million adults go birdwatching every year in the UK. Following *The Birdwatchers' Code* is good practice, common sense and will help everybody to enjoy seeing birds.

1. Welfare of birds must come first

Whether your particular interest is photography, ringing, sound recording, scientific study or just birdwatching, remember that the welfare of birds must always come first.

2. Habitat protection

A bird's habitat is vital to its survival and therefore we must ensure that our activities do not cause damage

3. Keep disturbance to a minimum

Birds' tolerance of disturbance varies between species and seasons. Therefore, it is safer to keep all disturbance to a minimum. No birds should be disturbed from the nest in case the opportunities for predators to take eggs or young are increased.

In very cold weather, disturbance to birds may cause them to use vital energy at a time when food is difficult to find. Wildfowlers impose bans during cold weather; birdwatchers should exercise similar discretion.

4. Rare breeding birds

If you discover a rare breeding bird and feel that protection is necessary, inform the appropriate RSPB Regional Officer, or the Species Protection Department at the RSPB, The Lodge, Sandy, Beds. SG19 2DL. Otherwise, it is best in almost all circumstances to keep the record strictly secret to avoid disturbance by other birdwatchers and attacks by egg-collectors.

Never visit known sites of rare breeding birds unless they are adequately protected. Even your presence may give away the site to others and cause so many other visitors that the birds may fail to breed successfully.

Disturbance at or near the nest of species listed on the First Schedule of the Wildlife and Countryside Act 1981 is a criminal offence.

5. Rare migrants

Rare migrants or vagrants must not be harassed. If you discover one, consider the circumstances carefully before telling anyone. Will an influx of birdwatchers disturb the bird or others in the area? Will the habitat be damaged? Will problems be caused with the landowner?

6. The law

The bird protection laws, as now embodied in the Wildlife and Countryside Act 1981, are the result of hard campaigning by previous generations of birdwatchers. As birdwatchers, we must abide by them at all times and not allow them to fall into disrepute.

7. Respect the rights of landowners

The wishes of landowners and occupiers of land must be respected. Do not enter land without permission. Comply with permit schemes.

If you are leading a group, do give advance notice of the visit, even if a formal permit scheme is not in operation. Always obey the Country Code.

8. Keeping records

Much of today's knowledge about birds is the result of meticulous record keeping by our predecessors. Make sure you help to add to tomorrow's knowledge by sending records to your county bird recorder.

9. Birdwatching abroad

Behave abroad as you would at home. This code should be firmly adhered to when abroad (whatever the local laws). Well behaved birdwatchers can be important ambassadors for bird protection.

(Reprinted with the permission of RSPB).

YOUR BIRDING YEAR IN NORTH WALES

THIS PART OF THE book is aimed at helping you plan your birding trips more effectively. For example, you may wish to observe migrating seabirds. By reading the monthly summaries you will be able to find out which species will be present, the best time of year to visit and which sites to head for. Then simply turn to the site page in the main section to find out how to get to your chosen birding venue.

January's calendar is very comprehensive, covering species which occur throughout the period from October to March and is intended to be complementary to the calendars for each of those months. Similarly, April is also very comprehensive, covering the months April to July for summer visitors.

JANUARY

The start of the birding year. The short winter days can still provide wonderful birding in North Wales. If we're lucky enough to have cold, calm conditions, a trip along the coast from RSPB Conwy westwards to Anglesey will produce enough birds to keep any observer more than happy!

Water Rails feed in the open at RSPB Conwy, divers and grebes can be seen from the promenade at Llanfairfechan, Little Egrets and Kingfishers at Aber Ogwen, Pale-bellied Brent Geese feed at Beddmanarch Bay, Black Guillemots dive in Holyhead Harbour and Chough swoop over the cliffs at RSPB South Stack.

Divers and grebes: Calm seas and a good telescope are the key to success with these groups of birds. Any coastal area can provide Red-throated Divers and Great Crested Grebes, but to see the scarcer species you will have to be more selective with your searching. Undoubtedly Llanfairfechan promenade is the prime site for observing these species.

Herons: Little Egrets have increased dramatically in North Wales over the last 20 years and can now be found throughout the year. Most reliable sites in the winter are Aber Ogwen, just east of Bangor and Foryd Bay, just west of Caernarfon.

In freezing conditions, you may be lucky enough to encounter a Bittern at one of the Anglesey wetlands, driven out of its usual hiding place deep in the reeds by the cold weather.

Swans and wildfowl: The winter months hold huge numbers of wildfowl in North Wales. Whooper Swans are declining as a winter visitor but small flocks can still be found on the Glaslyn Marshes near Porthmadog and at Llyn Alaw on Anglesey. The Anglesey wetlands also hold good numbers of duck: RSPB Valley Wetlands is a great place to see a wide cross-section of species.

For seaduck, Morfa Bychan near Porthmadog is the best site and often holds Long-tailed Ducks, Scaup, Eiders and Velvet Scoters among large numbers of Common Scoters. However, the area can be disturbed by jet-skis, particularly at weekends.

Birds of prey: The winter months are a good time to catch up with Hen Harriers at their coastal roost sites, the best location being the Cefni Estuary on Anglesey, where birds can be watched from the edge of Newborough Forest. Merlins are also around the coasts at this time of year, making them a little easier to find than when they are on their moorland breeding sites. Try Foryd Bay and the Cefni Estuary for this dashing raptor.

Passerines: Twite can be found in small numbers wintering along the coast – the most reliable site is Llanfairfechan saltmarsh, where they can be found among the Linnet flocks. Snow Buntings can be seen along the shingle beach at Pensarn where they are continually disturbed by dog-walkers but the birds don't seem to mind.

Rarities: Long-staying over-wintering birds are the most likely rarities at this time of year. Recent years have seen a drake Black Scoter habitually return to Llanfairfechan, where it has provided many with a quality year tick early in the year. A rare gull could also occur anywhere along the coast, so check those flocks carefully.

The relatively mild winters of North Wales have allowed the odd rare passerine to over-winter here, a recent example being the Hume's Yellow-browed Warbler at Caernarfon. Given luck, small parties of Waxwings may have filtered across to North Wales from the east coast of the UK by now.

With a determined effort it is quite possible to see more than 100 bird species in a single day in North Wales at this time of year – what a great start to your year list!

FEBRUARY

Wildfowl: Large numbers of wildfowl remain, so it's always exciting to get out to see these huge flocks before they begin their migration north. Foryd Bay, to the west of Caernarfon, is perhaps the easiest place to observe huge numbers of wildfowl; thousands of Wigeon can be seen here. On the Dee Estuary, RSPB Point of Ayr is a great place to visit on a rising tide, as huge numbers of wildfowl are pushed in front of the hide by the incoming waters.

Birds of prey: The raptors mentioned in January will still be in evidence.

Waders: This is a good month to catch up with Purple Sandpipers. The two prime sites are Trearddur Bay on Anglesey and Rhos Point in Conwy.

Passerines: Crossbills will be breeding in our upland conifer plantations. Try Clocaenog Forest and Gwydyr Forest for these charismatic finches.

Rarities: As previously mentioned in January.

MARCH

Swans and wildfowl: This is your last chance to see big concentrations of wildfowl before they begin their migration north.

Birds of prey: Many raptors begin to display this month and it is probably your best opportunity to catch up with the elusive Goshawk. These spectacular hunters indulge in fantastic undulating display flights high above their dark conifer homes. Choose a calm, sunny day around mid-morning to maximise your chances of this difficult species.

Gamebirds: Black Grouse will be in full display this month, with the impressive males lekking on traditional moorland sites. You will need to get up early as the best action takes place around dawn but it is well worth the effort. The mountain road over World's End is THE site to see this most amazing spring phenomenon. The same area should also produce displaying Red Grouse, giving their distinctive *'go-back, go-back'* calls.

Terns: Look for the first returning Sandwich Terns at any coastal site this month. Cemlyn Bay on Anglesey, where the species breeds in large numbers, is a good bet for your first of the year.

Woodland species: One woodland bird above all others is very difficult to pin down, not just in North Wales but in any part of the UK – the Lesser Spotted Woodpecker. In March, this diminutive woodland recluse announces its presence by drumming and displaying. Listen out for its piercing, rather raptor-like, calls to help you locate this much sought-after bird. The woodlands of the Conwy valley are as good a bet as any to find one.

Passerines: If there are any wintering Snow Buntings along the coast, March is a great time to see the males in their newly-acquired, handsome piebald breeding plumage. The beach at Pensarn has proven the most reliable site for these northern buntings in recent years.

Migrants: The first migrants of spring will be arriving around the coasts, the most likely candidates being Wheatears, Chiffchaffs and Sand Martins. Given warm southerly winds towards the end of the month, we may see a few other species arrive, including Ring Ouzel and perhaps the first Willow Warbler.

Rarities: With lots of gulls migrating north at this time, there is always the chance of something rare among the commoner birds. Iceland, Glaucous and Ring-billed Gulls have all occurred at this time of year. Mediterranean Gulls can be found among the large flocks of Common Gulls moving north, Pensarn and Llandulas beaches are the best sites to visit in late afternoon, as the gulls gather to roost.

APRIL

Divers and grebes: By April, the majority of divers and grebes will be well into their moult to breeding plumage, making them a spectacular sight. The promenade at Llanfairfechan is the best place to enjoy the show. Calm, sunny conditions allow you to enjoy the spectacle of more than 100 Red-throated Divers, up to half a dozen Great Northern Divers and, with luck, a dozen or so Slavonian Grebes. Another great place to see Great Northern Divers in breeding plumage is Aberdesach, south-west of Caernarfon.

Herons: Little Egret numbers increase at this time as birds from further south join the small over-wintering population. These graceful little herons can be encountered at almost any wetland site as they move north; the Glaslyn estuary around Porthmadog, Foryd Bay, Caernarfon, Aber Ogwen east of Bangor and RSPB Conwy are all sites that normally hold Little Egrets at this time.

Waders: With the ever-lengthening days of spring, wader migration increases and many of the species are now moulting into their superb breeding colours. Black-tailed Godwits exchange rusty red feathers for their drab grey-brown plumage of winter. Golden Plovers assume their stunning black, white and gold breeding coats and Turnstones become tortoiseshell beauties.

Some of the best sites for seeing spring waders include the Dee Estuary, River Clwyd, RSPB Conwy, Morfa Madryn, Foryd Bay, Beddmanarch Bay and the Alaw Estuary.

Gulls and terns: By late April, the majority of the breeding Sandwich Terns will be making a noisy spectacle back at Anglesey's Cemlyn Lagoon, where they are joined by smaller numbers of Common and Arctic Terns.

Passerines: This month sees the majority of our warblers, flycatchers and chats returning from their African wintering grounds. Our woodlands become alive with birds and a dawn visit will be rewarded with wonderful birdsong.

Those classic Welsh birds – Pied Flycatcher, Redstart and Wood Warbler – can all be found by the end of the month back on territory in the hanging oak woodlands. Hafod Woods in the Conwy valley is a good example of this habitat and contains a wide cross-section of woodland birds.

Migrants: With huge numbers of birds migrating at this time of year, birders should make for the headlands in search of new arrivals. The Great Orme at Llandudno, RSPB South Stack Reserve, Anglesey and the Aberdaron area on the Lleyn peninsula should all produce fantastic birding.

Rarities: With so many birds on the move, there is always the chance of something rarer being caught up in the massive movement. Birds overshooting their Mediterranean breeding grounds are most likely to occur. Perhaps a Hoopoe, Wryneck or Alpine Swift may add spice to an April birding day.

MAY

Swans and wildfowl: Lowland wetland sites are worth checking for an overshooting Garganey. RSPB Conwy records this species almost annually, May being the peak month. Other sites to check include RSPB Valley Wetlands Reserve and Cemlyn.

Birds of prey: The pair of Ospreys at Pont Croesor near Porthmadog should have well-grown young towards the end of the month, making it the best time to visit. The parents will be busy ferrying fish back the nest site. These spectacular birds should not be missed.

Waders: Migration will still be in full swing for many species of wader and the chances of something rare among them are relatively high. Cemlyn Lagoon on the north Anglesey coast is probably THE best site for a vagrant wader this month. This is also the month when Dotterel pass through, heading for northern breeding grounds. The Range near RSPB South Stack Reserve and the Great Orme, Llandudno are the two most accessible sites where the species are likely to be encountered.

Seabirds: For a real spectacle, visit RSPB South Stack Reserve to marvel at this fantastic seabird colony. Thousands of Guillemots pack the ledges below Ellins Tower Information Centre. Puffins should be seen bobbing about on the water below the cliffs, while Manx Shearwaters should be passing offshore. Chough and Peregrine will add to the excitement. The Great and Little Ormes at Llandudno also hold breeding Guillemots, Razorbills, Kittiwakes, Shags and Cormorants.

Migrants: Coastal headlands should be scoured for scarce and rare migrants. The Great Orme, Llandudno, Carmel Head and South Stack on Anglesey, and the Aberdaron area on the Lleyn Peninsula have all established good track records for turning up scarce migrants.

Rarities: May is one of the best months for rare birds to turn up in the region. Keep a sharp look-out wherever you are; rare birds can, and do, turn up anywhere. Birdline Wales has news of all the latest sightings updated throughout each day.

JUNE

Gulls and terns: Cemlyn Bay on the north Anglesey coast is a must-visit site this month. The tern colony, at its peak of activity, is a fantastic spectacle of sound, vision and smell – a real assault on the senses!

Hundreds of Sandwich Terns are crowded onto the islands in the lagoon where they breed along with Black-headed Gulls and small numbers of Arctic and Common Terns. With real luck, you may be fortunate enough to find a very rare Roseate Tern among them. This species formerly bred at Cemlyn and a recent increase in sightings suggests they may do so again.

The only Little Tern colony in Wales – Gronant Beach – will also be at its peak of activity and should not be missed. The colony is wardened, so please report to the staff on duty when you arrive.

Seabirds: Penmon Point on Anglesey will provide good views of Black Guillemots in the strait between the point and the adjacent Puffin Island. Small numbers of Puffins should also be seen with a very good chance of breeding Eiders here. Another great place for seeing Black Guillemots is Holyhead Harbour: view from the footbridge or the long stay car park. The seabird colonies on the Great and Little Ormes are also well worth visiting this month.

Nightjars: A calm warm evening is the best time to search for the mysterious Nightjar in our upland forests. Gwydyr and Clocaenog Forests offer the best chances to encounter one of these enigmatic birds. Look out for roding Woodcock at the same sites.

Rarities: Early June can still produce some outstanding rarities. Though the bulk of migration has finished, there is still the chance that an Eastern Mediterranean species in particular could overshoot to our coastline. A Black-headed Bunting is a possibility, or perhaps more likely, a Common Rosefinch. It was in early June when the famous Black Lark spent a week at RSPB South Stack Reserve.

JULY

Herons: Little Egret numbers in the region begin to increase. A high tide visit to Aber Ogwen just east of Bangor should produce a high count, perhaps as many as 100.

Birds of prey: The Osprey chicks at Pont Croesor should now be close to fledging.

Waders: Return wader passage begins in earnest this month. Look out for Green Sandpipers and Black-tailed Godwits, the latter still in their beautiful breeding plumage. Try the Point of Ayr, River Clwyd, RSPB Conwy, Beddmanarch Bay, Alaw Estuary, and Foryd Bay.

Gulls and terns: This is the last chance to visit our tern colonies before the birds begin their migration south.

Seawatching: July is the best month to catch up with a Storm Petrel in our region. Keep a close eye on the weather forecast for strong onshore winds and you should be rewarded. July can also be a good month for seeing good numbers of Manx Shearwaters offshore, particularly from The Range near South Stack. There is always the chance of something rarer among them, perhaps a Balearic or Sooty Shearwater.

Rarities: Some spectacular rarities have occurred in July, most notably in recent years a Sooty Tern at Cemlyn Lagoon, which stayed for almost a month. Remarkably, years earlier a Bridled Tern also spent July at Cemlyn, so perhaps this is the place to watch.

AUGUST

Herons: Numbers of Little Egrets increase, the highest counts usually occurring at Aber Ogwen, the North Wales Wildlife Trust Reserve just east of Bangor, where in excess of 100 birds have been recorded.

Waders: Wader passage steps up a gear with large numbers returning to estuaries. With luck, some scarcer species such as Curlew Sandpiper or Little Stint, may be located,.

Gulls and terns: August can be a good month for Mediterranean Gulls and it is worth checking through any concentration of Black-headed and / or Common Gulls for this charismatic visitor. The cob pools at Porthmadog and the high tide roost at Llanfairfechan saltmarsh have proven particularly productive for this species.

Large flocks of terns can be found at the mouth of the Dee Estuary at the RSPB Point of Ayr Reserve. The majority are Sandwich Terns mixed in with smaller numbers of Common, Arctic and Little Terns.

Seawatching: Keep an eye on the weather forecast for north-westerly winds and head for Point Lynas or Cemlyn on the Anglesey coast and you should be rewarded with some classic seawatching. Large numbers of Manx Shearwaters, Gannets, Kittiwakes and terns should be on the move. These concentrations attract skuas; Arctic Skuas are the most likely to be encountered but any of the four occurring species are possible. Carefully check any shearwaters, as this is the best time to encounter the globally threatened Balearic Shearwater off our coast.

Passerines: Migration gets underway in earnest this month with large numbers of birds on the move. The headlands at Uwchmynedd, Llyn Peninsula, Carmel Head, Anglesey and Great Orme, are all worth visiting to witness the spectacle of migration.

This is also the last chance to catch up with any summer visitors to our inland woodlands and upland areas, such as Pied Flycatcher, Wood Warbler, Whinchat and Ring Ouzel, all of which will soon be leaving their breeding grounds.

Migrants: Given east or south-easterly winds, any coastal cover is worth checking for grounded and lost migrants. Many scarce and rare species have been recorded at this time of year, including Wryneck, Red-backed Shrike, Melodious Warbler and Ortolan Bunting.

Rarities: Perhaps the best chance of a real rarity this month would be an adult wader, perhaps of American origin and hopefully still in its breeding plumage, making it that much easier to identify than the juveniles that occur later in the autumn.

SEPTEMBER

Swans and wildfowl: This month sees a huge influx of wildfowl from their northern breeding grounds. Foryd Bay near Caernarfon can hold several thousand Wigeon, a fantastic bird spectacle. The saltmarshes of the Dee Estuary also attract huge numbers of birds, including Pintails, Wigeon, Teal and Shelducks.

Waders: Wader passage reaches its peak this month with fresh-plumaged juvenile birds joining the adults on their migration south. This is the best month for getting to grips with these often difficult-to-identify birds, as it is possible to see a full range of plumage types all within one flock.

Again, the Dee Estuary is the place for spectacular numbers of waders. Pick a day when there is a high tide of 9m or more around midday for the best wader watching. Other sites to try for passage waders include River Clwyd, RSPB Conwy, Morfa Madryn, Foryd Bay and Alaw Estuary.

If water levels are low, try the freshwater lakes on Anglesey for species such as Wood, Green and Common Sandpiper. Check limestone pavements on the Great Orme for passage Dotterel. This species also occurs on The Range, RSPB South Stack, Anglesey.

Seawatching: Onshore winds should provide wonderful seawatching this month as huge numbers of birds make their way down the Irish Sea. Petrels, shearwaters and skuas will all be on the move. Your choice of seawatching venue will be dependent on the wind direction. Some of the best locations include Point Lynas and Cemlyn on Anglesey, Point of Ayr in Flintshire, and Criccieth and Porth Ysgaden in Gwynedd. Onshore winds are best at all these locations.

Migrants: Passerine migration will be in full swing this month. Bardsey Island Bird Observatory is without doubt the best place to witness bird migration (the same applies for October). The period around the new moon, when migrating birds are more likely to be disorientated by poor weather, is the best time to visit with an enhanced chance of something really exciting turning up. The list of vagrants and rarieties recorded on the island is enormous and mouthwatering.

Any coastal headland is worth checking at this time of year for lost migrants. Some of the most productive sites include the Point of Ayr, the Great Orme, Penmon Point, Cemlyn, RSPB South Stack and the Aberdaron area.

Rarities: September is a great month for rare birds with almost anything possible from any compass direction. The largest numbers of American waders have been recorded this month, so check carefully through all flocks of waders that you encounter.

OCTOBER

Swans and wildfowl: The bulk of the returning wintering swans and wildfowl will have returned by the end of this month. Impressive numbers can again be seen on the marshes of the Dee Estuary, Foryd Bay and on the Anglesey lakes.

Numbers of Brent Geese should have returned and are best looked for at Beddmanarch Bay and again at Foryd Bay. A small herd of Whooper Swans should have returned to the Glaslyn marshes near Porthmadog, however numbers here are in slow decline year by year.

Birds of prey: Hen Harriers and Merlins should have left their moorland breeding grounds and returned to coastal wintering areas. The best site to look for these two species at this time of year is the Cefni Estuary on Anglesey.

Waders: Huge numbers of wintering waders will now have returned to our estuaries and coasts. For sheer spectacle, visit the Dee Estuary where tens of thousands of waders will have gathered for the winter. Smaller numbers of Purple Sandpipers will be back at their traditional wintering sites – try Rhos Point or Trearddur Bay.

Seawatching: Seawatching at this time of year can still be very productive, given onshore winds. Again the best places to try are Point Lynas and Cemlyn on Anglesey, Point of Ayr in Flintshire, and Criccieth and Porth Ysgaden in Gwynedd.

Passerines: Small numbers of Snow Buntings begin to return, though numbers vary from year to year. One of the most reliable sites is the shingle beach at Gronant. This is a good month to look for Hawfinches at their traditional sites in the Conwy valley – Caerhun and Llanbedr-y-Cennin.

Migrants: October is the best month to witness visible migration as huge numbers of birds move west along the North Wales coast. Early mornings on calm days are the best conditions to witness this at sites such as the Great Orme, RSPB South Stack, and Uwchmynydd headland, Aberdaron. During this month it is worth checking any and all coastal headlands for scarce migrants. October is the month to be out in the field searching for exciting migrants.

Rarities: October has produced a fantastic array of rarities in the past, particularly on Bardsey Island where many of these have been trapped and ringed at the Bird Observatory. This only highlights how many rare birds must pass through North Wales at this time of year, so surely some of them must be awaiting discovery on the mainland?

Rarities from the east predominate, with birds drifting across from Siberia. These include such fantastic birds as Pallas's Warblers, Yellow-browed Warblers, Richard's Pipits and Red-breasted Flycatchers.

NOVEMBER

Divers and grebes: November and December are great months for gazing out to sea, hopefully on a calm day, to see wintering divers and grebes. Llanfairfechan Promenade is probably the best site, with an excellent chance of connecting with Great Northern and Red-throated Divers and Slavonian Grebes offshore. There will be the added bonus of seaduck, including large numbers of Common Scoters and in recent years a returning drake Black Scoter (still present April 2007 at least). Also try Holyhead Bay, nearby Beddmanarch Bay and Borth-y-Gest.

Passerines: This is the best month to witness the fantastic spectacle of a Starling roost, where hundreds of thousands of these birds gather just before dusk to swarm into their reedbed roost. RSPB Conwy Nature Reserve is the most accessible site to marvel at this wonder of nature.

Migrants: Migration is all but over, though some impressive movements can still be witnessed, given cold weather conditions further to the east. Species such as Fieldfare and Redwing can occur in large numbers. It is still worth covering the headlands, particularly early in the month, for those last few remaining straggler migrants. Species such as Garden Warbler and Firecrest can still be found.

Rarities: Perhaps surprisingly November has actually produced more rare birds in North Wales than October, and has included some unprecedented birds, including Green Heron in Red Wharf Bay and Laughing Gull in Porthmadog.

DECEMBER

Swans and wildfowl: This is a great month to visit Morfa Bychan beach to see wintering wildfowl in the shallow bay. Rafts of Common Scoters feed just beyond the breakers, giving amazing views. Scan carefully through the flocks and you may well be rewarded with other species, including Long-tailed Ducks, Scaup and Velvet Scoters.

During any spells of cold weather, check the Anglesey lakes for species which may have been displaced from further east. For example, check Llyn Coron for Smew.

Birds of prey: A late afternoon visit to the Cefni Estuary may well be rewarded with a sighting of Hen Harrier coming in to roost on the saltmarsh on the southern shore. Other raptors here could include Merlin, Peregrine and Barn Owl.

Passerines: A visit to the Dee Estuary at Flint Castle should produce a small flock of wintering Twite on the saltmarsh.

Rarities: You could try searching the vast conifer plantations of Clocaenog Forest for a wintering Great Grey Shrike, though few other birds are likely to be encountered during your visit. A better bet may be to search for vagrant wildfowl among the flocks of commoner wintering species eg: American Wigeon among Eurasian Wigeon, Surf Scoter among Common Scoter or if you are really lucky, a Lesser Scaup among Tufted Duck.

HOW TO USE THIS BOOK

HERE is a typical layout of the site guide pages. Once familiar with the layout, you will be able to extract the information you need quickly and painlessly.

Title of site. Sites are listed in alphabetical order and numbered.

Key points: Opening times, terrain, suitability for wheelchair users and other useful tips. ALWAYS check opening times with the site managers before you visit.

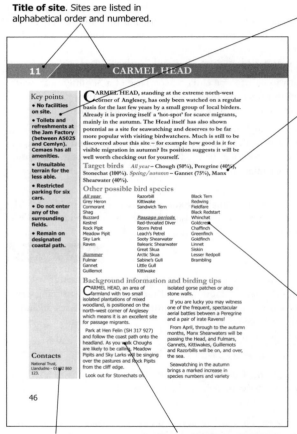

11 — CARMEL HEAD

Key points
- **No facilities on site.**
- **Toilets and refreshments at the Jam Factory (between A5025 and Cemlyn). Cemaes has all amenities.**
- **Unsuitable terrain for the less able.**
- **Restricted parking for six cars.**
- **Do not enter any of the surrounding fields.**
- **Remain on designated coastal path.**

CARMEL HEAD, standing at the extreme north-west corner of Anglesey, has only been watched on a regular basis for the last few years by a small group of local birders. Already it is proving itself a 'hot-spot' for scarce migrants, mainly in the autumn. The Head itself has also shown potential as a site for seawatching and deserves to be far more popular with visiting birdwatchers. Much is still to be discovered about this site – for example how good is it for visible migration in autumn? Its position suggests it will be well worth checking out for yourself.

Target birds   *All year* – Chough (50%), Peregrine (40%), Stonechat (100%). *Spring/autumn* – Gannet (75%), Manx Shearwater (40%).

Other possible bird species

All year	Razorbill	Black Tern
Grey Heron	Kittiwake	Redwing
Cormorant	Sandwich Tern	Fieldfare
Shag		Black Redstart
Buzzard	*Passage periods*	Whinchat
Kestrel	Red-throated Diver	Goldcrest
Rock Pipit	Storm Petrel	Chaffinch
Meadow Pipit	Leach's Petrel	Greenfinch
Sky Lark	Sooty Shearwater	Goldfinch
Raven	Balearic Shearwater	Linnet
	Great Skua	Siskin
Summer	Arctic Skua	Lesser Redpoll
Fulmar	Sabine's Gull	Brambling
Gannet	Little Gull	
Guillemot	Kittiwake	

Background information and birding tips

CARMEL HEAD, an area of farmland with two small isolated plantations of mixed woodland, is positioned on the north-west corner of Anglesey which means it is an excellent site for passage migrants.

Park at Hen Felin (SH 317 927) and follow the coast path onto the headland. As you walk Choughs are likely to be calling. Meadow Pipits and Sky Larks will be singing over the pastures and Rock Pipits from the cliff edge.

Look out for Stonechats on isolated gorse patches or atop stone walls.

If you are lucky you may witness one of the frequent, spectacular aerial battles between a Peregrine and a pair of irate Ravens!

From April, through to the autumn months, Manx Shearwaters will be passing the Head, and Fulmars, Gannets, Kittiwakes, Guillemots and Razorbills will be on, and over, the sea.

Seawatching in the autumn brings a marked increase in species numbers and variety

Contacts
National Trust, Llandudno - 01492 860 123.

46

Target birds and the likelihood of seeing them: Lists the species for which the reserve is most noted. The percentage figure gives a rough idea – based on our experiences at the site – of how likely you are to see the target species, provided you visit the site at the correct time and stay for a reasonable amount of time. Where you see 'winter raptors (25%)' this means that you have a 25% chance of seeing each species of raptor at the site.

Other possible species: Lists the commoner species you are likely to see. Phrases such as 'winter thrushes', 'common woodland birds', 'common waterfowl' are used to save space but please see pages 164 and 165 for a more detailed explanation of what is included. Occasionally, 'good' species are included in this section instead of the Target section if the chance of seeing that species is low.

Useful contacts: Phone numbers to confirm access details etc.

Background information: Generally, this section will take you through the walk, with details of the birds that you might see and handy tips to help you see them. It might contain more information on points which have been briefly mentioned in previous sections, e.g. more extensive bird lists, more detailed information about terrain etc.

Best time of year to visit.
There may be things to see at other times of year but this season is likely to produce the best results.

Relevant OS Landranger map number

Grid reference(s) of parking area(s) giving easiest access to site.

Site facility symbols:
£ Payment required
Parking available
Refreshments available
Toilets
Wheelchair access

Maps: The larger, more detailed map shows trails, hides and other key features for the reserve. (See key to symbols below). The small thumbnail map shows the reserve's position within North Wales.

Access: Detailed directions to the parking area(s) or reserve entrance (the harder a site is to find, the more detailed the description). For some sites, we have included the most straightforward route, for those unfamiliar with the area, not necessarily the quickest.

Other nearby sites: Not comprehensive but a selection of ideas for sites to visit in the general area of the reserve you have chosen. Refer to the North Wales map (inside back cover) for a complete list of sites in the area.

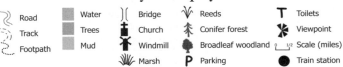

ALL YEAR   OS MAP 114   SH 317 927 & SH 329 930

with Red-throated Divers, Storm and Leach's Petrels, Sooty and Balearic Shearwaters, Arctic and Great Skuas, Sabine's and Little Gulls, and Black Tern all possible. A strong, persistent north-west wind will considerably enhance some chances.

The site can witness some amazing visible migration in autumn when thousands of thrushes and finches pass overhead.

Among the many Chaffinches, Greenfinches, Goldfinches and Linnets, the keen observer who is familiar with the calls should pick up Bramblings, Siskins and Lesser Redpolls, while Crossbills, Waxwings and Hawfinches all joined the party in 2005.

Several Firecrests have been spotted with the many passage Goldcrests, and Yellow-browed Warbler has also appeared on a couple of occasions.

Black Redstarts and Whinchats are regular in the autumn, while Richard's Pipits and Lapland Buntings have been seen so frequently in recent autumns as to almost qualify as regular!

With so many migrants around, raptors often put in an appearance, so there is always a chance of a Hen Harrier, Sparrowhawk, Merlin or Short-eared Owl. And of course during the summer months, there is a

Access details
(Approx 5.5 miles NE of Holyhead)
Leave A55 Expressway after crossing the Brittania Bridge onto A5025 to Amlwch. The junction is immediately after the bridge on the left. Continue on A5025 until one mile after Cemaes. Then take the right turn at Tregele on to an unclassified road that leads to Cemlyn. At S edge of Cemlyn Lagoon continue straight on until you see a small car park on

your right at Hen Felin (SH 317 927). This car park will accommodate no more than six cars. If it is full, go back to Cemlyn (SH 329 930), and from there follow the coast path to Carmel Head.

good chance of picking up a Hobby.

A North American vagrant Buff-breasted Sandpiper was recorded in 2005 and 2006 on the pastures, as were Dotterel, Wood Lark, Tawny Pipit and Wryneck.

Real rarities in recent times here have been Black Stork, Snowy Owl and Isabelline Wheatear – ample proof of the site's potential.

Other nearby sites
Cemlyn.

47

Key to map symbols

	Road		)(	Bridge		🌿	Reeds		T	Toilets
	Track		♁	Church		🌲	Conifer forest		❋	Viewpoint
	Footpath		✚	Windmill		🌳	Broadleaf woodland		0 ½	Scale (miles)
	Water								
	Trees		〰	Marsh		P	Parking		●	Train station
	Mud								

ACCESSIBILITY OF SITES

SITES FULLY ACCESSIBLE TO WHEELCHAIR USERS

Aber Ogwen
Beddmanarch Bay
Bodelwyddan Castle
Church Island
Clocaenog Forest (Bod Petrual)
RSPB Conwy
Criccieth
Holyhead Harbour/ Soldiers Point
Llanddulas and Pensarn Beaches
Nant Ffrancon Valley
Pont Croesor
Porthmadog
Rhos Point
Trearddur Bay

SITES PARTLY ACCESSIBLE TO WHEELCHAIR USERS

Aberdaron Area
Aberdesach and Pontllyfni
Borth-y-Gest
Caerhun Church
Cefni Reservoir
Connah's Quay
Dinas Dinlle
Flint Castle
Foryd Bay
Great Orme Country Park
Gwydyr Forest
Inland Sea
RSPB Lake Vyrnwy
Llanfairfechan and Morfa Madryn
Llyn Alaw
Llyn Brenig
Llyn Llywenan
Llyn Maelog
Malltraeth Cob Pool
Morfa Bychan (Black Rock Sands)
Penmon Point
RSPB Point Of Ayr
Porth Ysgaden
Red Wharf Bay
RSPB South Stack
Traeth Lligwy

RSPB Valley Wetlands
World's End
Wrexham Area Sites

SITES ACCESSIBLE BY PUBLIC TRANSPORT

Aberdaron Area
Aberdesach and Pontllyfni
Aber Ogwen
Beddmanarch Bay
Bodelwyddan Castle
Borth-y-Gest
Caerhun Church
Cefni Reservoir
Church Island
Coed Hafod
Connah's Quay
RSPB Conwy
Criccieth
Dinas Dinlle
Flint Castle
Foryd Bay
Great Orme Country Park
Gronant Beach
Gwydyr Forest
Holyhead Harbour/ Soldiers Point
Inland Sea
RSPB Lake Vyrnwy
Little Orme
Llanddulas and Pensarn Beaches
Llanfairfechan and Morfa Madryn
Llyn Coron
Llyn Maelog
Malltraeth Cob Pool
Morfa Bychan (Black Rock Sands)
Morfa Harlech NNR
Point Lynas
RSPB Point Of Ayr
Porthmadog
Red Wharf Bay
Rhos Point
River Clwyd
RSPB South Stack
Trearddur Bay
RSPB Valley Wetlands
Wrexham Area Sites

ABERDARON'S location at the west end of the Lleyn Peninsula makes it ideal to receive arrivals of migrant birds. Its remoteness means it is still very underwatched, so if you fancy some solitary birding with a better-than-average chance of finding your own scarce, or even rare, birds, this is the place to go in North Wales. Few real rarities have been found so far, but the Lesser Grey Shrike that frequented the village gardens (and washing lines!) for weeks in October - November 1986, and the second Red-eyed Vireo for Wales, discovered by the revered Welsh poet RS Thomas, hint at the potential.

Target birds   *All year* – Chough (100%), Peregrine (90%), Stonechat (100%), Raven (100%), Yellowhammer (80%). *Winter* – Great Northern Diver (60%), Black Redstart (40%).

Other possible bird species

All year	Gannet	Lesser Redpoll
Fulmar	Golden Plover	
Shag	Grey Plover	*Summer*
Sparrowhawk	Lapwing	Manx Shearwater
Buzzard	Sanderling	Gannet
Kestrel	Dunlin	Shelduck
Peregrine	Snipe	Cuckoo
Oystercatcher	Whimbrel	Swift
Ringed Plover	Common Sandpiper	Hirundines
Curlew	Turnstone	Wheatear
Commoner gulls	Arctic Skua	Grasshopper Warbler
Guillemot	Great Skua	Spotted Flycatcher
Razorbill	Mediterranean Gull	
Sky Lark	Little Gull	*Winter*
Meadow Pipit	Kittiwake	Red-throated Diver
Rock Pipit	Commoner gulls	Mallard
Grey Wagtail	Sandwich Tern	Golden Plover
Pied/White Wagtail	Common Tern	Lapwing
Stonechat	Hirundines	Turnstone
Blackcap	Whinchat	Mediterranean Gull
Chiffchaff	Wheatear	Common Gull
Goldcrest	Sedge Warbler	Fieldfare
	Reed Warbler	Redwing
Spring and autumn	Whitethroat	
Red-throated Diver	Lesser Whitethroat	
Manx Shearwater	Willow Warbler	

Background information and birding tips

A CAR or bicycle is an advantage if you intend to cover the area in a single day but if you want to make a weekend of it and cover the area on foot, there is a campsite and plenty of B&B establishments. If you are planning a longer visit, you will get the chance to take a boat trip from Aberdaron harbour around nearby Bardsey Island, with the chance to see dolphins, porpoises and seals as well as seabirds.

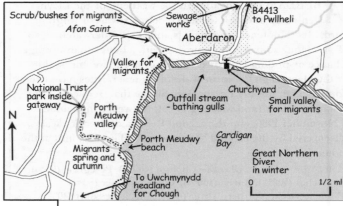

The village churchyard, right by the beach, makes a good starting point. There are always Wheatears and Meadow Pipits present on passage, but the specialities here are Black Redstarts, which are frequent on passage, with birds sometimes present during the winter months.

Just a little further along the beach is an outfall that crosses the beach to the sea, and this should always be checked for bathing and resting gulls.

From the village centre a track, marked on the accompanying map, leads to the small sewage works. There is an excellent amount of cover, and its position in a small valley means that it is usually sheltered and is attractive to warblers, flycatchers and Goldcrests on passage, with Stonechat throughout the year.

Now head up the hill west out of the village in the direction of Uwchmynydd. After less then half a mile you will see a small valley to the left leading down to the beach.

It has sparse cover, but

Access details.

(Aberdaron lies approx 16 miles SW of Pwllheli).

From Caernarfon take A487 to fourth roundabout, then A499 signed to Pwllheli. Continue SW out of Pwllheli following signs to Llanbedrog and Aberdaron. After five miles at Llanbedrog village, fork right onto B4413. Continue along this road, being sure not to deviate off it, for about 11 miles into the village of Aberdaron, where there is parking.

If coming from the south head for Portmadog, and take A497 to Pwllheli. Once in Pwllheli follow direction as above.

with its small stream (the Afon Saint) is still attractive to migrants, such as Grasshopper, Sedge, Reed, Willow and Garden Warblers, as well as both species of Whitethroat and Spotted Flycatcher in both spring and autumn.

Just a little further along the road there is a turn-off to the right. Do not follow this, but stop to view the dense willow bed. Watch for a while as it may appear dead at first glance, but perseverance has paid off a

number of times in the past with a handful of records of Yellow-browed Warblers among their commoner brethren.

In a further 250 metres the lane divides and you should take the left fork. In less than half a mile you will see a gate on your left. Go through it and park on the small National Trust car park (no charge) at the top of the Porth Meudwy valley.

Leave the car here and follow the rough track down

to the sea and back. It is little over half a mile each way, but too rough to be accessed by the less able.

This is the best site for migrants, with much dense cover, and is worth spending at least a couple of hours working it during passage times.

The common warblers, Spotted and Pied Flycatchers, Goldcrest, finches and buntings often add interest to the resident Stonechats, Linnets and Yellowhammers,

but Yellow-browed, Melodious and Subalpine Warblers have all occurred, as have Common Rosefinches and Firecrests.

On June 21, 1995, while waiting to cross over to Bardsey Island, North Wales birder Marc Berw-Hughes found the first Rüppell's Warbler for Wales (and the fifth for Britain) here, illustrating its potential even outside main passage times.

In winter, a Great Northern Diver is often present in the small bay at the valley bottom.

Leaving the valley, turn

left out of the car park and continue along the lane until you are overlooking the sea. This is Uwchmynydd Headland with its magnificent views out over Cardigan Bay and the island of Bardsey in the near distance. This is perhaps the best area in Wales to see Choughs, with some large flocks present outside the breeding season if you are lucky.

Peregrine and Raven are near certainties here too. All that remains is to retrace your steps back to Aberdaron village, where you can refresh yourself, or who knows, even celebrate your find, in one of its pubs or cafes!

The Uwchmynydd Headland is one of the best sites in North Wales to encounter Chough – after the breeding season, it is possible to see this charismatic crow in large family groups.

Key points

- **Open access at all times along public rights of way.**

- **Disabled birders can view from car parks in both villages.**

- **No toilet facilities – nearest Caernarfon, Pwllheli or Dinas Dinlle.**

- **Telescope useful.**

- **Birding from car possible in poor weather.**

LYING HALFWAY between historic Caernarfon and the resort town of Pwllheli, Aberdesach has recently been discovered as one of the most reliable sites in Wales for seeing divers in winter and early spring. In summer you can enjoy panoramic views of Caernarfon Bay, with Manx Shearwaters heading to their breeding colonies on the Pembrokeshire islands and Bardsey after feeding at sea. Nearby Pontllyfni has riverside vegetation and the added attraction of a nearby fish farm.

Target birds   *All year* – Dipper (80%), Chough (60%).
Spring/summer – Gannet (95%), Manx Shearwater (60%).
Winter/spring – Red-throated Diver (60%), Great Northern Diver (95%).

Other possible bird species

All year		
Common waders	Wheatear	Sand Martin
Common gulls		Wheatear
Sky Lark	*Summer*	
Grey Wagtail	Oystercatcher	*Occasional*
Rock Pipit	Ringed Plover	Little Ringed Plover
Stonechat		Black-throated Diver
	Autumn	Scarcer waders
	Sanderling	Mediterranean Gull
Spring	Whimbrel	Snow Bunting
Sanderling	Turnstone	
Whimbrel	Arctic Skua	*Recent scarce birds*
Turnstone	Sandwich Tern	Avocet
Sand Martin	Common Tern	

Winter-plumaged divers, like this Great Northern, are reliable birds in the early part of the year.

Background information and birding tips

ANYONE who enjoys the challenge of seeking out and identifying divers should head for Aberdesach and Pontllyfni, two small seaside villages southwest of Caernarfon, during the winter months or when the birds are on passage.

Both villages overlook Caernarfon Bay, which plays host to a variety of other seabirds, including Gannets and Manx Shearwaters. March and April have the highest numbers of divers present and Great Northerns regularly reach double figures.

It is also the best time for seeing Black-throated Divers, though they are by no means regular here. We recommend checking the *Birdwatcher's Yearbook* tide tables and time your visit to coincide with high tide, when the birds are closest to shore.

Choughs are sometimes to be seen on the boulder clay cliffs to the southwest of the village.

Nearby Pontllyfni has a wider variety of habitats and birds. By following the footpaths either side of the Afon (River) Llyfni to the beach you are likely to see Dippers and Grey Wagtails, while the neighbouring coastal fields are attractive to flocks of gulls. On occasion we have found a Mediterranean Gull among them.

There is a fish farm on the eastern side of the Afon Llyfni. Much of the site is out of view, but the settlement ponds can be viewed from the top of the

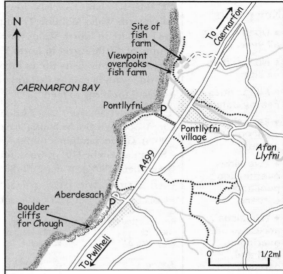

Access details

(Approx. 8 miles SW of Caernarfon).

Exit Caernarfon S on A487. At Llanwnda bear right onto A499. Pontllyfni is the first site you will reach, signposted off main road. There is limited parking at SH 434 525 near the Afon Llyfni, giving access to footpaths either side of the river to the beach.

Less than a mile further S, Aberdesach is also

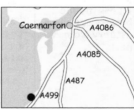

signposted off A499. There is ample parking, overlooking the beach at SH 424 514.

beach. This is a good area for seeing early spring migrants such as Sand Martins and Wheatears.

The ponds have attracted a wide variety of waders in the past, including Little Ringed Plover and Avocet. Unfortunately these waters are becoming over-vegetated, but are still worth a quick look.

On-shore winds between April and September may very well produce views of Manx Shearwaters. Plan your visits for early mornings or evenings to see the largest numbers of these exciting seabirds.

Other nearby sites

Dinas Dinlle.

Key points

- **Open access all year.**
- **No facilities on site.**
- **All facilities in nearby Bangor.**
- **Easy short walk on level ground.**
- **Two hides overlooking pool and estuary.**
- **Wheelchair access to hide overlooking pool and estuary.**
- **Less mobile birders can view estuary from car park.**

Contacts

North Wales Wildlife Trust - 01248 351 541.

THE RIVER OGWEN flows into the Menai Straits at this North Wales Wildlife Trust reserve, which is probably the best site in North Wales for Kingfisher. The highest counts of Little Egret in north Wales are regularly recorded here. Time your visits for an incoming or falling tide, as at low tide waders can be distant, and at high tide no mud is left exposed for birds to feed.

Target birds *All year* – Little Egret (100%), Kingfisher (70%). *Spring* – Greenshank (80%). *Autumn* – Greenshank (100%), Green Sandpiper (60%), Water Rail (50%). *Winter* – Slavonian Grebe (70%), Goosander (90%), Peregrine (60%), Greenshank (90%), Water Rail (80%).

Other possible bird species

All year	Sandwich Tern	*Autumn*
Grey Heron	Great Spotted	Passage waders
Red-breasted Merganser	Woodpecker	
Shelduck	White Wagtail	*Winter*
Grey Wagtail	Wheatear	Common wildfowl
		Waders
Spring	*Summer*	Gulls
Whimbrel	Great Crested Grebe	

Background information and birding tips

THE MAIN habitats at this site close by Bangor are foreshore and a small pool surrounded by trees. At the reserve's car park you have a fine view of the small estuary of the River Ogwen and the Menai Straits beyond, so it is possible to see some good birds – including some of the target species – from the cover of the car in inclement weather. However, be sure to time your visit for when the tide is neither too far in or out.

The make-up of the species present will vary greatly from season to season. Waders, gulls and wildfowl will make up the majority and Little Egret numbers can range from a handful to more than 100!

Scan offshore for wintering grebes. Great Cresteds should be easy to see, while Slavonian

Grebes are regular – up to three have been recorded in recent years. Check the exposed mud for waders, especially the area to the east of the car park, where a telescope would be useful. The main channel of the Ogwen should hold feeding Red-breasted Mergansers and, if you are lucky, Goosanders.

Check the hedge at the back of the car park for passerines, especially during migration times. Walk back along the access road, scanning the fields to the left for roosting waders, plus wagtails and pipits in spring and autumn. Further on, tall trees to the right should, with patience, produce sightings of Treecreepers, Nuthatches and Great Spotted Woodpeckers.

Take the path to the right to

reach the first hide overlooking a brackish pool. Little Grebes are usually present, along with Teal in winter but, with a bit of luck, you should enjoy close views of Greenshank, Water Rail and Kingfisher outside the summer months.

Back at the road, turn right and continue until you reach a farm on the left. Go through a gate on the right and follow the path alongside a high stone wall. Check for woodland species, including Jays, Long-tailed and Marsh Tits.

At the next gate turn right again until you reach the second hide, which overlooks the pool (less brackish at this end) and the Ogwen Estuary. Spend time here for good views of Grey Herons and Little Egrets which fish throughout the year. In any season other than summer you should enjoy first-class views of Greenshanks and Kingfishers. Also in winter there will be Snipe, Teal and probably a Water Rail.

Once you have given the pool some time, turn to the other side of the hide overlooking the Ogwen Estuary. Red-breasted Mergansers and smaller numbers of Goosanders are present here all year. From September through to April there are large numbers of Wigeon and Teal, with smaller numbers of Goldeneyes and more occasional Pintails and Shovelers.

At high tide many waders roost on the bank on the far side of the estuary. A telescope is needed to provide the best views. The majority will be Oystercatchers, Curlews and Redshanks, together with small numbers of Greenshank from August to May and, more occasionally, Bar-tailed

N

Little Egret/Grey Heron roost trees

Channel of *Ogwen* for Goosander and Red-breasted Merganser

Damp fields for waders at high tide and migrants

Aber Ogwen
The Spinnies Reserve

Hide overlooking pool and estuary

Viewpoint for straits

Hide

Pools

Footpath to hide for woodland species

River *Ogwen*

0   1/4ml

To A55
(Bangor)

Access details

(Two miles E of Bangor).

Leave A55 North Wales Expressway four miles west of Llanfairfechan at the sign for Tal-y-Bont (junction 11). Continue N on minor road for half a mile to a large lay-by on right. Just beyond take right turn, signed Nature Reserve. Drive carefully

along single track road to the car park at end.

and Black-tailed Godwits. Whimbrels are regular during both passage periods.

Gulls are always present in varying numbers and should be checked for less usual species. Mediterranean Gull is regularly recorded among the large numbers of Black-headed Gulls. Strangely, considering the proximity of breeding colonies in the Menai Strait, terns are not often seen, with Sandwich

Terns being the most likely.

Raptors hunt the estuary and there is a good chance of Buzzard, Sparrowhawk and Peregrine sightings. Osprey has been recorded several times on passage. Now retrace your steps to the car park, checking for new arrivals.

Other nearby sites

Aber Valley, Llanfairfechan.

29

Key points

- **Open access all year.**

- **Spectacular walk with waterfall at head of valley.**

- **Car parking £2.**

- **Free toilet facilities.**

- **Paths not suitable for wheelchairs.**

- **Walking boots and outdoor clothing advised.**

- **Public toilets and picnic area by main car park.**

- **Pub and cafe in village.**

Grid references:

Park at SH 663 720 for Valley Walk

Park at SH 676 716 for Hillside Walk

Contacts

Countryside Council for Wales - 0845 130 6229.

THIS VERY scenic site, complete with a wooded valley, fast-flowing river and mountainside, is delightful to visit early on a spring morning when the woodland is full of birds. Redstarts, Pied Flycatchers and Wood Warblers are particular targets but the common birds all add to the magical birdsong performance. The hillside at the end of the road is probably the best site in Wales for seeing Chough at any time of the year.

Target birds
All year – Peregrine (70%), Dipper (80%), Grey Wagtail (90%), Chough (80%), Raven (100%). *Spring* – Tree Pipit (80%), Redstart (100%), Pied Flycatcher (100%), Wood Warbler (70%), Ring Ouzel (50%).

Other possible bird species

All year	Stonechat	Garden Warbler
Buzzard	Jay	Wheatear
Sparrowhawk	Siskin	
Great Spotted Woodpecker	Common woodland birds	*Occasional*
		Crossbill
Nuthatch	*Spring*	
Treecreeper	Willow Warbler	

Background information and birding tips

THE WALK to the waterfall in this beautiful valley is always a pleasure, regardless of the birds you may encounter, but an early morning walk in spring can produce great birding, with the air full of birdsong.

The valley, much of which is managed as a nature reserve by Countryside Council for Wales, has extensive areas of mixed deciduous woodland in the lower section. Acid oak woodlands on the upper slopes give way to hawthorn scrub even higher. Sheep walk (unfenced open country where sheep roam freely) and heavily grazed grassland dominates above the treeline. Many of the conifer plantations have been felled.

After parking near the stone hump-backed bridge, check the river for Dippers and Grey Wagtails. Keep a look out for both these species wherever the path,

travelling southwards, allows views of the fast-flowing water.

In spring you should encounter Redstarts, Pied Flycatchers and Wood Warblers in the woodland. It is a good idea to swot up on songs and calls before your visit, as finding woodland birds is so much easier if you can identify their voices. Nuthatches, Treecreepers and Great Spotted Woodpeckers are all likely in this first section of the walk.

As the path enters more open areas, keep an eye on the sky. Buzzards should be easy to see. Sparrowhawk is also very likely and if your luck is in, a Peregrine may grace the air. Garden Warblers may well be found in the scrub areas along with Blackcaps, Willow Warblers and Chiffchaffs. Listen for the raucous calls of Jays and you may get a glimpse of one of these gaudy crows.

Further on still, the path runs alongside recently coppiced alders, so stop to check them for Siskins and, possibly, Lesser Redpolls.

As you near the spectacular waterfall, the mature trees are left behind and replaced with scattered hawthorns. Tree Pipits can be found giving their parachute song flights over the scree slopes from April to June.

In spring, scan the dark cliffs either side of the falls for Ring Ouzels. These cliffs hold Peregrines and Ravens all year round and Choughs are possible flying over.

Enjoy a well-deserved rest below the waterfall and take time to scan the cliffs; birds can be difficult to spot here. Rested, return to the parking area. Drive on up the road beyond the stone hump-backed bridge.

After about one mile, the tarmacadam ends in a small rough parking area. The hillside here is one of the best sites in Wales to see Chough, particularly in autumn and winter when a pre-roost flock of up to 50 birds can gather in the late afternoon. Chough can be found here all year round and a short walk around the area should produce a sighting.

In spring, the stone walls and hawthorn bushes can often hold Ring Ouzels, while Wheatears are common. Stonechats are resident and usually easy to find, occasionally joined by Whinchats in spring. Ravens and Peregrines are encountered regularly, while Buzzards and Kestrels should be seen on most visits.

The views from the hillside

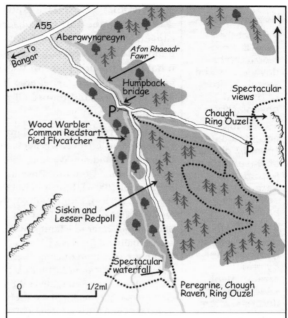

Access details

(Eight miles W of Conwy).

Aber Valley lies midway between Bangor and Conwy just S of A55 North Wales Expressway. Leave A55 at Abergwyngregyn (junction 13) and head S through village, following signposts to 'The Falls'.

The valley sides rise steeply just beyond the village so it is easy to see where you should be heading. Follow minor road for 0.75miles to car parking on right just before a stone hump-backed bridge.

Alternatively, cross bridge, then take first right. Follow the road round the bend to the additional parking area, picnic tables and toilets.

To reach the open hillside area, continue over the stone hump-backed bridge and climb steeply to the dead end. A small rough parking area lies at the end of the road, about one mile beyond the bridge.

following the North Wales Coastal Path up from the car park are spectacular – both across to Anglesey and eastwards along the North Wales coast.

31

Contacts

Bardsey Island Trust,
Hon. Bookings Secretary:
Mrs Alicia Normand,
46 Maudlin Drive,
Teignmouth, Devon,
TQ14 8SB.
Tel. 01626 773 908
www.bbfo.org.uk
www.bardsey.org

BARDSEY ISLAND, a National Nature Reserve and home to the only bird observatory in Wales, is a small, rugged island off the south-western tip of the Lleyn Peninsula. Only accessible by boat in the best of weather, it holds an historic place in Welsh ornithology because its geographic position, sheltered habitats and the influence of the 130-year-old lighthouse all serve to attract a wide variety of migrants every year.

Target birds

Spring – Manx Shearwater, Osprey, Hobby, Dotterel, Turtle Dove, Wryneck, Short-toed Lark, Black Redstart, Melodious Warbler, Firecrest, Woodchat Shrike, Golden Oriole, Common Rosefinch (all 20%). *Summer* – Manx Shearwater (100%), Storm Petrel (90%), Peregrine (100%), Razorbill (100%), Puffin (100%), Kittiwake (100%), Little Owl (90%), Long-eared Owl (50%), Chough (100%). Note percentages refer to island stays: chances of seeing Storm Petrel are virtually nil for day visitors and those for Little Owl and Puffin are greatly reduced. *Autumn* – Sooty Shearwater (20%), Balearic Shearwater (20%), Leach's Petrel (20%), Woodcock (80%), Pomarine Skua (20%), Long-tailed Skua (20%), Little Gull (80%), Wryneck (20%), Richard's Pipit (20%), Black Redstart (80%), Ring Ouzel (70%), Firecrest (60%), Lapland Bunting (60%), Snow Bunting (70%).

Other possible bird species

Spring		Guillemot
Red-throated Diver	Reed Bunting	Sky Lark
Great Northern Diver	*Spring/summer*	Rock Pipit
Common Scoter	Fulmar	Stonechat
Sanderling	Gannet	Wheatear
Whimbrel	Shag	Grasshopper Warbler
Turnstone	Sparrowhawk	Other warblers
Sandwich Tern	Kestrel	Spotted Flycatcher
Common Tern	Peregrine	
Whinchat	Oystercatcher	*Summer*
Raven	Ringed Plover	Great Black-backed Gull
Linnet	Kittiwake	Lesser Black-backed Gull
Lesser Redpoll		

Background information and birding tips

ORNITHOLOGISTS have recognised the importance of the island both as a staging post for migrants, and scarce resident birds since the early 1900s.

The sole Welsh bird observatory was set up in 1953 and is open to weekly visitors from March to November. Exciting birding can be found at any time of the season, but is very weather dependent.

The island's landscape can be

neatly divided in two; a steep-sided 500 foot hill on the east side and a flatter agricultural area to the west. This is predominantly well draining sheep pasture but there is an abundance of more inviting areas to birds, including well-vegetated gardens around all the houses on the island and the observatory.

A series of willow beds or 'withies' lie in the centre, together with two or three permanent ponds. A rough area of gorse and bracken on the west coast and round the lighthouse on the south end also regularly hold migrants. A small Sitka spruce plantation to the north is the only real woodland on the island and is used by many migrants. The sandy beaches at the south end are often good for a variety of waders, pipits and wagtails.

A walk around the whole west side, looking at all the above habitats, will usually take a maximum of four hours. A walk around the mountain to the east will occupy a maximum of two hours, so it is easy to cover the whole island thoroughly in a day.

The light beams from the striking red and white operational lighthouse regularly attract thousands of birds at night and it has a fascinating history of bird 'attractions'. The reasons for this are not fully understood, but it is undoubtedly linked to the phases of the moon and poor visibility.

If poor weather obscures the birds' view of the moon and stars while they are flying over the Irish Sea, they will head towards the nearest light source, namely Bardsey lighthouse.

There were many fatalities in

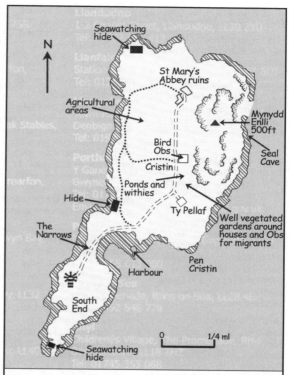

Access details

(14 miles W of Pwllheli).
Observatory visitors are transported by boat from Aberdaron, a 20-minute journey.
Day visitors should contact the Bardsey Island Trust which runs boats from Pwllheli (tel 08457 112 233), the journey taking about an hour. The terrain on the island is unsuitable for

wheelchairs. Dogs are not allowed on the island.

the past – indeed the log makes gruesome reading – but a system is now in place to draw birds to the ground beneath the

light, rather than letting them crash straight into it. History has shown that a week either side of a new moon is the best period for

attractions, so this is a good time for visiting birders.

Spring migration begins in mid-March and can continue until mid-June. The first migrants to arrive are large numbers of Meadow Pipits and wagtails, with the first falls of Chiffchaffs and Wheatears. Numbers increase steadily to early April, when good counts of Goldcrests can occur.

From the middle of April to the end of May, migration can be spectacular and large falls of common migrants occur most years.

A fall of 360 Grasshopper Warblers occurred in 2004 and counts of more than 1,000 Willow Warblers are regular. Daily counts of more than 100 Whitethroats and Sedge Warblers have also been recorded.

With this volume of migration, rarities such as Song Sparrow (1970), Rock Bunting (1967), Collared Flycatcher (1957), Crested Lark (1982), Yellow Warbler (1963), Summer Tanager (1957), Pine Bunting (2001), Common Yellowthroat (1996), American Robin (2003) and Blyth's Pipit (2005) are bound to occur.

In June and July attention moves to the resident island birds. Bardsey is home to about 16,000 pairs of Manx Shearwaters, the fifth largest colony in the world. It has also recently been discovered that about 100 pairs of Storm Petrels nest on the island in the summer.

There are also six pairs of Choughs breeding around the cliffs and resident pairs of Ravens, Peregrines and Little Owls. There are small colonies of Razorbills, Puffins and Kittiwakes around the inaccessible eastern side of the island.

A calling male Corn Crake has been seen for the last two years and hopes are high that this once-common breeder will return soon. However the variety and number of breeding passerines on the island is relatively small. Passage waders are frequently seen in small numbers at this time also.

From August to October, autumn migration begins apace. As in spring, large falls of warblers leaving their breeding areas can occur. Counts of 1,000-plus Willow Warblers are not uncommon, usually attracted to the lighthouse along with other warblers, waders and seabirds in suitable conditions.

Seawatching can be excellent at this time when the wind veers from west to north-west. There are two well-placed seawatching hides on the island at the south and north ends, which give good views as birds pass south along the west coast into Cardigan Bay. Large shearwaters, petrels, gulls, terns and skuas are all recorded annually in variable numbers.

In September, passerine migration is still in full swing and falls of warblers, flycatchers and chats are regular, with huge numbers of hirundines moving south. Bardsey is probably the best place in Wales to find scarce European migrants at this time, with Wryneck, Icterine and Melodious Warbler, Common Rosefinch and Ortolan Bunting all nearly annual in occurrence.

October is probably the most exciting month of the year but the migration patterns are very weather-dependent. Huge numbers of finches, thrushes and Starlings can be seen moving south of the end of the island.

Attractions to the lighthouse can be spectacular and fatal for some. Redwings, Blackbirds, waders, Goldcrests, warblers and Starlings can all occur in large numbers and every area of cover is alive with birds.

With the large numbers of birds and species passing through the island, rarities are found every year and Bardsey holds a lot of the only Welsh and a few of the only British records of some Eastern and American migrants. Such records include Summer Tanager (1957), River Warbler (1969), Common Yellowthroat (1996) and Eye-browed Thrush (1999).

Other nearby sites

Aberdaron, Porth Ysgaden

Key points

- **Access at all times.**
- **Free car park.**
- **Toilets by car park.**
- **Whole bay viewable from car park, no walking required.**
- **Telescope an advantage.**

VISITORS keen to see Slavonian Grebes should head for this large shallow bay close to Holyhead, as it is Anglesey's best site for the species and also for Pale-bellied Brent Geese. It is mainly a site to visit in the winter months as it holds a good mixture of waders and wildfowl but, being so accessible, it is worth calling in at any time.

Target birds   *Winter, spring and autumn* – Slavonian Grebe (85%), Pale-bellied Brent Geese (80%), Bar-tailed Godwit (60%), Grey Plover (60%), Goldeneye (50%).

Other possible bird species

Summer
Sandwich Tern
Common Tern
Arctic Tern

Winter
Great Crested Grebe

Red-breasted Merganser
Shelduck
Wigeon
Knot
Dunlin

Ringed Plover
Curlew
Redshank
Turnstone
Common Gull

Slavonian Grebes appreciate the relative shelter offered by Beddmanarch Bay in winter.

Background information and birding tips

THE BAY is adjacent to the A5 trunk road, two miles east of Holyhead. There is a large car park and all the birds in the bay can be observed from here. Obviously a telescope is a big advantage but plenty can be seen at close range, especially on rising and falling tides.

From November through to March, this is the best site on Anglesey to obtain views of Slavonian Grebes: usually around four birds will be present but up to nine have been recorded.

Also you should get very close views of Pale-bellied Brent Geese, as numbers of this species have been increasing steadily over the past 20 years, and more than 100 birds are quite regular here.

Have a good look at them as you may find a dark-bellied bird among them, and in March one year a Black Brant was discovered here.

It is often easier to find the Slavonian Grebes and other wildfowl such as Goldeneyes, Red-breasted Mergansers and Great Crested Grebes when the tide is out. At these times all birds are concentrated in a narrow deep-water channel that runs through the centre of the bay.

To get the best views of waders, it is preferable to be here an hour or two either side of high tide. In winter good numbers of Dunlin and Ringed Plovers will be swirling round with Oystercatchers, Redshanks, Curlews, Knot, Turnstones, Grey Plovers and Bar-tailed Godwits.

Shelduck and Wigeon are regularly seen and there is usually a gathering of gulls as the tide goes out.

They are mainly Black-headed, Herring and Common Gulls, but a close inspection could be rewarded with something completely out of the ordinary – remember that Forster's Tern, Bonaparte's, Glaucous, Iceland

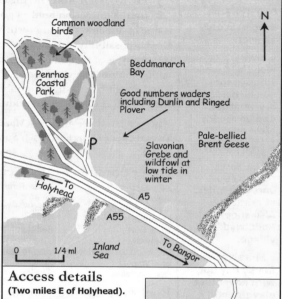

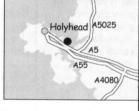

Access details

(Two miles E of Holyhead).

Leave A55 just before Holyhead and follow signs to Penrhos Coastal Park. Turn right onto A5 at the roundabout near Tesco's supermarket, and the bay is on your left just beyond the woodland, about one mile distance.

and Mediterranean Gulls have all been found here in the past.

You can, if you wish, spend an hour or two wandering around the woodlands in the Penrhos Coastal Park; generally only the very common species are to be found here.

Other nearby sites

Holyhead Harbour, Inland Sea, Trearddur Bay.

37

Key points

- **Open access all year.**
- **Easy woodland walk suitable for wheelchairs in dry weather. Can be muddy after rain.**
- **Free parking.**
- **Tea-shop, restaurant, bars and toilets at castle. Also shops in Bodelwyddan village.**
- **Suitable for a family day out, with adventure playground, garden maze, Victorian games room and gift shop.**

Contacts

Bodelwyddan Castle – 01745 584 060.

THE WOODLAND on the estate of this wellknown tourist attraction holds a good selection of birds and is one of the few sites in North Wales where Marsh Tit is a good possibility. A relatively short woodland walk means you don't need to spend a long time at the site – unless other family members are exploring the Castle's other attractions – and a visit can easily be combined with other sites nearby, such as River Clwyd or Llanddulas and Pensarn Beach.

Target birds: *All year* – Marsh Tit (70%), Nuthatch (90%), Treecreeper (90%), Jay (90%). *Spring/summer* – Blackcap (90%).

Other possible bird species

All year		
Buzzard	Mistle Thrush	House Martin
Sparrowhawk	Coal Tit	Willow Warbler
Pheasant	Goldcrest	Chiffchaff
Stock Dove	Siskin	Whitethroat
Tawny Owl	Bullfinch	Garden Warbler
Great Spotted Woodpecker		Spotted Flycatcher
Grey Wagtail	*Spring/summer*	
Pied Wagtail	Swift	
	Swallow	

Background information and birding tips

THE PRESENT DAY Bodelwyddan Castle (pronounced *Bod-el-with-an*) is a creation of Sir John Hay Williams dating from between 1830 and 1852. It is situated in 260 acres of magnificent parkland and makes a good destination for a family outing.

As well as formal gardens, the grounds hold a lovely area of mixed woodland, with easy access, so the keen birdwatcher can explore for birds while his/her family enjoy the attractions of the gardens and the castle (now an outstation of the National Portrait Gallery).

Follow the road uphill to the car park on your right. Park here and

The castle woodlands offer birdwatchers one of their best chances to encounter Marsh Tit in North Wales.

walk uphill with the castle on your left. Continue straight on and the road becomes a level track into the wood.

This leads to a bird hide, which overlooks a small clearing with bird feeders. Sadly the feeders are often left empty and at these times few birds are present. However, when the feeders are full, the area is alive with birds, so it is a good idea to take food with you and top up the feeders. You will be amazed at how quickly the birds discover they are full!

Marsh Tits are scarce birds in North Wales and the woods here are perhaps the best location to catch up with this charismatic tit. By slowly walking along the track and listening carefully for calls, you should be able to locate a good selection of other birds.

Nuthatches and Treecreepers should be easily seen, while Great Spotted Woodpeckers will certainly be heard and perhaps seen. In spring and summer, warblers join the resident birds and Blackcaps should be seen with relative ease and both Willow Warblers and Chiffchaffs are common.

Listen carefully for the songs of warblers to help you locate individual species. Blackcaps and Garden Warblers sound very similar, so can be tricky. Garden Warbler song is more subtle and melodious and sounds a little softer, but visual sightings are still the best way to ensure you can honestly claim both species.

Spotted Flycatchers may be found making aerial sorties through the canopy in pursuit of insects. Be aware that you

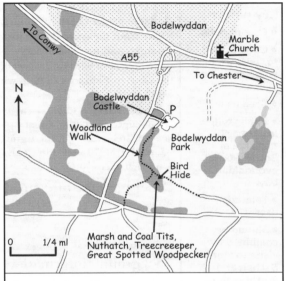

Access details

(Approx four miles S of Rhyl).

Access is very easy, as the site is just off A55 North Wales Expressway (junction 25), two miles W of St Asaph or 2.5 miles E of Abergele, signposted Bodelwydden.

From the east: Turn left at the end of slip road, at the roundabout, into the Castle entrance.

From the west: At the top of the slip road, turn right

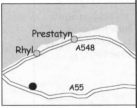

at the roundabout. Cross A55 down to another roundabout where you will see the entrance to the castle.

might see fallow deer in the woodland rides and at dusk in summer you may be lucky and spot a badger on one of the paths or even from the hide.

After visiting the bird hide, you can retrace your steps or walk back down to the castle on a small path off to your right. This brings you into the castle gardens.

Other nearby sites

Gronant Beach, Llanddulas and Pensarn Beach, Point of Ayr, River Clwyd.

39

Key points

- **Free parking.**
- **Good access for all, including wheelchair users.**
- **Scenic village.**
- **Public toilets in car park and café at Borth-y-Gest overlooking the bay.**
- **Telescope essential.**
- **Should be combined with visits to Morfa Bychan and Porthmadog.**
- **Allow around two hours to scan the estuary thoroughly.**

Contacts

Porthmadog Tourist Information Office – 01766 512 981

BORTH-Y-GEST is a small, pretty village on the west side of the Glaslyn Estuary, just south of Porthmadog. Views from the coastal path just south of the village are stunning and give the observer a great chance to check the whole area with limited walking required. In winter, the Glaslyn Estuary can hold wintering divers, grebes and wildfowl.

Target birds

Winter – Great Northern Diver (60%), Slavonian Grebe (80%), Great Crested Grebe (100%), Black-necked Grebe (20%), Little Egret (80%). *Spring/summer* – Little Egret (70%), Osprey (20%), Mediterranean Gull (40%), Sandwich Tern (70%).

Other possible bird species

Winter		Curlew
Wigeon	Shelduck	Knot
Teal	Cormorant	*Occasional*
Goldeneye	Buzzard	Peregrine
Red-breasted Merganser	Oystercatcher	Merlin
	Redshank	

Background information and birding tips

THE SPECTACULAR views across the Glaslyn Estuary from the footpath at Borth-y-Gest are always worthwhile at any time of year but in winter, there is the added bonus of some good birding.

The main interest is provided by divers and grebes, so a telescope will be very advantageous in combating the often distant views.

Careful scanning of the estuary should produce Slavonian Grebes and with luck, a Great Northern Diver. Black-necked Grebe has been recorded occasionally.

Little Egrets are now regular fixtures at Borth-y-Gest in winter, so check the edge of the saltmarsh.

During the winter months, Slavonian Grebes resemble diminutive winter-plumaged Great Crested Grebes, being black-and-white and intermediate in size between Little and Great Crested Grebes.

The only other confusion species is Black-necked Grebe. To separate them, concentrate on the head patterns – Slavonian has a clean clear-cut pattern with the white cheek patches ending in a straight line where they meet the black crown under the eye. In Black-necked Grebe there is a greyish bulge between the black crown and white cheeks, giving the bird a 'dirty face'.

If you are able to get a close-up view you may be able to detect the bill shape – in Slavonian it is straight and in Black-necked the lower mandible tilts upwards. Slavonian heads are flat, while Black-necked shows a steep forehead but again you will need to be close to see these features clearly.

In terms of posture, Black-necked Grebes tend to fluff up their feathers, rather like Little Grebes, while Slavonian Grebes have a far sleeker, smoother appearance.

If the tide is not fully in, check the sandbanks and mudflats for waders, which may include small parties of Knot. Raptors occasionally hunt the area and a Merlin or Peregrine are both possible.

The far shore of the estuary should be checked for Little Egrets, which regularly fish the edge of the distant saltmarsh. The tidal channels should hold Wigeon, Teal, Shelducks,

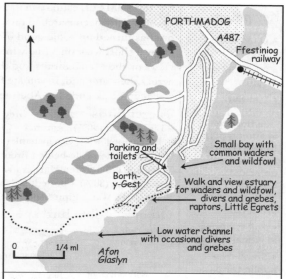

Goldeneyes and Red-breasted Mergansers. If the tide is low, check the channel to the north of the viewpoint for grebes and divers.

Access details

(One mile S of Porthmadog).
From centre of Porthmadog, head S on minor road signposted Borth-y-Gest. Follow for half a mile, uphill past a church on right. Just over the brow of the hill, fork left for Borth-y-Gest.
After small bay on left as you enter the village, turn left into car park. From here walk along the road at far end of parking area out to the coast. The road ends after 100m.

A footpath starts here and after 50m, brings you out to a wonderful viewpoint across the estuary.

Other nearby sites

Criccieth, Morfa Bychan, Pont Croesor, Porthmadog.

41

Key points

- **Open access all year.**

- **No facilities on site.**

- **Limited facilities in Newborough, including public toilets (though not always unlocked). Spar shop has good range of produce.**

- **Full facilities in Menai Bridge.**

- **Small free public car park.**

- **Unsuitable terrain for the less able.**

- **Wellingtons advisable in winter or after rain.**

THIS SMALL estuary in the southern part of Anglesey has only been watched on a regular basis in recent years but has turned up some good birds in that time. You can enjoy a short walk on a fine winter's day with spectacular views of the Menai Straits and the Snowdon mountains across the water and, if you are feeling more energetic, the walk can be extended to Abermenai Point.

Target birds

All year – Grey Partridge (60%). *Spring* – Little Egret (90%). *Summer* – Cuckoo (90%). *Autumn* – Peregrine (70%), Greenshank (90%), Spotted Redshank (80%). *Winter* – Pale-bellied Brent Goose (100%), Merlin (70%), Peregrine (70%), Hen Harrier (60%), Golden Plover (70%), Greenshank (80%), Spotted Redshank (70%), Twite (Abermenai Point 50%), Water Pipit (Abermenai Point 30%).

Other possible bird species

Spring/autumn
Passage waders

Winter
Great Northern Diver
(Abermenai Point)
Wigeon

Pintail
Tree Sparrow
Brambling

Recent rare and scarce birds
Great White Egret

American Wigeon
Shore Lark
Little Bunting
Snow Bunting

Background information and birding tips

FOR A WALK in winter, begin by thoroughly checking the area around the car park for finches, sparrows and buntings. Such diligent searching revealed a Little Bunting among the ever-present Reed Buntings during a recent winter.

An obvious path leads across the saltmarsh from the car park to the estuary – good footwear is recommended as it can get very wet in places.

It will take you around ten minutes to reach the estuary. On the way, look out for Grey Partridge in the fields to the left.

The estuary of the Braint is very small – more a glorified channel than a fullblown river – and a careful approach is required to

avoid disturbing the waders that will be present.

Upstream from where you will stand, there will almost certainly be Greenshanks and Spotted Redshanks (with both species often present in autumn too), and there is at least one Little Egret here in winter.

Now walk right towards the river mouth, where a small flock of Brent Geese will be with other common wildfowl, including Wigeon and Pintail, throughout the winter.

At this time Hen Harriers, Merlins and more occasionally a Short-eared Owl, will frequent the saltmarsh, the adjacent fields and muddy flats. At the point where the Braint flows into the Menai Strait you are likely to find Bar-tailed

Contacts

Countryside Council for
Wales - 0845 130 6229

Godwits, Knot and Grey Plovers.

For the more energetic, try the three mile tramp across the dunes and mudflats to emerge at Abermenai Point. On the way, Twite can sometimes be found on the saltmarsh, together with the commoner Goldfinches and Linnets. Occasionally a Water Pipit is reported among the many Rock Pipits.

At the Point itself, both Snow Buntings and Shore Larks have occured. More likely are sightings of Great Northern Divers just offshore and Sanderlings on the seaward side of the spit. The walk to the estuary and back can take as little as 30 minutes but allow four to five hours if you tackle the walk to Abermenai Point.

Birds are fewer in spring and summer but Grey Partridges are still to be seen in the fields and Little Egrets are more frequent on the estuary at these times. Sky Larks are everywhere and it is one of the best places in North Wales to see a Cuckoo.

Grasshopper Warblers sing from the more vegetated areas, especially around the car park where Sedge Warblers and Whitethroats are common.

At the mouth of the estuary, Sandwich Terns will be fishing, sometimes with Arctics and Commons, while Great Crested Grebes and Red-breasted Merganisers will be on the sea.

Other nearby sites

Malltraeth Cob, Newborough Forest.

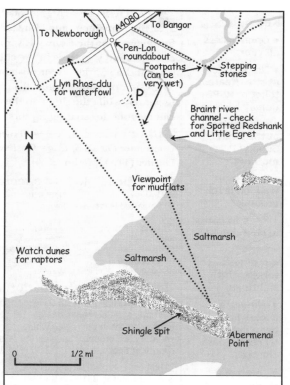

Access details

(Approx one mile SW of Newborough village).

Cross to Anglesey on A55 North Wales Expressway, turning left immediately after the Britannia Bridge, then left again towards Llanfair PG.

As you enter that village turn left again onto A4080. After Birdworld the road is long and straight, passing a model village to the left. Eventually you will come to a mini-roundabout.

The A4080 goes to Newborough village, but go straight on and immediately after the roundabout turn left. This lane leads to the car park for the Braint Estuary.

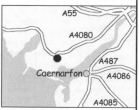

Key points

- **Open access all year.**

- **No facilities at site. Nearest toilet at RSPB Conwy reserve.**

- **No parking at the church Sunday morning.**

- **Easy short walk on level ground.**

- **Keep to paths in churchyard.**

- **Early mornings best for Hawfinch sightings.**

- **Wheelchair access has been improved by recent path changes.**

- **Telescope useful.**

A FAVOURITE HAUNT of that most elusive of species, the Hawfinch, this 13th Century church also offers fine views over the Conwy River and valley. Check the centuries-old yew trees in the churchyard and the attractive surrounding parkland for this chunky, heavy-billed species. The water meadows below the church have wildfowl species in winter, while the ridge on the opposite side of the valley can be good for soaring raptors.

Target birds

All year – Hawfinch (50%), Peregrine (60%), Goosander (90%). *Spring* – Goshawk (30%). *Winter* – Hen Harrier (40%), Merlin (30%).

Other possible bird species

All year	Nuthatch	Teal
Red-breasted Merganser	Raven	Redshank
Buzzard		Redwing
Lapwing	*Winter*	Fieldfare
Redshank	Mute Swan	
Curlew	Greylag Goose	*Spring*
Great Spotted	Canada Goose	Common Sandpiper
Woodpecker	Wigeon	Whimbrel

Background information and birding tips

HAWFINCHES are much-sought birds and Caerhun is one of the few places in the region where you will have probably an even chance of finding one.

The best approach, if time allows, is to park on the B5106 in the lay-by just south of the church entrance. Walk to the gate and follow the single-track lane down to the church. If time is limited, drive to the church (other than on Sunday mornings when a service will be in progress). However, by walking the lane you'll definitely increase your chances of seeing birds, and especially Hawfinches.

At the first bend in the lane, scan the upper parts of trees to your left, which are regularly used by Hawfinches. Once round the bend you should also check several tall trees lining the lane.

As you near the church keep an eye on the dead branches at the top of the yew trees as these make great perches for several species, including our target bird. If you haven't yet struck lucky, try scanning the tops of trees close to Caerhun Hall, which you can see from the church gate. A telescope is useful because of the distance involved.

Also check the trees to the north where the wood that borders the sheep field is another possible spot. Having checked all the surrounding tree tops, quietly enter the churchyard, as Hawfinches could be feeding on the ground or in the yews. Be careful not to flush them. Check all the trees carefully. Having done this you can relax, hopefully with Hawfinch on your list, and enjoy the stunning views over the Conwy Valley.

The water meadows below

the church hold a flock of Wigeon in winter, which, in the past, has attracted American Wigeon. The main channel is likely to hold both Goosanders and Red-breasted Mergansers throughout the year. Waders such as Common Sandpiper and Whimbrel may be seen in spring with the resident Lapwings, Redshanks and Curlews.

The wooded ridges on the far side of the valley are good for soaring raptors and, with patience, you should see a good selection. Most likely are Buzzards, with double figures likely in good weather. Peregrine Falcons are regular, often engaging in 'dog fights' with the numerous local Ravens. Sparrowhawks and Kestrels are resident and on a fine, sunny spring morning from mid-February to mid-April you just might be rewarded with a displaying Goshawk.

A visit in winter could produce a Hen Harrier or Merlin hunting the marshy areas to the south of the church. Also check the pylons here for a roosting Peregrine.

The gulls that come to bathe on the sandbanks in the river are always worth checking, as Iceland, Ring-billed and Mediterranean Gulls have all been recorded.

If you have the time it is worth walking north from the church, taking the footpath with the river on your right. It takes about an hour to work the church and river meadows – add another hour for the walk north.

This leads to an area of mixed woodland where a good variety of the commoner species typical

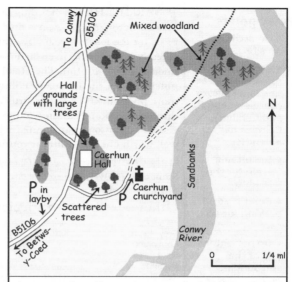

Access details

(Approx. 3.5 miles S of Conwy).

From A55 North Wales Expressway (junction 19), turn onto A470 signed for Betws-y-Coed, passing the Bodnant Gardens National Trust property. The road then runs alongside the Conwy River to your right.

Take the first right onto B5279 over a level crossing, and then the Tal-y-Cafn bridge over river and keep left. After three-quarters of a mile turn left at a T-junction onto B5106. After just under a mile look carefully for a

finger post to Caerhun 13th Century Church. The sign is on right, the entrance on the left. Continue past the entrance 100 metres, and park in the lay-by on your right. Walk back north to the entrance lane.

of the habitat can be seen. Hawfinches and Lesser Spotted Woodpeckers have been seen in the past, and it might prove interesting with better coverage. Retrace your route to the

car remembering to keep your eye on those tree tops!

Other nearby sites

RSPB Conwy, Great Orme, Little Orme.

45

Key points

- **No facilities on site.**

- **Toilets and refreshments at the Jam Factory (between A5025 and Cemlyn). Cemaes has all amenities.**

- **Unsuitable terrain for the less able.**

- **Restricted parking for six cars.**

- **Do not enter any of the surrounding fields.**

- **Remain on designated coastal path.**

CARMEL HEAD, standing at the extreme north-west corner of Anglesey, has only been watched on a regular basis for the last few years by a small group of local birders. Already it is proving itself a 'hot-spot' for scarce migrants, mainly in the autumn. The Head itself has also shown potential as a site for seawatching and deserves to be far more popular with visiting birdwatchers. Much is still to be discovered about this site – for example how good is it for visible migration in autumn? Its position suggests it will be well worth checking out for yourself.

Target birds

All year – Chough (50%), Peregrine (40%), Stonechat (100%). *Spring/autumn* – Gannet (75%), Manx Shearwater (40%).

Other possible bird species

All year		*Black Tern*
Grey Heron	Razorbill	Black Tern
Cormorant	Kittiwake	Redwing
Shag	Sandwich Tern	Fieldfare
Buzzard		Black Redstart
Kestrel	*Passage periods*	Whinchat
Rock Pipit	Red-throated Diver	Goldcrest
Meadow Pipit	Storm Petrel	Chaffinch
Sky Lark	Leach's Petrel	Greenfinch
Raven	Sooty Shearwater	Goldfinch
	Balearic Shearwater	Linnet
Summer	Great Skua	Siskin
Fulmar	Arctic Skua	Lesser Redpoll
Gannet	Sabine's Gull	Brambling
Guillemot	Little Gull	
	Kittiwake	

Background information and birding tips

CARMEL HEAD, an area of farmland with two small isolated plantations of mixed woodland, is positioned on the north-west corner of Anglesey which means it is an excellent site for passage migrants.

Park at Hen Felin (SH 317 927) and follow the coast path onto the headland. As you walk, Choughs are likely to be calling, Meadow Pipits and Sky Larks will be singing over the pastures and Rock Pipits from the cliff edge.

Look out for Stonechats on

isolated gorse patches or atop stone walls.

If you are lucky you may witness one of the frequent, spectacular aerial battles between a Peregrine and a pair of irate Ravens!

From April, through to the autumn months, Manx Shearwaters will be passing the Head, while Fulmars, Gannets, Kittiwakes, Guillemots and Razorbills will be on, and over, the sea.

Seawatching in the autumn brings a marked increase in species numbers and variety

Contacts

National Trust, Llandudno - 01492 860 123.

with Red-throated Divers, Storm and Leach's Petrels, Sooty and Balearic Shearwaters, Arctic and Great Skuas, Sabine's and Little Gulls, and Black Tern all possible. A strong, persistent north-west wind will considerably enhance your chances.

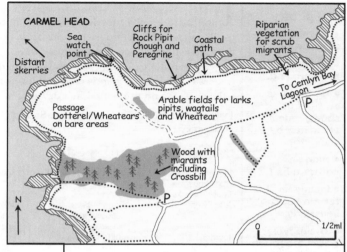

The site can witness some amazing visible migration in autumn when thousands of thrushes and finches pass overhead.

Among the many Chaffinches, Greenfinches, Goldfinches and Linnets, the keen observer who is familiar with the calls should pick up Bramblings, Siskins and Lesser Redpolls, while Crossbills, Waxwings and Hawfinches all joined the party in 2005.

Several Firecrests have been spotted with the many passage Goldcrests. Yellow-browed Warbler has also appeared on a couple of occasions.

Black Redstarts and Whinchats are regular in the autumn, while Richard's Pipits and Lapland Buntings have been seen so frequently in recent autumns as to almost qualify as regular!

With so many migrants around, raptors often put in an appearance, so there is always a chance of a Hen Harrier, Sparrowhawk, Merlin or Short-eared Owl. Of course during the summer months, there is a

Access details

(Approx 5.5 miles NE of Holyhead).

Leave A55 Expressway after crossing the Brittania Bridge onto A5025 to Amlwch. The junction is immediately after the bridge on the left. Continue on A5025 until one mile after Cemaes. Then take the right turn at Tregele on to an unclassified road that leads to Cemlyn. At S edge of Cemlyn Lagoon continue straight on until you see a small car park on

your right at Hen Felin (SH 317 937). This car park will accommodate no more than six cars. If it is full, go back to Cemlyn (SH 329 936), and from there follow the coast path to Carmel Head.

good chance of picking up a Hobby.

A North American vagrant Buff-breasted Sandpiper was recorded in 2005 and 2006 on the pastures, as were Dotterel, Wood Lark, Tawny Pipit and Wryneck.

Real rarities in recent times here have been Black Stork, Snowy Owl and Isabelline Wheatear – ample proof of the site's potential.

Other nearby sites

Cemlyn.

47

Key points

- Open access at all times.

- Car park at northern end.

- No facilities on site but shops, toilets etc in nearby Llangefni.

- Hide on northern half.

- Mainly level terrain but can be muddy.

- The gravel tracks are rough – wheelchair users will find them hard going.

- Allow two hours to give the reservoir thorough coverage.

Contacts

Welsh Water – 01443 245 2300

IF YOU INTEND to visit this Anglesey site in the winter months to see the roosting flock of Whooper Swans, you'll will have to get up early – the birds fly off to graze in the fields shortly after dawn on most days. A trip in autumn may well produce passage waders or Garganey, but finding waders on passage depends on water levels being low enough – the eastern end drops first in a dry spell to expose mud.

Target birds   *Winter* – Whooper Swan (75%). *Autumn* – Garganey (25%).

Other possible bird species

All year	Common woodland	Spotted Redshank
Little Grebe	species	Ruff
Great Crested Grebe		
Mute Swan	*Summer*	*Winter*
Buzzard	Sedge Warbler	Teal
Coot	Blackcap	Wigeon
Moorhen	Chiffchaff	Pochard
Tawny Owl	Willow Warbler	Tufted Duck
Great Spotted Woodpecker		Goldeneye
Common thrushes	*Autumn*	Ruddy Duck
Goldcrest	Common Sandpiper	Coot
Coal Tit	Green Sandpiper	Siskin
	Wood Sandpiper	Redpoll

Background information and birding tips

THIS WELSH WATER Reservoir features two areas of water separated by a disused railway line. From the car park at the northern end you can walk around both halves, or cut your walk short by going along the railway track to do just half the area.

At the southern end there is limited parking by the gated entrance.

In the car park, you should find Goldcrests and Coal Tits at most times of year and in winter a mixed flock of Siskins and Redpolls is often present.

You may also see a Great Spotted Woodpecker or Crossbills at this end of the reservoir.

A few hundred yards along the track on the right there used to be a hide but it was burnt down in 2007. At the time this book went to press there had been no announcements about a replacement hide being built and you will need to contact Welsh Water to check on progress.

From the point where the hide stood you should see Little and Great Crested Grebes, Coot, Tufted Ducks and Pochard.

In autumn, check out the flock of Teal foraging along the edges for the elusive Garganey. Late August/September is the best time to find the summer migrant before it leaves for Africa.

Wildfowl numbers increase in winter and you may find a Scaup or Long-tailed Duck among the commoner species.

Buzzards and Sparrowhawks are regularly seen, and a Goshawk is reported here occasionally. Gulls feeding in nearby fields in winter months come in to bathe or roost, and close scrutiny could produce a Glaucous or Mediterranean Gull.

If water levels drop, the late summer/autumn period could produce some passage waders. Common Sandpipers are regular along the railway embankment in most years and Green and Wood Sandpipers, Spotted Redshank and Ruff can all occur too.

Check both ends of the reservoir for exposed mud as this is likely to attract any hungry waders passing through the area.

If you stop here during summer, check the vegetation surrounding the water as it harbours plenty of breeding warblers.

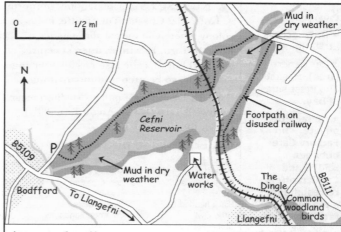

Access details

(Approx 6.5 miles NW of Menai Bridge).

From A55 (junction 6), turn off to Llangefni on A5114. In Llangefni, take B5111 NW towards Llanerchynedd. The reservoir's car park is on your left after about two miles.

If you intend exploring the southern end of the reservoir, turn left out of car park and take next left. Park carefully in the gateway on left just before the village of Bodffordd.

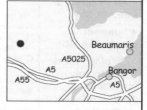

Other nearby sites

Malltraeth, Newborough Forest.

49

Key points

- **Open access at all times.**

- **Car parks (free) on east and west sides of bay.**

- **No facilities on site. Jam Factory Cafe between A5025 and Cemlyn offers refreshments and toilet facilities.**

- **All facilities in Cemaes Bay.**

- **Summer warden on site.**

- **Display boards (April to July) in west car park give basic information.**

- **Part of shingle ridge closed during breeding season, follow on-site instructions. Not accessible to wheelchairs.**

- **Coastal footpath can be muddy in places – wear appropriate footwear.**

ANGLESEY'S coastal lagoon, immortalised in the books of artist Charles Tunnicliffe, holds an important tern colony where you have a slim chance of seeing the rare Roseate Tern. In winter, interest centres on waders and wildfowl but this site also has an amazing ability to draw in rare birds, so be prepared for anything.

Target birds *Summer* – Mediterranean Gull (40%), Sandwich Tern (100%), Arctic Tern (80%), Common Tern (80%), Roseate Tern (5%).

Other possible bird species

All year	Gannet	Common Scoter
Mute Swan	Shelduck	Arctic Skua
Ringed Plover	Red-breasted	Great Skua
Redshank	Merganser	Kittiwake
Black-headed Gull	Oystercatcher	
Little Owl	Common Sandpiper	*Winter*
Stonechat	Sand Martin	Little Grebe
	Swallow	Wigeon
Spring	Sedge Warbler	Teal
Whimbrel	Whitethroat	Goldeneye
Meadow Pipit		Coot
Wheatear	*Autumn*	Golden Plover
Grasshopper Warbler	Manx Shearwater	Purple Sandpiper
	Storm Petrel	Turnstone
Summer	Leach's Petrel	Kingfisher
Manx Shearwater	Gannet	

Background information and birding tips

THE AMAZING movement and noise of the terns at this site in spring and summer is a beauty to behold and you can dream of finding Whiskered, Caspian, Bridled or Sooty Tern – all birds recorded by some lucky people at this magical site on the north coast of Anglesey.

Now a Local Nature Reserve managed by the North Wales Wildlife Trust, this site is good enough to merit a whole day's attention.

The longer you stay, the more birds you will discover. Despite covering only one square kilometre, it packs a lot into every corner. No two visits are the same and we guarantee you will never tire of birding this area.

There is a car park on the east side of the bay and from here you will be able to walk along the shingle ridge to view the tern colony – please remember to walk below the skyline, otherwise you will risk flushing all the birds.

Part of this ridge is roped off in the breeding season to protect the nests of Ringed Plovers and Oystercatchers.

The dominant species in the colony is Sandwich Tern, whose numbers have increased to about 1,500 pairs in recent years; small numbers of Arctic and Common Terns also nest on the islands and though Roseate Terns have not lived here for a few years, one or two are still seen annually.

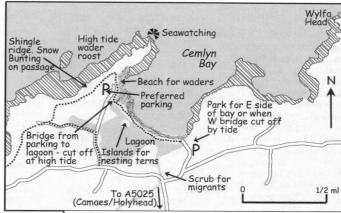

Among the Black-headed Gull colony look out for Mediterranean Gulls which are becoming more regular nowadays. Shelduck, Red-breasted Mergansers and Redshanks are also nesting around the lagoon.

If you opt for the car park at the western end, be aware that you can only access the shingle ridge at low water as the bridge is submerged at high tide (and so is the car park on very big tides)! From here, you can walk out onto the headland. Check the beach for waders: Ringed Plover, Dunlin, Turnstone, Purple Sandpiper, Curlew, Whimbrel, Golden Plover and Grey Plover are all regular visitors.

On the short turf of the headland, Wheatears will dash around, flashing their white rumps in spring, while Meadow and Rock Pipits as well as Stonechats should also be seen. Snow Buntings are generally passage visitors here and seldom stay in winter.

There is a footpath leading over the fields along the coast. This is a good vantage point to try a little seawatching in the autumn (July to October), but remember you will need a westerly or even

Access details

(Approx 15 miles NE of Holyhead).

Leave A55 at junction 3 and head NE for Valley. Turn right at trafic lights onto A5025. After about 11 miles, turn left in Tregele onto unclassified road, signposted Cemlyn. There are car parks at both ends of the shingle ridge.

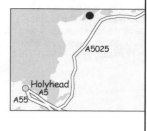

better, a north-westerly, wind to get the best results.

July is the best month to see Storm Petrels and in the ideal conditions mentioned, they could be very close – just off the rocky coast.

Manx Shearwaters, Gannets, Kittiwakes, auks and Common Scoters should all be seen on most watches, and as the month passes into August, you can expect to add sightings of Arctic Skuas and Great Skuas too.

During September, numbers of all these species will increase, along with the chance of seeing Balearic and Sooty Shearwaters, Leach's Petrel, Sabine's Gull and Black Tern.

October is another good month for Leach's Petrel and possible Pomarine and Long-tailed Skuas. This is also one of the best places

Other nearby sites

Carmel Head.

51

in North Wales to see Atlantic grey seal.

Continuing along the coastal path, from the top of the hill you will see some flooded fields below you. These are particularly attractive to passage waders and either here or around the lagoon some exciting birds such as Squacco Heron, Blue-winged Teal, Black-winged Stilt, American Golden Plover, Pectoral Sandpiper, Buff-breasted Sandpiper, Lesser Yellowlegs and Terek Sandpiper have been found.

When you reach the large round stone pillar, turn left and walk down towards the farm; be sure to wear stout footwear as the path is often very muddy here.

Lapwings, Snipe and Redshanks are often among the rushes here, and look out for a Little Owl sometimes perched on the dry stone walls.

On reaching the road, turn left back towards the lagoon. Sedge Warblers, Whitethroats and Reed Buntings should be seen along this road with Swallows and Sand Martins overhead during summer.

Whinchat and Yellow Wagtails are occasionally seen here on passage and as we've said before, you never know what 'goodies' are to be found here among the commoner fare. Shore Lark, Red-backed Shrike, Great Grey Shrike, Woodchat Shrike, Isabelline

Contacts

National Trust, Llandudno – 01492 860 123.

North Wales Wildlife Trust, Bangor – 01248 351 541.

Shrike, Melodious Warbler, Rose-coloured Starling, Common Rosefinch and Black-headed Bunting have all been recorded!

At the end of this track you will return to the lagoon – make sure you stop near the bridge to have another look over that impressive tern colony.

Raucous Sandwich Terns dominate the Cemlyn tern colony, but occasionally rarer species turn up, so check through the birds carefully.

HERE'S A SITE where you can stroll along well-surfaced paths through an area of mixed woodland which tumbles downhill to meet the shoreline of the Menai Straits. A causeway over the tidal mud connects the Isle of Anglesey to the tiny Church Island, which as the name suggests, holds a church and cemetery covering the whole area. From the footpath that runs around the perimeter you can enjoy outstanding views of the Straits and the two spectacular bridges that connect Anglesey to the mainland.

Target birds
All year – **Little Egret (90%), Peregrine (50%).** *Winter* – **Red-breasted Merganser (90%), Shag (80%), Kingfisher (40%).**

Other possible bird species

All year		
Cormorant	Nuthatch	Redshank
Grey Heron	Treecreeper	Curlew
Greylag Goose	Jay	
Shelduck		*Summer*
Oystercatcher	*Winter*	Common Tern
Buzzard	Little Grebe	Arctic Tern
Great Spotted	Wigeon	Sandwich Tern
Woodpecker	Teal	
	Sparrowhawk	

Background information and birding tips

BEFORE LEAVING the small car park, scan the surrounding trees for woodland species, as this is one of the few sites where you can add Nuthatch to your Anglesey list.

Take the path downhill through the woodland, keeping a sharp eye out for any additional species – perhaps a Great Spotted Woodpecker or Treecreeper?

At the bottom of the hill, the path reaches the shoreline and the views open up. It is worthwhile to scan any areas of exposed mud for waders and check the water's edge for feeding wildfowl before walking across the causeway and taking the circular walk around the island.

Little Egrets may well be feeding in the shallows or roosting, often with Grey Herons, on the islet offshore. Cormorants should be easy to see, joined in winter by Shags.

In summer, Common Terns should be feeding over the Straits but check carefully for other species among them. The most likely candidates are Sandwich and Arctic Terns, but a lucky few observers have seen a Roseate Tern here on more than one occasion.

Check out the Britannia Bridge, (the road/rail bridge to the west), for Peregrine Falcons, as these hunters use the gantries as lofty lookout posts.

In winter, check the rocky shoreline for a hunting Kingfisher;

Key points

- **Open access all year.**
- **No facilities at the site itself.**
- **All facilities, including cafes and pubs, in Menai Bridge village.**
- **Beautiful view of Menai Straits.**
- **Wheelchair-friendly Tarmac paths.**
- **Close views of birds.**

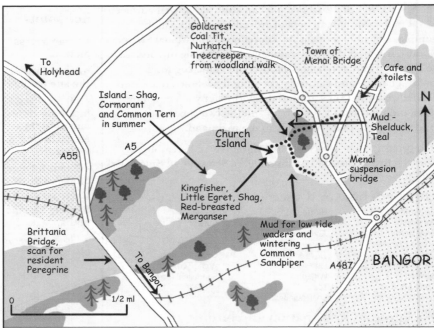

To Holyhead

Goldcrest, Coal Tit, Nuthatch Treecreeper from woodland walk

Town of Menai Bridge

Cafe and toilets

N

Island - Shag, Cormorant and Common Tern in summer

A5

Church Island

P

Mud - Shelduck, Teal

A55

Menai suspension bridge

Kingfisher, Little Egret, Shag, Red-breasted Merganser

Mud for low tide waders and wintering Common Sandpiper

A487

BANGOR

Brittania Bridge, scan for resident Peregrine

To Bangor

0   1/2 ml

Access details

Approx 1.5 miles W of Bangor on N shore of Menai Straits).

Take A5 onto Anglesey over the Menai Suspension Bridge. Go straight on at roundabout, following A5.

Continue past the supermarket and Chinese restaurant and park in the car park on your left. If you reach another roundabout, you have gone too far and need to retrace your steps.

Beaumaris

A5025

Bangor

A5

A55

it is always a thrill to see this gorgeous bird, especially when it is perched.

Red-breasted Mergansers are another winter visitor here and you would be unlucky not to see one after giving the waters a good scan.

On a fine day, you are very likely to see Buzzard soaring overhead and perhaps a Sparrowhawk over the woods.

A Tarmac path runs south-east from the island towards the Menai Bridge, giving you further views of the area.

Other nearby sites

Aber Ogwen, Penmon Point.

THE BREATH-TAKING walk to the top of Craig Bron Banog, a hill of more than 500 metres, is equally matched by the commanding views across the Clocaenog Forest. A good forest track makes the steep walk up from the metalled road fairly easy. As with most upland areas, bird populations are at low levels but include some spectacular rewards for the patient. Early morning visits on calm clear days will produce the best results.

Target birds
Winter/early spring – Goshawk (40%), Black Grouse (30%), Willow Tit (20%), Great Grey Shrike (40% in years when it occurs), Crossbill (60%), Siskin (90%), Brambling (40%).

Other possible bird species

Winter/early spring		
Buzzard	Great Spotted Woodpecker	Treecreeper
Sparrowhawk	Meadow Pipit	Jay
Kestrel	Goldcrest	Raven
Peregrine	Coal Tit	Bullfinch

Background information and birding tips

TO ENHANCE your chance of seeing the forest's most special birds, aim to arrive at the parking area as early as possible on a calm, clear day. Leave it later in the day and it is likely that other people will have walked the tracks and possibly disturbed some of the birds. High winds always make inland birding tough and if the visibility is poor, you can wave goodbye to raptor sightings.

Walking uphill through the conifers from the parking area, listen hard. Calls are the best way to find birds in dense forest. Walk slowly, giving yourself the chance to locate any feeding flocks. Check any areas of willow scrub – there aren't many – for the very elusive Willow Tit and listen for its nasal *'zi zi taah taah, taah'* call.

Make sure you can familiarise yourself with likely bird calls before you go. Check out Crossbill, Siskin, Brambling and Willow Tit – learning these will definitely improve your chances of connecting. Keep looking up to check for over-flying raptors, the views on the way up are limited but you may be lucky.

As you near the summit the track emerges from the dark conifers onto an open area of heather moorland. The early visitor may be lucky enough to come across a magnificent Black Grouse. Small numbers of these amazing birds are in the area and have been encountered lekking on Craig Bron Banog. The view will be of a bird bursting from the heather and heading off across the forest like a black-and-white Exocet missile, so keep your wits about you!

Once out on the heather moor you can begin to scan in earnest for the site's real speciality, the Great Grey Shrike, a species that has been annual in recent years! The hill is without doubt the best

Key points

• **Open access all year.**

• **Not accessible to wheelchair users: terrain is too demanding.**

• **Upland forestry area, so boots, warm clothing and waterproofs needed.**

• **Telescope desirable.**

• **No facilities on site. Caerdigion on A5 has a café, pub and public toilets. Ruthin has full range of facilities.**

• **Limited parking, free.**

Contacts

Forest Enterprise, Coed y Brenin Centre, Dollgellau – 01341 440 666.

place in North Wales to find one of these rare butcher birds. Luckily, the Great Grey Shrikes like to perch on exposed treetops, so if one is around, it should be found.

However, Great Greys have large territories and are very mobile, so if you don't see one at first scan, don't give up: it can literally pop up at any moment. Having a telescope will help greatly, so find the best vantage point and patiently scan. Being so pale and liking to sit on top of trees means you can spot a shrike at very long range.

Check any thorn bushes in the area for signs of a shrike. Like other members of the shrike family, Great Greys keep a larder of excess food, a pretty grizzly sight of small mammals and birds impaled on long thorns! But find a larder and you know that a shrike is active in the area, so just wait long enough and you should be rewarded.

The best chances of seeing a Goshawk are, again, to scan and scan again! The fantastic views from the top give a 360 degree panorama of airspace over the vast forest. Any raptor moving around above the trees should be seen. You will no doubt see many Buzzards before you score a Goshawk, but with patience you will have an excellent chance.

Mid-morning can be a good time for soaring raptors, so if you are planning to remain on the site for several hours, ensure you are well-prepared with warm clothing, hot drinks and food. A hilltop in winter can be a very cold place to stand still.

On your return, walk down the

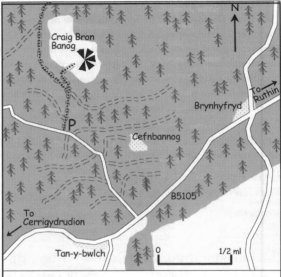

Access details.

(Clocaenog turn-off lies approx 8.5 miles SW of Ruthin).

Craig Bron Banog hill is best accessed from S, off B5105 (Cerrigydrudion to Ruthin) road. Turn N off B5105 at SJ 025 502, approximately five miles E of Cerrigydrudion or 8.5 miles west of Ruthin.

The minor road runs N through the conifer wood uphill for just under a mile. Just after a left bend, look carefully for a track entrance/lay-by on the right. Park carefully, ensuring you do not block access to the forest track at SJ 017 512.

Walk uphill on forest track through the conifers. Ignore forest tracks on either side and after just over half a

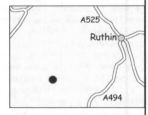

mile of steady climbing, the track bends round to the right and opens out onto heather moorland. Another 200 metres and you reach the mast and panoramic views across Clocaenog Forest. Retrace your steps to return to your vehicle.

hill again checking carefully for Crossbills and Siskins and any other birds that may be moving through the forest.

THIS PICNIC SITE gives easy access to an area of mixed woodland on the south side of the vast Clocaenog Forest, just off the B5105. The variety of trees and relatively easy viewing gives birders the chance of seeing a good cross-section of woodland birds, including Crossbills. Early mornings are best, as many species will be in song, making them so much easier to locate.

Target birds

All year – Grey Wagtail (90%), Crossbill (75%), Siskin (90%). *Spring/early summer* – Woodcock (40%), Tree Pipit (70%), Redstart (90%), Wood Warbler (75%), Pied Flycatcher (90%).

Other possible bird species

Spring/early summer		
Buzzard	Blackcap	Nuthatch
Sparrowhawk	Willow Warbler	Treecreeper
Great Spotted	Chiffchaff,	Jay
Woodpecker	Goldcrest	Goldfinch
	Long-tailed Tit	Bullfinch
	Coal Tit	

Background information and birding tips

HERE'S a site where you can begin birding the moment you've stepped out of your car. Use your ears to help you locate which species are in the area and scan the tree-tops around the parking area for feeding Crossbills and Siskins. In spring/early summer many additional species may well be present.

By arriving as early as possible, you will find more birds are in song and with luck you'll soon find Pied Flycatchers and Redstarts in the trees adjacent to the car park.

While this site has been chosen for its ease of access and a representative selection of coniferous woodland bird species, it is but a small part of the huge forest area that is Clocaenog.

If you don't succeed in spotting particular species at either of the two sites we highlight, it is always worth exploring other likely looking areas of the forest. The key species – Wood Warbler, Pied Flycatcher, Siskin and Crossbill – are widely distributed, so you could encounter them anywhere.

To continue your walk from the Bod Petrual picnic site, head south along the metalled road and you soon reach a woodland pool on your left.

The trees around the pool are again a good location to look for Crossbills; listen out for their *'chup-chup'* calls and watch for falling debris as the birds dismember pine cones.

Siskins are very regular here and in spring and early summer Pied Flycatcher can be seen flitting through the overhanging branches. Scan the water's edge for feeding Grey Wagtails. These beautiful birds are usually present and fairly easy to see.

Key points

- **Open access at all times.**

- **Free parking.**

- **Public toilet at car park.**

- **Both Cerrigydrudion and Ruthin have a full range of cafés, pubs and accommodation.**

- **Flat walk suitable for less able and wheelchair users.**

- **Early morning best**

Contacts

Forest Enterprise, Coed y Brenin Centre, Dollgellau – 01341 440 666.

It is well worth walking slowly right round the edge of the lake. You should find Redstarts on the far side in spring and early summer. Look out for resident woodland species such as Sparrowhawk, Buzzard, Great Spotted Woodpecker, Goldcrest and Long-tailed Tit.

Continue along the Tarmac road past the lake and the road drops gently downhill. You soon reach a forest track off to your right. The junction of track and road is a good place to stand, listen and scan. In spring and early summer the distinctive 'spinning coin' song of the Wood Warbler may well be heard from the deciduous trees. This area is also the best place to see Jays and Coal Tits.

If you visit at dusk in spring and early summer, you will have an excellent chance of seeing a roding Woodcock and hearing calling Tawny Owls.

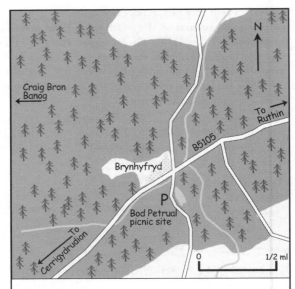

Access details.

(Approx seven miles W of Ruthin).

Bod Petrual picnic site lies on the southern edge of the Clocaenog Forest approximately six miles E of Cerrigydrudion at SJ 037 512. The picnic site is clearly signed on S side of B5105. The car park has ample parking.

Other nearby sites

Llyn Brenig

IN WINTER, birds can be hard to find but in spring, an early morning visit to this beautiful ancient woodland on the edge of the Snowdonia National Park can be a joy. At this time of year the woodland holds a great variety of birds, including the Welsh classics – Pied Flycatcher, Redstart and Wood Warbler. Hawfinches are also here and can be found with luck or persistence.

Target birds *All year* – Hawfinch (40%). *Spring* – Lesser Spotted Woodpecker (20%), Pied Flycatcher (100%), Redstart (100%), Wood Warbler (100%).

Other possible bird species

All year	Common woodland birds	*Winter*
Buzzard		Brambling
Sparrowhawk	*Spring*	
Great Spotted	Tree Pipit	*Occasional*
Woodpecker	Garden Warbler	Goshawk
Nuthatch	Blackcap	Marsh Tit
Treecreeper	Willow Warbler	Firecrest

Background information and birding tips

HAFOD WOODS or Coed Hafod (Coed is the Welsh word for a wood) is a beautiful site and worth a visit for the walk alone. Rocky ridges, several small streams and gorges add habitat diversity to a mainly broadleaf woodland.

Ideally, the wood is best visited in spring when birdsong is at its peak, making the birds that much easier to locate. A really early start will ensure the dawn chorus, a wonderful experience, is in full swing.

Walk a short distance north from the lay-by and turn right over the stile to enter the woodland. In spring, bluebells and wood anemones carpet the floor.

Move slowly and listen hard; birds will be singing and calling everywhere and with care you can quickly filter out the commoner species to track down the target birds.

As you move uphill, you will have to cross two more stiles but once beyond the second of these, you are in the heart of the wood and the noise of the busy A470 is a little less intrusive. A level section of path bends round to the right and this can be a productive area for Wood and Garden Warblers.

From this point, take the first left turn off the path, uphill. This is a particularly good section for Pied Flycatchers. Stand, wait, and watch, and you should be rewarded and if you keep listening for the soft *'tic'* call of the elusive Hawfinch you might strike lucky.

These chunky finches can be encountered anywhere in the wood but they usually prefer to stay high in the canopy where they can be tough to spot, even if you do hear one call!

The path climbs up, then levels out and reaches some stone walls.

Key points

- **Open access all year from adjacent A470.**
- **Scenically beautiful woodland walk.**
- **Free parking.**
- **Not suitable for wheelchairs, due to stiles and rough terrain.**
- **Walking boots advised, paths can be muddy.**
- **No facilities on site.**
- **Betws-y-Coed and Llanrwst have public toilets, cafes and a range of accommodation.**
- **Do not confuse this site with the Woodland Trust site at Maentwrog.**

Contacts

FSC Rhyd-y-Creauau (Drapers Field Centre – 01690 710 494

The area on the right of the path is good for Redstarts and a Wood Warbler usually holds territory here.

The next section of path has beech trees. Again, look carefully for a Hawfinch, and in winter a flock of Bramblings could be present.

Listen for the rather raptor-like calls of Lesser Spotted Woodpecker but bear in mind that you will be very lucky indeed to see one of these diminutive peckers.

Open areas on the west side of the wood can hold Tree Pipits and allow you to scan the skies for raptors. The path then turns south along the ridge, descending the slope back to the path on which you entered the wood, completing your circular walk.

Allow a good two hours to do justice to the area; patience is a great ally in woodland birding. Scarce birds that have been recorded include Goshawk and Marsh Tit at all times of year, while in winter there have been records of Firecrest, usually in areas with holly trees.

For anyone interested in exploring the area in more detail, the Field Studies Council Rhyd-y-Creauau centre, just outside Betws-y-Coed, offers a variety of residential courses for students and adults interested in natural history.

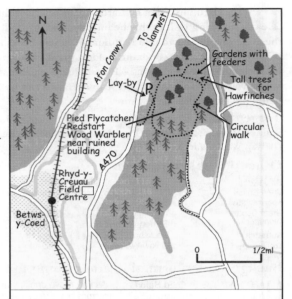

Access details

(Approx 2.5 miles S of Llanrwst).

Coed Hafod lies on E side of Conwy Valley midway between Llanrwst and Betws-y-Coed alongside A470.

Park in lay-by approximately two miles north of Betws-y-Coed (same distance from Llanrwst). From here, walk 20 metres N, towards Llanrwst to a stile on your right. The footpath begins here.

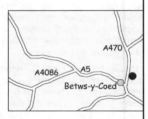

It is possible to complete a circular walk through the wood or, if time is limited, a shorter walk should produce most species.

Other nearby sites

Gwydyr Forest, Nant Ffrancon Valley.

DESPITE the industrial setting on land occupied by a power station, the nature reserve's varied habitats adjacent to the bird-rich Dee Estuary attract wintering wildfowl and waders, as well as being noted for passage waders. It is, to quote from Deeside Naturalists Society's own website "a splendid example of what can be achieved when industry and conservation groups work together in partnership".

Target birds
Autumn – Little Egret (100%), Black-tailed Godwit (100%) Greenshank (80%), Spotted Redshank (80%), Curlew Sandpiper (50%), Kingfisher (50%). *Winter* – Little Egret (100%), Pintail (100%), Merlin (40%), Peregrine (60%), Black-tailed Godwit (100%).

Other possible bird species

All year	Dunlin	Whitethroat
Mute Swan	Ruff	
Cormorant	Snipe	*Autumn*
Grey Heron	Black-tailed Godwit	Pink-footed Goose
Shelduck	Bar-tailed Godwit	Common duck species
Oystercatcher	Whimbrel	Ringed Plover
Lapwing	Black-headed Gull	Little Stint
Curlew	Lesser Black-backed Gull	Green Sandpiper
Redshank	Sandwich Tern	Common Sandpiper
Herring Gull	Common Tern	Whimbrel
Great Black-backed Gull	Swift	Other common waders
Sky Lark	Sand Martin	
Starling	House Martin	*Winter*
Reed Bunting	Swallow	Wigeon
	Wheatear	Gadwall
Spring	Sedge Warbler	Goldeneye
Little Egret	Reed Warbler	Common wader species
Wigeon		Common Gull
Teal	*Summer*	Meadow Pipit
Ringed Plover	Oystercatcher	Grey Wagtail
Grey Plover	Reed Warbler	Raven
Knot	Sedge Warbler	Fieldfare
		Redwing

Background information and birding tips

A KEY FEATURE of this reserve, managed jointly by the Deeside Naturalists Society and power company E.ON, is the 17-acre Bunded Pool complex. The pools were created on an area of saltmarsh by the Dee Estuary, and can be observed from one of three hides.

During much of the year they are home to species such as Grey Heron, Shelduck, Mallard, Teal, Oystercatcher and Redshank, with Little Egret, Black-tailed Godwit, Greenshank, Spotted Redshank and Curlew Sandpiper all regular in the late summer, autumn and early winter periods.

Key points

• **Normal access restricted to DNS members.**

• **Public access available on Open Days publicised in local press and on DNS website (see contacts overleaf).**

• **Non-member group visits can be arranged (see contacts overleaf).**

• **Visit at high tides when wildfowl and waders are pushed off estuary.**

• **Five bird hides are wheelchair accessible.**

• **Telescope useful.**

• **Field centre with toilets (including disabled) on site.**

• **Nearby Flint and Connah's Quay have all facilities.**

Access details.

(Connah's Quay lies five miles W of Chester).

From England: Take A550 from Liverpool/N Wirral or A5117 from Ellesmere Port/M56, following roads to Queensferry. Turn left 200m after junction of A550 and A5117 at A548, following signs to Flint. Go over the Dee Bridge and turn off dual carriageway at B5129, Connah's Quay exit.

Turn right under A548, then left, following signs to the power station. After a sharp turn right over the railway you will reach a mini-roundabout. The left hand exit has a barrier across the road – this is the entrance to the reserve. On open days there will be someone to let you through and give directions to the hides.

From Flint: Take A548 towards Connah's Quay/Queensferry. After two and a half miles take B5129 Connah's Quay exit off the dual carriageway. Turn left following signs to the power station. See above for reserve entrance details.

From Connah's Quay: Take B5129 towards Flint. Where the road meets A548, go under the dual carriageway. Turn left following signs to the power station. See above for reserve entrance details.

The Ash Pool and adjacent wet meadows should be visited. This area is an 11-acre compound created to attract wintering and passage waders. The area is overlooked by a superb double storey hide, and provides feeding and roosting sites for Wigeon, Mallards, Teal, Redshanks, Curlews, Snipe and Lapwings.

The wet meadows are attractive to breeding Sky Larks, Meadow Pipits and Lapwings in the spring and summer months.

Give yourself enough time to explore the nature trail at the eastern end of the reserve. This passes through a rough scrub area of bramble, hawthorn, birch and elderberry and holds good numbers of breeding Sedge Warblers, Whitethroats and Reed Buntings. In winter thrushes find the area much to their liking.

Contacts

Deeside Naturalists Society – www.deeestuary.co.uk

For group visits, contact DNS Secretary, 21 Woodlands Court, Hawarden, Deeside, Flintshire CH5 3NB or e-mail: deesidenaturalists@btinternet.com

Other nearby sites

Flint Castle, Gronant, RSPB Point of Ayr.

ONE OF THE best birdwatching sites in the whole of Wales, the RSPB's visitor-friendly reserve should not be missed. Lying alongside the A55 coastal route, the reserve could not be easier to access and provides year-round interest. Waders and wildfowl are the main attraction, but the reserve has a reputation for turning up the unexpected.

Target birds

All year – Little Grebe (100%), Little Egret (100%), Gadwall (80%), Red-breasted Merganser (100%). *Spring* – Garganey (20%), Osprey (20%), Little Ringed Plover (40%), Yellow Wagtail (40%). *Summer* – Ruddy Duck (50%), Lesser Whitethroat (70%). *Autumn* – Starling roost (100%). *Winter* – Goldeneye (100%), Peregrine (50%), Water Rail (90%), Jack Snipe (20%), Kingfisher (70%), Grey Wagtail (80%).

Other possible bird species

All year
Cormorant
Grey Heron
Shelduck
Common wildfowl
Buzzard
Sparrowhawk
Kestrel
Oystercatcher
Black-tailed Godwit
Curlew
Herring Gull
Great Black-backed Gull
Lesser Black-backed Gull
Stock Dove
Great Spotted Woodpecker
Pied Wagtail
Chiffchaff
Long-tailed Tit
Linnet

Reed Bunting

Spring
Dunlin
Whimbrel
Common Sandpiper
Black-tailed Godwit
Mediterranean Gull
Other commoner gulls
Grey Wagtail
White Wagtail
Whinchat
Stonechat
Wheatear
Grasshopper Warbler
Common warblers

Summer
Hirundines
Reed Warbler
Sedge Warbler

Whitethroat

Autumn
Goosander
Pintail
Sanderling
Curlew Sandpiper
Little Stint
Bar-tailed Godwit
Greenshank
Green Sandpiper
Whimbrel
Kingfisher
Hirundines
Wheatear
Siskin

Winter
Whooper Swan
Goosander
Dunlin
Rock Pipit

Background information and birding tips

WHENEVER you visit Conwy you should see more than 40 species by completing the circular route of this outstanding reserve, – we have recorded as many as 80 in less than two hours in the autumn, which goes to show its potential. Though it is a site that can be visited for a few minutes or a full day, if you linger you will see a lot more.

The reserve, which opened in 1996, was created from spoil excavated during the construction of the Conwy Tunnel, where the A55 by-passes the historic town of Conwy. The reserve has since

Key points

• Limited access at all times.

• Full access from visitor centre (open 9am to 5pm).

• Free entry to RSPB members – small charge otherwise.

• Easy, flat walking on two miles of trails.

• Three hides and viewing screens.

• On-site shop with drinks and light snacks.

• Cafe open 10am - 5pm.

• Daily updated noticeboard, plus sightings logbook.

• Toilets, including disabled.

• Full wheelchair access.

• Ample free parking.

• Conwy Castle nearby.

Contacts

RSPB – 01492 584 091
e-mail: conwy@rspb.org.uk
Visit www.rspb.org.uk for site information.

established a reputation for good birds.

We recommend starting your visit at the reserve centre (open every day from 9am to 5pm). Here there is a recent sightings board, which will give you an idea of what to expect.

It is worth checking the tide-tables here too, as high tides push birds from the adjacent Conwy estuary onto the reserve to roost.

The views from the visitor centre are stunning, with Conwy Castle, the Conwy Valley, the mountains of the Carneddau, the estuary and reserve lagoons making a fine panorama.

Through the centre's big plate glass windows you overlook lagoons giving close views of many species of wildfowl, waders and gulls.

The feeders attract a good variety of passerines in winter, but also provide amazingly close views of usually elusive Water Rails as they forage underneath on the spilt food.

From the visitor centre walk out onto the trail to a boardwalk alongside a large reedbed, which, in summer, is a good place to see Reed and Sedge Warblers and Reed Buntings close-up.

In autumn and winter the reedbeds provide a roost for thousands of Starlings, whose pre-dusk displays are a spectacle not to be missed.

You'll then reach the Tal-y-Fan hide, a double hide, each half overlooking one of the two lagoons. This is a great vantage point, and if time is limited, the visitor centre and this hide will generally provide a good cross-section of the birds of the reserve. Again the views are superb.

Waders and wildfowl will be present on the lagoons, but the species composition will depend on the season and tide.

Reed and Sedge Warblers are easy to see in summer, while Wigeon graze the causeway between the lagoons in winter. Leave the hide and follow the trail right over a wooden bridge by a pool, which is good for Kingfisher in autumn and winter, but only if you can spot it before it spots you!

Stand on the bridge for a while and watch the poolside bushes that are good for passerines, including Whitethroats and Lesser Whitethroats in spring and summer and Goldcrests and the occasional Blackcap in winter.

At the path's next T-junction you will see the Carneddau hide overlooking the deepest lagoon. This is the best place for Red-breasted Mergansers, Pochards and Tufted Ducks, with Great Crested Grebes in summer. Canada and Greylag Geese should be conspicuous on the islands. Gulls from the adjacent estuary use this lagoon to rest and bathe and should be checked for scarcer species.

Quickly turning right, the path runs alongside dense bramble that is good for warblers in spring and summer and has held Firecrest on several occasions in winter.

From here a scan of the distant ridges for raptors should reveal Buzzard, probably Sparrowhawk, possibly Peregrine, and if your luck's really in, a Goshawk.

Take the next right turn through an area of rough grass, reed and scrub that is again good for warblers in season and, with a bit of luck, Stonechat.

The small creek can hold Water Rail in winter and the occasional Little Egret at any time of the year.

In spring look out for breeding Lapwings but if the birds seem distressed move quickly on, as they probably will have young close to the path.

The trail brings you to the Conwy Estuary with more stunning views over Snowdonia.

If the mud flats are exposed, look for waders and gulls but at high tide wildfowl will be present, including large numbers of Shelduck. Follow the trail alongside the estuary, enjoying spectacular views of Conwy Castle.

Other nearby sites

Caerhun, Great Orme, Little Orme, Llanfairfechan.

Two viewing screens to the right overlook the lagoon and should produce similar species as the Carneddau hide but also look to the right for Kingfisher on the sluice gate in winter.

Next is the Benarth hide, set back from the path a little. Do spend some time here – it has a reputation for turning up unusual birds.

Ask any local birder and you will hear tales of Terek Sandpiper, Little Crake, two Bluethroats together, Black-headed Wagtail and Ortolan Bunting.

It could be you who finds the next mega-rarity but more likely are wildfowl and waders according to season. In winter Wigeon often graze by the hide and Water Rails are regular.

In autumn Snipe give close-up views and Jack Snipe are seen on occasions.

Now you can head back to the track and continue along the estuary on the last leg of the two mile circuit to the visitor centre. This will take you through the car park, where the bushes are often alive with passerines.

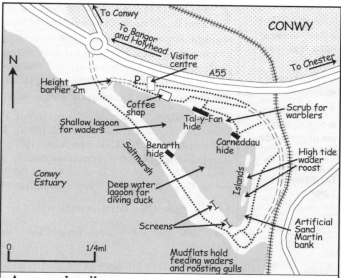

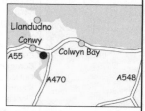

Access details

(Half mile E of Conway town centre, on E bank of river).

The reserve lies alongside A55 North Wales Expressway. From E, leave A55, at turn signposted Deganwy. There is also a brown information sign for the reserve. Get in left hand lane of slip road and turn immediately left at the roundabout. Continue down hill for 200 metres and round to the left, under a two-metre height barrier. Phone the centre if you need it opening. At the far end of the large car park you will find the visitor centre.

The car park has speed ramps, so please drive slowly.

Early autumn is the time when Redstarts are often seen. Chiffchaffs overwinter and have on occasions been joined by a Firecrest.

Call in at the centre to check that nothing has been found while you were on the trails and add your sightings to the logbook. A well-earned cup of tea or coffee can be enjoyed as you have a last scan of the lagoon.

65

Key points

- **Easy access, view from car park.**
- **Telescope essential.**
- **Free parking.**
- **Public toilets on promenade W of car park.**
- **All other facilities in the town.**

CRICCIETH is a very scenic site for birding – to the west lies historic Criccieth Castle, while across the bay, mountains rise from the sea. It is also an easy site to bird as you simply view from the car park at the east end of the promenade. The birding prospects change according to the season, but it is the bay offshore that holds the main interest throughout, and a telescope will be a huge help.

Target birds

All year – Gannet (80%), Fulmar (80%). *Winter/spring/autumn* – Little Gull (60%). *Winter* – Red-throated Diver (90%), Common Scoter (100%), Eider (50%), Purple Sandpiper (90%), Turnstone (100%). *Spring* – Pomarine Skua (50%). *Autumn* – Common Scoter (100%), Arctic Skua (50%), Great Skua (10%), Purple Sandpiper (70%).

Other possible bird species

All year
Red-throated Diver
Cormorant
Shag
Sparrowhawk
Buzzard
Kestrel
Peregrine
Oystercatcher
Ringed Plover
Curlew
Common gull species
Guillemot
Razorbill
Sky Lark
Meadow Pipit
Rock Pipit
Grey Wagtail
Pied Wagtail
Stonechat

Raven
Common thrushes and finches

Spring
Manx Shearwater
Gannet
Grey Heron
Knot
Purple Sandpiper

Spring/autumn/winter
Great Crested Grebe
Fulmar
Shelduck
Wigeon
Teal
Red-breasted Merganser

Grey Plover
Knot
Sanderling
Bar-tailed Godwit
Turnstone
Mediterranean Gull
Little Gull
Common Gull

Summer
Fulmar
Manx Shearwater
Gannet
Mallard
Lesser Black-backed Gull
Kittiwake
Sandwich Tern
Common Tern
Hirundines
Whitethroat

Background information and birding tips

ON A WINTER birding visit, seaduck and divers offshore will provide the main focus. Try to pick a calm, overcast day as viewing birds will be much easier if you are not looking into reflected glare from choppy waters.

Large numbers of Common Scoters will be in the bay but the flocks can be distant so a telescope will be a great help.

Careful checking of the flocks may produce small numbers of Eiders. Red-throated Divers will also be offshore, though you would be very fortunate indeed to find any other species of diver.

Other possibilities are Velvet Scoters and Scaup but bear in mind that though both species are probably annual visitors, they remain scarce. Cormorant, Shag,

Contacts

Pwllheli Tourist Information – 01758 613 000.

Guillemot and Razorbill should be found without too much difficulty.

Check the boulder beach below the car park for waders. The main targets are Purple Sandpipers and they should be found easily enough alongside the commoner Turnstones and Oystercatchers also feeding here.

The crumbling cliffs to the east of the car park regularly have Stonechats and Rock Pipits and if your luck is really in, a Black Redstart.

The bay offshore has recently been discovered as an area to observe skuas on their northward migration during spring. May is the peak month with a few records from April and June but much is still to be learned about this exciting passage.

Check the weather forecasts for strong south-westerly winds which push the skuas into the north-east corner of Cardigan Bay where they can be seen from Criccieth promenade. Pomarine Skuas are the species most likely to be blown in, sometimes in tight flocks of up to 30 birds!

Small numbers of Arctic and Great Skuas have also been seen and one Long-tailed Skua to date – surely more to come with more coverage. Little Gulls are regular,

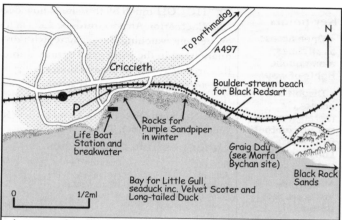

Access details

(Five miles W of Porthmadog).

Take the A497 from Porthmadog to Criccieth. In the centre of the town, a minor road passes directly in front of the castle. Follow this road heading eastwards out of the town as it follows the coast along the line of the bay.

Just before the road bends inland to go over a railway, there is a car park on the right hand side. Park here to view the beach and shoreline.

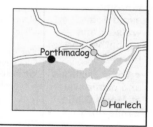

sometimes in good numbers, offshore.

During autumn, strong south-westerly winds are again the key to the best birdwatching. Seabirds migrating down the Irish Sea are blown into the north-east corner of Cardigan Bay in gales, meaning any seabird could be recorded. We are certain that if the site received better coverage, more records would come.

Little Gulls are one of the most likely species to be seen feeding over the surf. Kittiwakes are also likely, along with Gannets, Fulmars

and terns. There have been several records of Grey Phalaropes riding the stormy seas just off the car park, so check carefully as these tiny waders are easy to overlook.

Purple Sandpipers should be found on the boulder beach. Rock Pipit and Stonechats are resident, and keep an eye out for Black Redstarts, particularly in November.

Other nearby sites

Borth-y-Gest, Morfa Bychan beach, Porthmadog.

Key points

• **Open access at all times along public rights of way.**

• **Disabled access via metalled roads but not footpath from Morfa Lodge to Fort Belan.**

• **High tide visits are most productive.**

• **Visit early morning to avoid dog walkers and sunbathers on beach.**

• **Toilet facilities and picnic site at Morfa Dinlle, a mile north.**

• **Refreshments available in Dinas Dinlle or nearby Caernarfon.**

• **Strictly no access to airfield.**

Contacts

RSPB Bangor office
– 01248 363 800

THOUGH much of this site is now occupied by Caernarfon Airport, birdwatchers can still find plenty of excitement watching the sea here, with divers more or less guaranteed in the winter and spring. Raptors flying around this area of rough fields and dunes lying to the west of Foryd Bay are also good in those seasons.

Target birds   *Winter/spring* – Red-throated Diver (95%), Great Northern Diver (90%), Hen Harrier (50%), Merlin (60%), Golden Plover (100%), Twite (20%).

Other possible bird species

All year	Common Tern	Arctic Skua
Buzzard	Hirundines	Kittiwake
Kestrel	White Wagtail	Sandwich Tern
Common gulls	Wheatear	Common Tern
Common seabirds		Hirundines
Lapwing	*Summer*	White Wagtail
Curlew	Oystercatcher	Wheatear
Sky Lark	Ringed Plover	
Stonechat	Lapwing	*Recent scarce birds*
Linnet		Osprey
	Autumn	Dotterel
Spring	Manx Shearwater	Sharp-tailed Sandpiper
Sanderling	Gannet	Hoopoe
Whimbrel	Sanderling	Richard's Pipit
Sandwich Tern	Whimbrel	Ortolan Bunting

Background information and birding tips

THE SMALL seaside resort of Dinas Dinlle is positioned on the south-western side of Morfa Dinlle, a peninsula which comprises a dune system in the north, a complex of low-lying fields in the interior, including Caernarfon Airport airfield, and boulder clay cliffs to the southwest.

The area around these cliffs is worth checking for Chough. The red-billed member of the crow family has also been seen in fields opposite the airfield.

Flocks of Lapwings and Curlews are a familiar sight on the peninsula during the autumn and winter months , while the airfield and neighbouring pastures are especially noted for sizable flocks

of Golden Plover. This area, which will need at least half a day to cover thoroughly, attracts a variety of migrants, often including large numbers of White Wagtails and Wheatears.

Raptors, including Merlins and Hen Harriers, occur regularly during the autumn and winter.

The western shore overlooks Caernarfon Bay, which hosts good numbers of divers and a variety of seabirds in season. Both Great Northern and Red-throated Divers winter offshore in small numbers, but during March and April their numbers increase and well over 100 Red-throated have been recorded on several occasions. Black-throated Divers are infrequent visitor during these months.

Late summer can produce Arctic Skuas, which are attracted by the flocks of terns. The beach supports passage waders, which include good numbers of Whimbrels and Sanderlings.

The road between the resort and the airfield is worth checking in winter for small numbers of Twite as well as ubiquitous Rock Pipits. Snow Bunting is an occasional species in winter along the beach towards Fort Belan (constructed in 1775 to counter any invasion threat by Napoleon's troops).

High tide is the best time to view divers and other seabirds from anywhere along the road between the village and the airfield.

To see waders you'll have to be prepared for a bit of a trek along the cobbled beach but your reward will be shorebirds such as Turnstones, Whimbrels and Sanderlings.

The airfield, which can be viewed from the top of the beach, is the best area for Golden Plovers and other grassland waders but get there before the dog walkers and sunbathers arrive.

In 2007 the RSPB acquired an area of wet fields and shallow pools between Morfa Dinlle and Foryd Bay to manage for breeding waders (Lapwings in particular) and winter wildfowl. The area can be viewed from the public footpath running from south of the airfield on a metalled road to Blythe Farm (no vehicular access).

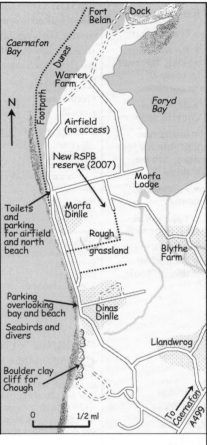

Other nearby sites

Aberdesach, Foryd Bay, Pontllyfni.

Access details

(Approx. three miles SW of Caernarfon).

Drive S from Caernarfon on A487 to Llanwnda. Bear right onto A499 and after about two miles take a minor road on right, signposted Llandwrog.

Proceed through Llandwrog village to the small coastal resort of Dinas Dinlle, where there is road/beachside parking at SH 436 566.

For the airfield and the northern section of beach, proceed N along coast road to park at SH 431 582. Viewing opportunities are generally limited to the coast road and beach. Though there is a public footpath that runs through the saltmarsh on the opposite side of the road from the picnic site at SH 434 575, it is rarely productive.

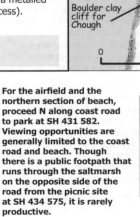

69

Key points

- **Free parking.**
- **No facilities at site. Nearest in town of Beaumaris.**
- **Beautiful coastal scenery.**
- **Paths not suitable for less able, can be muddy.**
- **Telescope useful.**
- **Take great care near cliff edge.**
- **Owned by National Trust.**

THE OPPORTUNITY to get sightings of Black Guillemots and other seabirds, swathes of wildflowers on the cliff-top heath and outstanding coastal scenery make this stretch of cliffs, three miles north of Beaumaris on Anglesey, a 'must visit' destination in spring.

Target birds   *April to July* – Peregrine (80%), Black Guillemot (100%), Rock Pipit (90%), Stonechat (100%), Raven (100%).

Other possible bird species

All year	Starling	Swift
Fulmar	Chaffinch	Sky Lark
Shag	Greenfinch	Hirundines
Cormorant	Linnet	Meadow Pipit
Sparrowhawk		Whinchat
Buzzard	*Spring*	Wheatear
Kestrel	Manx Shearwater	Grasshopper Warbler
Peregrine	Gannet	Sedge Warbler
Oystercatcher	Eider	Whitethroat
Herring Gull	Common Scoter	Lesser Whitethroat
Great Black-backed Gull	Red-breasted Merganser	Chiffchaff
Rock Pipit	Common gull species	Willow Warbler
Stonechat	Kittiwake	Goldfinch
Common thrushes	Sandwich Tern	Reed Bunting
Magpie	Guillemot	
Carrion Crow	Razorbill	
Raven	Cuckoo	

Background information and birding tips

FOR BIRDWATCHERS the main attraction here is Black Guillemot, the elegant auk species that breeds along this beautiful rocky coastline. Scan the sea from the car park, as very often you can see one of them straightaway.

A footpath runs from the car park to the cliff top, then west for about a quarter-of-a-mile. With patience, you should see Black Guillemots along this stretch reasonably easily but take great care along the cliff edge, as the grass can be slippery and a tumble is always a possibility.

Calm days are best for visiting, as the birds tend to spend more time

loafing about just offshore. Look out for the vivid red legs as the birds dive.

Stiff-winged Fulmars should be easy to see as they patrol at eye level along the cliffs and it is worth scanning the sky regularly here for a hunting Peregrine, or Ravens, as they are commonly sighted here.

Additional birds on the sea should include Guillemots, Cormorants and Shags. Scanning further offshore may well produce passing Gannets and Kittwakes and, with luck, Manx Shearwaters.

The flower-clad heathland around the car park has a good population of Stonechats, and even

Contacts

National Trust, Llandudno – 01492 860 123.

occasionally a Chough, while the bushes provide cover for migrants in season.

Both Common and Lesser Whitethroat can be found in the hedgerows, while steps down from the car park provide access to the beach frequented by Rock Pipits.

Very few birdwatchers visit this site outside the April-to-July period (the time that the Black Guillemots are known to be in residence). However, there is still a good chance of seeing the auk species at other times of year – after all, it is a species that is resident throughout the year at other sites.

The coastline looks suitable for wintering Turnstones and maybe even Purple Sandpipers – both species overwinter at nearby Penmon Point to the east.

In the opposite direction, Red Wharf Bay holds wintering Red-throated Divers and Common Scoters, so it is worth scanning for both from the cliffs of Fedw Fawr.

Peregrines and Ravens are both residents in the area and as Choughs are regularly seen at Penmon Point, it is perfectly possible you may spot the charismatic corvid here too.

Why not try a visit outside the 'peak' season and let us know what you find? The site is very compact and can be comfortably covered in an hour, so it won't take too much effort to add to the world's overall knowledge of the site.

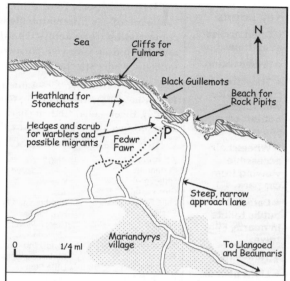

Access details

(Three miles N of Beaumaris).

From Beaumaris, take B5109 coast road NE for two miles to Llangoed. Turn left just before the only pub and continue along minor road for one mile.

Turn right, downhill, then first left into the single-track lane that leads down to the small car park. Please drive slowly and be prepared to reverse some way to find a passing place should you meet another vehicle.

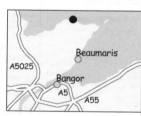

Park here, then continue on foot along the path that runs down to the cliff top. Walk W as far as the fence; then retrace your steps to the car park.

Other nearby sites

Penmon Point, Red Wharf Bay.

Key points

- **Open access at all times.**

- **Free parking.**

- **Stay close to car or ensure valuables are not left on show.**

- **Wheelchair-accessible viewing from car park.**

- **Cafes and public toilets in nearby Flint town.**

- **Tidal site.**

- **Light best in afternoon.**

- **Telescope useful.**

THE REMNANTS of Flint Castle, lying on the west bank of the internationally important Dee Estuary, gives commanding views across the tidal mudflats and salt marsh and if you time your visit correctly you'll be able to enjoy a fantastic wader spectacle.

Target birds
Winter – Little Egret (100%), Pintail (100%), Peregrine (70%), Merlin (50%), Grey Plover (100%), Knot (100%), Black-tailed Godwit (100%), Bar-tailed Godwit (100%), Mediterranean Gull (40%), Twite (80%).

Other possible bird species

All year	*Autumn*	
Cormorant	Great Crested Grebe	Common Tern
Little Egret	Wigeon	Meadow Pipit
Grey Heron	Teal	
Mute Swan	Red-breasted Merganser	*Winter*
Shelduck	Hen Harrier	Great Crested Grebe
Buzzard	Golden Plover	Wigeon
Peregrine	Lapwing	Teal
Sparrowhawk	Sanderling	Goldeneye
Kestrel	Curlew Sandpiper	Red-breasted Merganser
Oystercatcher	Little Stint	Hen Harrier
Ringed Plover	Dunlin	Sanderling
Black-tailed Godwit	Snipe	Grey Plover
Curlew	Bar-tailed Godwit	Knot
Redshank	Whimbrel	Dunlin
Great Black-backed Gull	Spotted Redshank	Snipe
Lesser Black-backed Gull	Greenshank	Common gull species
Herring Gull	Common Sandpiper	Yellow-legged Gull
Sky Lark	Yellow-legged Gull	Meadow Pipit
Linnet	Mediterranean Gull	Rock Pipit
Reed Bunting	Sandwich Tern	Grey Wagtail
		Raven

Background information and birding tips

THE DEE ESTUARY holds internationally important populations of waders and wildfowl, and watching from alongside the ruins of Flint Castle, is a great place to witness their impressive numbers.

Originally built by Edward I in the late 13th Century to help subdue the rebellious Welsh population, the castle was partly demolished after the English Civil War.

On arrival it can be rather daunting looking out across the vast expense of mudflats, sandbanks and salt marsh but if you have timed your visit well, a spring tide (9m-plus), will just be coming in.

Set up your telescope on the dirt track bordering the car park near the lifeboat station, just south of the castle and you are now ready to catch the action created by the incoming tide.

At first, the flocks of waders, wildfowl and gulls will be distant and scattered. As the tide floods the creeks and creeps across the mud flats, birds move ever closer and flocks are concentrated.

In autumn and winter, thousands of Black-tailed Godwits make a breathtaking spectacle as they sweep back and forth across the rising tide in tight flocks, perhaps buzzed by a Peregrine.

Huge rafts of beautiful Pintail ride the incoming water, while hundreds of colourful Shelduck are pushed closer inshore and ranks of Knot and Dunlin shuffle ahead of the fast advancing tide. Flocks of commoner gulls are marooned on sandbanks before being flooded off and moving to the disappearing shoreline.

It all makes a fast-moving scene involving thousands of birds that is spellbinding to watch. Time flies as the tide marches ever closer and soon you will be panicking to make sure you have checked every flock for something even rarer.

With luck the flood waters will push a flock of Twite out of the marsh up to the tideline or onto the adjacent rugby pitch, where great views can be enjoyed. Little Egrets are also likely to be pushed out of the creeks by the rising tide.

With so many birds on the move, there is always the chance of something special and if the site was better watched, it would no doubt produce a good few rarities. As it is, you are unlikely to meet many other birders here.

In the autumn, careful checking of the Dunlin flock should produce Curlew Sandpipers and perhaps a Little Stint, and with more luck, who knows what?

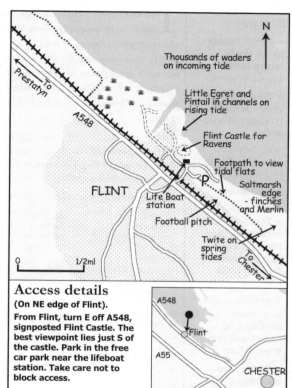

Access details

(On NE edge of Flint).

From Flint, turn E off A548, signposted Flint Castle. The best viewpoint lies just S of the castle. Park in the free car park near the lifeboat station. Take care not to block access.

Masses of Wigeon, Teal and Mallard add to the colour and sound of the scene.

The rising tide is a good time to encounter hunting raptors, particularly Peregrines, Merlins and Sparrowhawks.

If visibility is good, and you have a high quality telescope, you can scan the English side for hunting Hen Harriers, or perhaps a Marsh Harrier or Short-eared Owl, though, even with the best optical equipment, the views are pretty poor.

Gull flocks should be checked, as there are regular sightings of Mediterranean and Yellow-legged Gulls here. Given the numbers of gulls on the Dee, just about anything is possible!

Other nearby sites

Connah's Quay, Point of Ayr.

73

Key points

- **Open access at all times along public rights of way.**
- **Disabled and pram access to eastern side only.**
- **Toilets and other facilities in Caernarfon.**
- **Telescope useful.**
- **Terrain flat – hard surface road on east can be covered on foot or in vehicle.**
- **Path to west is usually muddy and too rough for wheelchair use.**
- **Allow three hours to cover the site in depth.**

THIS IS a site close to Caernarfon's splendid castle, with year-round birding interest, easy access and good viewing conditions. It makes an ideal retreat in poor weather as the east side can be birded entirely from a car. With the possible exception of high summer, there is always a good selection of wildfowl and waders and it is one of the easiest places in Wales to see a Jack Snipe at the spot indicated on the map.

Target birds

All year – Little Egret (80%). *Spring* – Greenshank (80%). *Autumn/winter* – Dark and pale-bellied Brent Goose (90%), Greenshank (80%), Spotted Redshank (40%), Jack Snipe (80%).

Other possible bird species

All year	Summer	
Cormorant	Sandwich Tern	Kingfisher
Common wildfowl	Whitethroat	Rock Pipit
Shelduck	Stonechat	Grey Wagtail
Goosander		Stonechat
Red-breasted Merganser	Autumn	
Buzzard	Grey Plover	Occasional
Sparrowhawk	Turnstone	Hen Harrier
Kestrel	Dunlin	Curlew Sandpiper
Oystercatcher	Black and Bar-tailed	Little Stint
Ringed Plover	Godwits	Ruff
Redshank	Snipe	Arctic Skua
Curlew	Sandwich Tern	Mediterranean Gull
Common gulls	Common Tern	
Sky Lark	Kingfisher	Recent scarce and rare birds
	Grey Wagtail	Spoonbill
Spring		American Wigeon
Great Crested Grebe	Winter	Black-winged Stilt
Common Sandpiper	Pintail	Pectoral Sandpiper
Black-tailed Godwit	Wigeon	Ring-billed Gull
Sandwich Tern	Peregrine	Glaucous Gull
Wheatear	Merlin	Iceland Gull
	Lapwing	Forster's Tern
	Snipe	Hoopoe
		Shore Lark

Background information and birding tips

FORYD BAY, a shallow estuary at the southern end of the Menai Strait, is bounded on its western side by a dune-covered shingle spit that constricts the entrance to the bay. The intertidal area within the bay consists of mud and sand flats.

A large saltmarsh stretches along the western shore in front of a flood defence embankment.

As part of a network of estuaries at the southern end of the Menai Strait, it is used by large numbers of wintering wildfowl and

Contacts

Key to hide and leaflet available from Gwynedd County Council (tel. 01286 672 255).

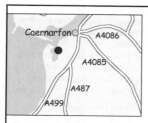

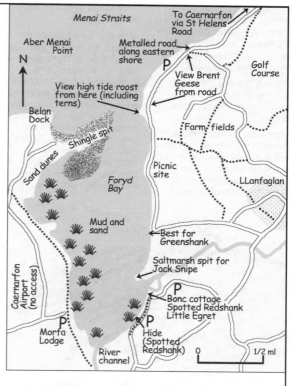

Access details

(Approx. 2 miles SW of Caernarfon).

There are several access points to E side of bay, all via minor roads that lead off A487 and A499 S of Caernarfon. Roadside parking along foreshore road can be accessed by taking the first right turn into St. Helens Road after crossing river bridge on A487 on S side of Caernarfon. It runs adjacent to the river and the shore before turning inland at SH 453 598. There is a picnic site at SH 453 603.

At next T-junction a left turn will take you back to your starting point. For views of the southern bay and access to roadside parking and bird hide located at SH 452 586), turn right and then first right again through Saron. More parking near mouth of Afon Gwyfai at SH 453 588.

The W side can only be accessed on foot via a footpath, which

runs in both directions from the campsite at Morfa Lodge (SH 444 587). Follow signs to Caernarfon Airport off

A499 through Llandwrog and Dinas Dinlle. There is roadside parking at the Airport (SH 443 585).

waders. Birds can often be seen commuting between Foryd Bay and the Braint.

The site holds large numbers of wintering Wigeon, which start to return from late July onwards, with a peak of more than 3,000 birds in November. Numbers decrease from January onwards with just a few small flocks remaining into April.

It is one of the few sites in

North Wales where both the *bernica* (dark-bellied) and *hrota* (pale-bellied) races of Brent Geese occur in reasonable numbers, with mixed flocks of more than 100 birds in mid-winter.

Time spent checking the wildfowl flocks has been rewarded in the past with the occasional Greater Scaup or even American Wigeon,

which has occurred in several winters.

Greenshanks are another speciality here and they can occur in every month of the year, though most are seen on return passage from July to October, when up to 30 can be present. During the winter months expect to find up to ten birds. Spotted Redshank is a regular

75

passage visitor in small numbers, and one or two birds often over-winter. Ruff, Curlew Sandpipers and Little Stints are regular in small numbers from August to October.

During the late 1980s, the bay was one of the few reliable sites for Little Egret in Britain.

Following its recent dramatic increase the species may have lost a little of its attraction, but is still always worth seeing. At this site Little Egrets are found in every month of the year,

occasionally in double figure numbers.

The site is best visited two to three hours either side of high tide. At these times wildfowl will move close inshore and wader flocks will be concentrated on restricted areas of mud and sand, while at high tide most birds roost on the western side of the bay. Oystercatchers, Dunlins and other waders tend to roost along Belan Point, which can be viewed from the foreshore road or picnic

site on the eastern side. Terns regularly roost on Belan Point, especially Sandwich, but also Common and Arctic. Little and Roseate Terns have also occurred in recent years here. Arctic Skuas are sometimes attracted to these tern flocks.

On an incoming tide Redshanks and Wigeon get squeezed onto the saltmarsh, which is best viewed from the hide on the south-eastern side of the Bay. It is also possible to get a closer look from a public footpath along the embankment on the western side.

In winter the saltmarsh is also a haven for many Snipe, with a few Jack Snipe, plus good numbers of Sky Larks and Rock Pipits. Water Pipit is an occasional, usually hard-to-locate, winter visitor.

At low tide wildfowl and waders can be seen all along the bay and are best viewed from the eastern shore. Most birds tend to congregate along the main channel, which meanders from the mouths of the Afon Gwyfai and Afon Carrog down towards the entrance of the bay.

Low tide is best for locating feeding flocks of Brent Geese. They tend to occur around the bay entrance and along the foreshore towards Caernarfon.

The muddier inner estuary near the mouth of the Afon Gwyrfai has been good in the past for scarcer waders and gulls, with both Iceland and Glaucous Gulls reported in recent winters.

Elegant Greenshanks frequent Foryd Bay for most of the year.

Other nearby sites

Afon Seiont for wildfowl and gulls (best vantage points are MANWEB Offices/Depot at SH481621 and Age Concern Centre at SH481623), Dinas Dinlle.

HEAD FOR this magnificent peninsula to enjoy superb views of Anglesey and the North Wales coast. For birdwatching the best months to visit are from March to November, when a whole day can easily be spent exploring the headland. The facilities of Llandudno, the premier resort town of Wales, are adjacent.

Target birds

All year – Peregrine (70%), Stonechat (95%), Chough (50%). *Spring/summer* – Fulmar (100%), Kittiwake (100%), Guillemot (100%), Razorbill (100%).

Other possible bird species

Spring
Hirundines
Wheatear
Whinchat
Ring Ouzel
Redstart
Tree Pipit
Grasshopper Warbler
Whitethroat
Willow Warbler
Siskin
Lesser Redpoll

Autumn
Dotterel
Short-eared Owl
Black Redstart

Richard's Pipit
Snow Bunting
Lapland Bunting
Common thrushes
Common finches
Occasional rarities

Winter
Red-throated Diver
Great Northern Diver
Common Scoter
Black Redstart
Snow Bunting

Recent rare and scarce birds
Osprey

Red Kite
Marsh Harrier
Hobby
Bee-eater
Hoopoe
Shore Lark
Short-toed Lark
Richard's Pipit
Woodchat Shrike
Isabelline Shrike
Sardinian Warbler
Yellow-browed Warbler
Pallas's Warbler
Arctic Redpoll

Background information and birding tips

AT FIRST SIGHT this great whaleback of a peninsula can seem a daunting place for birdwatching but over the years local birders have discovered those areas that produce good sightings and those that rarely seem to do so.

The two main reasons for a birder to visit the site are to see the breeding specialities, and to see visible migration taking place. During spring and summer the seabird colony has several hundred pairs of both Guillemots and Razorbills, with large numbers of Kittiwakes.

Nesting Fulmars, Cormorants and Shags can be easily seen from the Marine Drive toll road, which goes all the way around the outer perimeter of the peninsula.

To walk it at a leisurely pace takes around three hours, or you can pay the toll and drive, stopping at likely spots to view the cliffs.

The best vantage point is by the old lighthouse from which you can overlook the auk/Kittiwake colony below. Peregrines breed in this area and the short grass clifftop is a favourite of Choughs.

A little further on you come to the 'Rest and Be Thankful' café. From here, follow the concrete path to the left which takes you onto the

Key points

- **Open access at all times.**

- **Drivers' toll charge (£2) does not cover summit.**

- **Pay car park at summit but free elsewhere.**

- **Extremely busy during summer months.**

- **Summit can be reached from Llandudno by car, tram or, if you are very fit, on foot.**

- **Toilet facilities by cemetary (SH 769 839).**

- **Disabled access to Marine Drive and St Tudno's churchyard.**

- **Paths around limestone pavement not accessible by wheelchair.**

- **Food and drink in nearby Llandudno.**

Contacts

Conwy Countryside Services – 01492 575 200.

Stiff-winged Fulmars soar on the thermals of the Great Orme.

area known as the Limestone Pavement, which is exactly what it is to the geologist. In summer there will be breeding Stonechats, Sky Larks and Meadow Pipits, and you should also keep a look out for the unique sub-species of silver-studded blue butterfly that is found here.

Offshore from this high point Manx Shearwaters and Gannets should be seen with a little perseverance, while a strong northerly will produce a small chance of a skua or Storm Petrel.

The Great Orme protrudes a long way into the sea and as a result it attracts many tired migrants during the spring and autumn seasons. The best time of day to witness this is definitely early morning, the sooner after daylight the

better. There are two main migrant traps – the Limestone Pavement and the area in, and around, St Tudno's churchyard.

The best route, which takes two to three hours to cover on foot, starts on the grassy slope overlooking St Tudno's churchyard. This area often has Wheatears, chats and pipits in spring and autumn.

Walk down into the graveyard, which is good for Black Redstarts, and check the bushes behind it, as these can shelter good numbers of thrushes (including Ring Ouzels), warblers and crests during both migrations.

Walk back to where you parked on the grass and head up to a dry stone wall at the top of the gentle slope. Follow

the dirt track, viewing the heather on your right and the sheep fields to your left. Listen for pipits, finches and buntings calling as they pass overhead in a westerly direction.

It is always worth checking the hawthorns by the wall, as they have held good birds in the past, including Red-breasted Flycatcher, Firecrest, and, more regularly, Ring Ouzel in spring.

At the end of the wall you will have reached the Limestone Pavement. Explore this area thoroughly as it will usually be alive with Sky Larks, Meadow Pipits and Wheatears, with rarer species such as Dotterel, Richard's Pipit and Lapland Bunting found among them every autumn.

Access details

(Alongside Llandudno).

From E take the Llandudno turn (junction 20) off A55 North Wales Expressway, following signs to the promenade. From W, take Junction 20 to the same point. Keeping the sea immediately on your right, head to the Great Orme toll booth. After paying, follow Marine Drive around headland until it returns to Llandudno at West Shore.

[Map showing Great Orme area: GREAT ORME, Main seabird colony, Marine Drive, Toilets, Cemetery, St Tudno's church, Limestone Pavement, Summit, Tramway, Cable car, Toll booth, Very steep, Visitor Centre Parking (fee payable), Marine Drive, Empire Hotel, Mostyn Street, LLANDUDNO. Scale 0 – 1/2 ml. North arrow.]

To reach parking area above St Tudno's church turn left off Marine Drive after one and a quarter miles, clearly signposted to church. To reach lighthouse area and Limestone Pavement continue along Marine Drive.

To avoid paying the toll, drive to the top of Mostyn Street, which runs parallel to the Promenade and can be easily accessed from it. Turn right at Empire Hotel, then immediately left by the side of the hotel, and proceed up the very steep hill to the summit alongside the tram tracks. From here, reach St Tudno's church by turning right on the road that crosses the tracks. Marine Drive is not usually accessible from this route without payment of the toll. Though free, this route is not for the faint-hearted as the road is very steep and narrow in places.

All of the Great Orme can be accessed on foot or cycle from Llandudno, though you would certainly have to be fit

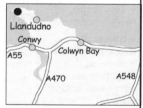

[Location map: Llandudno, Conwy, Colwyn Bay, A55, A470, A548]

to follow the tram lines. Much easier, follow signs for the Tramway from the town, catch the Victorian tram all the way up to the summit, and then walk down!

When you feel you've exhausted the area, walk back to the wall and follow it further around the sheep fields. Snow Buntings favour the grassy area around an obvious cairn in both early spring and autumn.

Keep following the wall to the Orme's summit, where you will find the Country Park visitor centre with its list of recent bird sightings. From here follow the path back to your car.

Please note that outside the summer months, when the birds mentioned are more or less guaranteed, the Great Orme can be a somewhat frustrating place for birdwatchers!

Most days are quiet but if conditions are calm and clear you could see thousands of birds moving overhead, or after bad weather, hundreds of tired birds sheltering upon it.

Other nearby sites

RSPB Conwy, Little Orme.

79

Key points

- Only Little Tern colony in Wales.
- Follow wardens' on-site instructions to minimise disturbance.
- Shingle beach with dunes and stream outfall.
- Free parking.
- Paths not suitable for less able.
- Warm clothes essential in winter.
- Telescope recommended.
- Shops at Gronant village and Prestatyn. Rhyl has many cafes and eating places.
- Inland, Rhuddlan is more pleasant and has all facilities.

Contacts

Debighshire County Council Countryside Services – 01824 708 261.

Prestatyn Tourist Information – 01745 889 092.

THE RAISED shingle beach at Gronant Beach, near Prestatyn is famous for being the last remaining nesting site for Little Terns in Wales. It is a good site in autumn for seeing passage waders, while in winter, the exposed beach is often home to Snow Buntings and healthy numbers of gulls at the stream outfall.

Target birds

Spring/summer – Little Tern (100%). *Autumn* – Jack Snipe (50%), Curlew Sandpiper (50%), Little Stint (50%), Arctic Skua (70%), Mediterranean Gull (70%). *Winter* – Merlin (70%), waders (100%), gulls (100%), Short-eared Owl (50%), Snow Bunting (80%). *Occasional* – Shore Lark, Glaucous Gull.

Other possible bird species

Spring/summer		*Winter*
Ringed Plover	Reed Bunting	Peregrine
Oystercatcher		Sanderling
Sandwich Tern	*Autumn*	Knot
Sky Lark	Seabirds	Grey Plover
Grasshopper Warbler	Waders	Dunlin
Whitethroat	Gulls	
	Terns	

Background information and birding tips

THE MAIN spring and summer attraction of this site, located one mile east of Prestatyn, is the last remaining Little Tern colony in the principality.

It is best to park at Presthaven Caravan Park and report to reception that you are there to see the Little Terns. From the main gate, head across the road to a footpath gate. Follow the path and then turn right over the footbridge across the dyke and head north through the dunes.

This path leads to the warden's hut on the edge of the shingle ridge and he will be able to show you the birds without disturbance. In the unlikely event that the site is not wardened, view the ridge from the dunes.

Take great care not to disturb these rare breeding birds and under no circumstances enter the fenced-off areas.

Also look for Ringed Plovers nesting among the Little Terns. Sky Larks should be seen and heard in the dunes, while the area around the footbridge can hold singing Grasshopper Warblers, Whitethroats and Reed Buntings.

For the best autumn and winter viewing, park at the end of the road just before the entrance to Presthaven Caravan Park, taking care not to block any access. Take the footpath opposite the park entrance and turn right over the footbridge across the dyke and continue north through the dunes.

Check any wet areas for Snipe or, with luck, a Jack Snipe, and keep an eye open for hunting raptors. On reaching the open beach, carefully check the shingle ridge for Snow Buntings, which are easy to overlook on this large open habitat. Gronant Beach has held Shore Larks in the past but

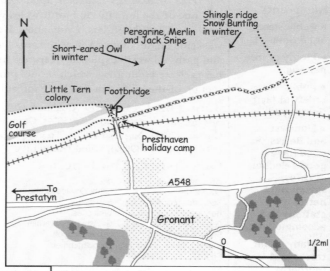

more likely are parties of wintering Sky Larks along the tide line and dune edge.

At high tide, a large wader roost may assemble on the shingle ridge. Take care not to disturb these birds – view from a distance with a telescope. Most will be Dunlin and Ringed Plovers, but Knot, Grey Plovers and Sanderlings should all be present.

Check the shoreline for gulls and scan offshore for Red-breasted Mergansers, Common Scoters and perhaps a Red-throated Diver. Retrace your steps through the dunes, looking out for Stonechats, back to the road.

Continue your walk eastwards through Presthaven Caravan Park past the offices, bearing left onto a sandy track behind the caravans. This path runs along the border between the dunes and a marsh.

Snipe, Jack Snipe and Reed Buntings are all possible sightings, while occasional Short-eared Owls, Merlins and Peregrines hunt the marsh and dunes beyond.

After half a mile, a freshwater stream runs onto the beach, attracting large numbers of gulls to bathe. Climb the high dune overlooking the outfall and find a spot out of the wind for an excellent view. Spend a long time scanning with a telescope as scarce species, particularly

Access details

(Approx one mile E of Prestatyn).

Leave Prestatyn heading E on A548. After just over one mile, turn left in Gronant on minor road signposted for Presthaven. Continue over the railway.

In summer: **Report to the Presthaven Caravan Park reception. Free parking is available if you ask. Stay well back from the fenced-off Little Tern nesting area and view with a telescope.**

In winter: **Park carefully on the road before the entrance to the Presthaven Caravan**

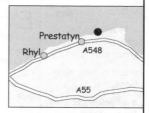

Park. Check signs to ensure parking is permitted at this time of year.

At other times of year: Follow the footpath through the sand dunes onto the shingle beach and carefully check the whole area.

Mediterranean Gulls, are regular visitors. Waders often feed at low tide and can often include Knot, Grey Plovers and Sanderlings.

For seawatching, the Point

of Ayr, just to the east, is a much better site to try your luck.

Other nearby sites

Flint Castle, Llanddulas, Pensarn, Point of Ayr.

81

Key points

- **Public access at all times.**
- **Plenty of free parking.**
- **Public toilets at Llyn Geirionydd.**
- **Llanrwst and Betws-y-Coed have a good selection of cafes, restaurants, petrol stations and accommodation.**
- **Many public tracks and footpaths.**
- **Great scenery.**
- **Many birds can be seen from the road.**
- **Early morning best.**
- **Weekends and Bank Holidays can be very busy.**

Contacts

Forest Enterprise, Gwydyr Uchaf, Llanrwst, Conwy – 01492 640 578.

THIS BEAUTIFUL area of upland conifer woodland is one of the few sites in North Wales where it is possible to see and hear Nightjars. Lying above Betws-y-Coed on the west side of the Conwy Valley, the area has numerous tracks and paths all worth exploring in spring and summer. We have selected four areas which should provide a good cross-section of the birds that this huge forest holds.

Target birds   *All year* – Goshawk (20%), Crossbill (70%). *Spring/summer* – Woodcock (50%), Common Sandpiper (90%), Cuckoo (70%), Nightjar (70%), Tree Pipit (90%), Pied Flycatcher (80%), Redstart (90%), Wood Warbler (90%).

Other possible bird species

All year	Spring	Occasional
Goosander	Great Crested Grebe	Osprey
Red-breasted Merganser	Snipe	Honey Buzzard
Buzzard	Whinchat	
Peregrine	Grasshopper Warbler	
Sparrowhawk	Lesser Redpoll	
Raven	Yellowhammer	
Coal Tit		

Background information and birding tips

EARLY MORNING is the best time to visit the forest, which is mostly owned by the Forestry Commission. Your birding begins as soon as you turn off the B5106, north of Betws-y-Coed, because the tall trees on the right-hand side of the road just beyond the junction are a good spot to look for Wood Warblers.

Continue into the forest and the road begins to climb uphill. It is worth stopping at any convenient lay-by to check for woodland species, which could include Crossbills and, more likely, Siskins.

Shortly after the brow of the hill, park on your left by the small lake, Llyn y Sarnau. This is a good vantage point to scan the treetops for parties of Crossbills, while the surrounding trees may well hold Siskins, Coal Tits and in spring, Willow Warblers, Chiffchaffs and

perhaps a Redstart or Tree Pipit.

A footpath begins on the opposite side of the road to the parking area and leads you into the forest. Follow this path to search for Crossbills, which are regularly encountered in this area.

Look out for any puddles or small pools from which the birds may come down to drink. How far you walk depends upon your time constraints and how quickly you find the Crossbill flocks.

Back at the car, continue along the minor road and after approximately 300m just beyond a small rise, park on your right taking care not to block the forest track. This is a good area for Tree Pipits.

Continuing along the minor road again, take a right turn signposted Llyn Geirionydd. Continue slowly, stopping at any convenient lay-by

Access details

(Approx five miles N of Betws-y-Coed).

From A5 in Betws-y-Coed, turn N onto B5106. After approximately three miles, after passing Gwydyr Castle on right, turn left onto minor road just before you reach a 'T' junction. Take minor road uphill through forest for just over a mile-and-a-half. After the road levels out, you reach a small lake on left, Llyn y Sarnau. Note: this can evaporate completely in a dry summer. Park on left, overlooking lake. A footpath starts on the opposite side of the road, which takes you into the forest.

Continue along minor road for a further half-mile, turning right where it is signposted Llyn Geirionydd to a small car park on left (0.5miles further on). Take footpath on left side of car park across heath area to Llyn Bodgynedd.

To Conwy
A470
Llanrwst
Gwydyr Castle
To Trefrw and Conwy
B5106
N

Llanrychwyn

Goosander, Common Sandpiper

Beech trees hold Wood Warbler

Llyn Geirionydd

Track along shore

PT

Open area for Tree Pipit, Grasshopper Warbler. Listen for Nightjar from small car park

Llyn Bodgynydd

P

Llyn y Sarnau - good area for Siskin, Crossbill

P

Recommended route through forest: good asphalt single track road with passing places

To viewpoint

0   1/2 ml

To Betws-y-Coed

Park at:
SH 777 592 For Llyn Y Sarnau
SH 766 597 For Llyn Bodgynydd
SH 763 603 For Llyn Geirionydd
SH 764 583 For View Point

From car park, drive onto Llyn Geirionydd and park on right by a public toilet block, soon after the road runs alongside the lake.

Retrace your route to the 'T' junction and turn right. Continue on this minor road for half a mile until you reach

A470
A4086   A5
Betws-y-Coed

a parking area on your left. This spot gives a panoramic view across the forest.

to check for forest birds, which again could include Crossbills, Siskins, Redstarts and Tree Pipits.

You soon reach a small car park on your left. Park here and take the footpath through the wooden gate. This path leads to Llyn Bodgynedd and takes you across

a heathland area, which in spring should hold Cuckoos, Tree Pipits and Redstarts.

On reaching the lake, scan carefully for Common Sandpiper around the rocky shore, while the open water may well hold Great

Crested Grebes. All the time, keep scanning the skies for raptors; Buzzard should be easy to see; Sparrowhawk, Kestrel and Peregrine are all possible; but you would be very fortunate indeed to sight a Goshawk.

Retrace your steps to the car, stopping frequently at likely looking spots. Eventually the road brings you to Llyn Geirionydd. Park by the public toilet block on your right and bird this area. Pied Flycatchers, Redstarts and Wood Warblers should be found in the surrounding trees. Scan the lake for Goosanders, Red-breasted Mergansers and Common Sandpipers. If time allows, it may be worth continuing on foot alongside the lake, checking the hillside on your right for Whinchats and Yellowhammers.

Back at the car, retrace your route up the hill and as far as the 'T' junction. Turn right here and continue on this minor road for half a mile until you reach a parking area on your left.

Park here and scan the panoramic view of wooded hills for raptors. A warm spring morning is best as raptors could well be displaying over the woodland. Buzzards should be very easy to see and patience may well be rewarded with views of a Goshawk.

This area is little watched, so better coverage may well produce more regular sightings of scarce raptors. Both Osprey and Honey Buzzard have been seen on spring migration.

Other species to look out for

Other nearby sites
Hafod Woods, Nant Ffrancon Valley.

Migrant Pied Flycatchers are key players in the spring bird spectacle.

include Raven, Pied Flycatcher, Redstart, Wood Warbler, Siskin, Lesser Redpoll and Crossbill.

The Gwydyr Forest is one of the few sites in North Wales where it is possible to see and hear Nightjars. The best place to look is at the small car park near Llyn Bodgynedd (see above for details). You will need to arrive about an hour before dusk; calm warm evenings will give you the best chance.

Walk a little way along the path towards the lake and climb up onto one of the small hills on your right for a panoramic view over the heathland and forest edge.

Wait quietly and patiently

for the Nightjars to begin their bizarre churring call. Please do not be tempted to use tape lures: these are rare breeding birds and as such, the use of tapes is not only illegal but potentially damaging to the birds.

Given luck, you may well see a Nightjar hawking over the heath or along the forest edge.

Dusk here may well produce reeling Grasshopper Warblers, singing Snipe and roding Woodcock. Tawny Owls should be heard calling and perhaps glimpsed. Take plenty of insect repellent and cover up well as the insects can be a real pain on still nights. A torch will be useful to find your way back to the car.

THE HARBOUR, sheltered by a very long breakwater, is a good site to visit in winter months for divers and Black Guillemots. Soldiers Point at the western end of the harbour is a migration hotspot and depending on weather conditions, can produce anything (or nothing)!

Target birds
Winter – Great Northern Diver (40%), Water Rail (60%). *All year* – Black Guillemot (60%), Rock Pipit (70%).

Other possible bird species

All year	Lesser Whitethroat	Blackcap
Oystercatcher	Whitethroat	Goldcrest
Black-headed Gull	Chiffchaff	Spotted Flycatcher
Herring Gull	Willow Warbler	
Stonechat		*Winter*
Jackdaw	*Autumn*	Red-throated Diver
	Fulmar	Little Grebe
Spring	Manx Shearwater	Great Crested Grebe
Collared Dove	Gannet	Cormorant
Meadow Pipit	Merlin	Shag
Wheatear	Arctic Skua	Red-breasted Merganser
Goldcrest	Great Skua	Redshank
	Kittiwake	Turnstone
Summer	House Martin	Linnet
Grasshopper Warbler	Meadow Pipit	
Sedge Warbler	Garden Warbler	

Background information and birding tips

HOLYHEAD HARBOUR used to be frequented by Europe's three commonest divers and five species of grebe, but nowadays sailing activity means the full range of species is no longer certain.

However it is still a good birding spot in winter months, with Great Northern as the most frequently-seen diver species. Red-throated Divers are recorded quite regularly but Black-throateds are now very scarce. Little and Great Crested Grebes should be seen but other grebes are now rare.

Black Guillemots on the other hand are increasing, with three or four pairs breeding in the area. Guillemots and Razorbills are also present in winter. Red-breasted Merganser is the only regular wildfowl species seen, but in very

cold weather, when nearby lakes are frozen, Tufted Ducks and Pochards may be found.

Waders are never numerous but Oystercatchers, Redshanks, Turnstones and Purple Sandpipers are best observed from the small car park at the eastern end of the harbour (SH 250 829) at high tide when they roost on the rocks to the right of the car park. Rare and scarce visitors seen here include White-billed Diver, Ring-necked Duck, Mediterranean, Little and Ring-billed Gulls, Forster's and Black Terns.

Soldiers Point is the area at the west end of the harbour. Park on the road opposite the Boathouse Hotel alongside the yachts and proceed along the tree-lined lane leading out onto the breakwater.

Key points

- All facilities available in Holyhead – nearest public toilets S of harbour, W of coastguard station (SH 245 832)

- Harbour can be viewed from the car.

- Telescope an advantage.

- Summer leisure activity on the water – but Black Guillemots still breed.

85

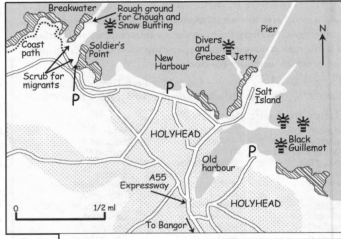

The first field on the left is sometimes waterlogged in winter and up to four Water Rails have been found here or in the wet area just beyond the pumphouse. Goldcrests are often found along the high bank with the occasional Chiffchaff and Firecrest in winter.

In spring, Willow Warblers, Blackcaps, Whitethroats, Lesser Whitethroats, Garden Warblers and Spotted Flycatchers all occur. As you continue along the lane you will pass a large former M.O.D. building on your right. Just beyond this there is a clump of willows by a gate, which is a favourite spot for finding Yellow-browed Warblers in late autumn, with more than a dozen occurrences here.

As you go on, you will pass some horse paddocks on your left – these are good for migrants, as is the area of scrub just behind the beach, which you will see when you arrive at the top of the lane.

Many scarce migrants have been found here, including Hoopoe, Wryneck, Richard's Pipit, Marsh, Icterine, Melodious, Barred, Pallas's, Hume's Yellow-browed and Dusky Warblers, Serin, Red-breasted Flycatcher, Isabelline Shrike and Common Rosefinch.

In winter the area of rough

Access details

From A55, continue into Holyhead, keeping straight on at the traffic lights and continue under the new footbridge, turning left at the end of the road. The harbour can be viewed from pull-ins on the right, then continue on for Soldiers Point.

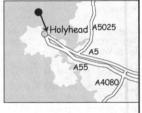

ground before you reach the breakwater attracts Linnets and you can sometimes find Twite, Snow Buntings and Lapland Buntings.

This is also the best place for Rock Pipits, with many pairs breeding and wintering. Behind the breakwater there is a small rocky beach, where a Killdeer was found in December 1993, but usually a few Turnstones and Redshanks are all you'll find.

If you cross the beach and go out onto the headland, seawatching can be good from here in a west, or preferably north-west, wind. Fulmars, Gannets, Manx Shearwaters, Kittiwakes and auks are regular.

Arctic and Great Skuas, with the occasional Pomarine Skua, Sabine's Gull and Leach's Petrel seen in September/ October. Balearic, Sooty, Cory's and Great Shearwaters have all been seen from this point.

Other nearby sites

Beddmanarch Bay, Inland Sea, RSPB South Stack.

THE INLAND SEA is a large tidal expanse of water between Holy Island and the main expanse of Anglesey and its sheltered aspect means it is very attractive to wildfowl and waders, especially during the winter months. Surprisingly, its potential has yet to be discovered by many birdwatchers, so there is the chance to make some exciting finds for, and by, yourself.

Target birds

Winter – Great Northern Diver (80%), Little Egret (80%), Pale-bellied Brent Goose (80%), Greater Scaup (25%), Red-breasted Merganser (100%).

Other possible bird species

All year	Common Tern	*Winter*
Grey Heron	Willow Warbler	Great Crested Grebe
Sparrowhawk	Sedge Warbler	Little Grebe
Stonechat	Blackcap	Gadwall
Raven		Teal
Finches	*Passage*	Shoveler
	Lapwing	Pintail
Summer	Black-tailed Godwit	Wigeon
Shelduck	Redshank	Pochard
Buzzard	Greenshank	Tufted Duck
Sandwich Tern	Common Sandpiper	Goldeneye

Background information and birding tips

THIS RELATIVELY unknown and very under-watched site, isolated from the sea by the A55 road, is at its best during the winter months when Pale-bellied Brent Geese are regular, as are good numbers of Wigeon.

They are often joined by Mallards, Teal, Shovelers, Gadwall and Pintails around the shallow edges. Goldeneye will be out on the deeper water, while Red-breasted Mergansers are ever-presents.

Smaller numbers of Tufted Ducks and Pochards are joined in most years by a few Scaup and the occasional Long-tailed Duck.

At least one Great Northern Diver is usually at this site, while Red-throated and Black-throated Divers do occur more occasionally. You should be able to see up to

50 each of Little and Great Crested Grebes, though Black-necked, Slavonian and Red-necked Grebes are much scarcer. However, singletons of each often remain for some time most winters. The herd of Mute Swans is sometimes joined by passing Whooper Swans. Coot occur in ever-increasing numbers.

The B4545 crosses the Inland Sea on a causeway and a footpath originating in Four Mile Bridge gives good access to the western side of the water.

Grey Herons roost in the conifers on the west shore and in recent years they have been joined by Little Egrets, with up to a dozen now seen regularly. Raptors are often present, with Buzzards and Sparrowhawks over the wooded area, and Peregrines and Merlins

Key points

• Public footpath on eastern shore flooded at high water.

• No facilities on site but shops etc in nearby Valley. Holyhead is only a five minute drive away.

• Wellingtons required if walking.

• Keep sun behind you by visiting in mornings.

• Telescope desirable as birds often distant.

• No access to western side.

• Path unsuitable for less able.

• Area distantly viewable from road at Four Mile Bridge.

often creating disturbance among the small, and not so small, birds on and around the water.

As the tide drops waders come in to feed. Dunlins, Knot, Ringed Plovers, Curlews and Redshanks are the regulars, but cold weather can mark the arrival of hundreds of Lapwings and Golden Plovers, though these seldom remain throughout the winter.

Walking the footpath through the saltmarsh you are sure to flush many Snipe, while Jack Snipe, Woodcocks and Water Rails are distinct possibilities if luck is on your side.

During spring and autumn passage periods, Black and Bar-tailed Godwits, Whimbrels, Greenshanks, Common and Green Sandpipers are all seen with some regularity. Garganey have been known to drop in and the occasional Osprey flies though.

In summer the scrub and gorse around the edges of the water hold Stonechats, Willow, Grasshopper and Sedge Warblers, Blackcaps, Whitethroats and Linnets.

On the open water you will see families of Shelduck, Greylag Geese, Mallards, Gadwalls and Red-breasted

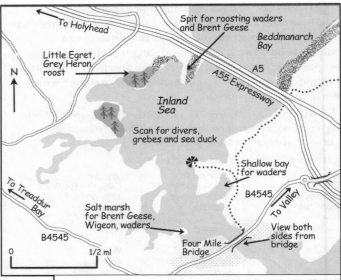

Access details

(Two miles SE of Holyhead).

Leave A55 at Junction 3 and head into the village of Valley. Turn left at lights, cross the level crossing before going over A55. After the mini-roundabout turn right, then right again into a cul-de-sac where you should park at SH 287 789. Follow public footpath to the water's edge, then continue left along the shoreline.

Alternatively, go straight on at the mini-roundabout and continue to Four Mile Bridge. Park by roadside near bridge and join the public footpath at SH 281 784.

Mergansers. Sandwich, Common and Arctic Terns from nearby colonies often visit to feed.

Scarce visitors in recent times have been Spoonbill,

Crane, Forster's Tern and Red-backed Shrike, but it must be emphasised the area is very underwatched and doubtless there are more goodies to be found.

Other nearby sites

Beddmanarch Bay, Holyhead Harbour, RSPB South Stack, Treaddur Bay.

LYING in the scenic Berwyn Mountains, the RSPB reserve of Lake Vyrnwy forms part of the largest remaining heather moorland in Wales. The best time to visit is May-June for breeding birds, including Hen Harrier, Merlin, Black and Red Grouse, but the area is worth a visit at any time of year. With an expanse of 26,000 acres to cover, the scenery is always inspiring.

Target birds

Spring – Goshawk (50%), Hen Harrier (50%), Merlin (50%), Black Grouse (20%), Red Grouse (40%), Redstart (100%), Tree Pipit (100%), Wood Warbler (70%), Pied Flycatcher (100%), Crossbill (50%).

Other possible bird species

All year	Siskin	Goldeneye
Goosander	*Spring*	
Buzzard	Woodcock at dusk	*Possible*
Peregrine	Wheatear	Red Kite
Dipper	Whinchat	Osprey on passage
Grey Wagtail		Short-eared Owl
Stonechat	*Winter*	
Raven	Whooper Swan	

Background information and birding tips

THE RESERVE, which lies in a remote part of the Berwyn Mountains, just east of the Snowdonia National Park, covers a huge area and a whole day will be needed to explore it.

Designated as a National Nature Reserve, SSSI and Special Protection Area, the reserve is managed by RSPB in conjunction with Severn Trent Water, which owns the reservoir itself.

Lake Vyrnwy is one of the few sites in Wales where you have a reasonable chance of seeing that phantom of the forests – Goshawk. The best chance presents itself in late February and March when these huge hawks indulge in display flights over the reserve's conifer forests.

Personally we have had the most success viewing over the valley on the north side of the lake (see map). Mid morning is often a good time to catch the display action.

An early start in spring may well be rewarded with some of the reserve's special birds. By driving along the minor roads north and west of the lake, both grouse species and a selection of raptors can be seen, given luck.

The local Black Grouse, Hen Harrier and Merlin populations are prospering, thanks to active habitat management by the RSPB.

These moorland areas are also great for Wheatears and Whinchats and displaying Curlews should be seen. Check streams for Dippers and Grey Wagtails.

The southern road meets the B4393 at Pont Eunant (SH 963 224) and climbs to more than

Key points

- **Largest area of heather moorland in Wales.**

- **Free parking.**

- **RSPB Visitor Centre (inc disabled toilet) open Apr to Oct (10.30am to 5.30pm); Nov to Dec 24 (10.30am-4.30pm); Jan to Mar (10.30am to 4.30pm Saturday and Sunday only)**

- **Café, toilets and bird hide near dam.**

- **Much of area can be viewed from roads.**

- **Walking boots and outdoor clothing required if exploring on foot.**

- **Footpaths not suitable for wheelchairs.**

- **Coed y Capel hide accessible to wheelchair users.**

Contacts

Warden – 01691 870 278. For details of events and guided walks, go to: www.rspb.org.uk

Access details

(Just over 20 miles W of Oswestry).

Take A495 SW from Oswestry for 12 miles, then turn W onto A490. Continue for just over four miles through Llanfyllin, then turn left onto B4393 which leads to Lake Vyrnwy. To reach the RSPB Visitor Centre, cross dam and turn left.

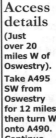

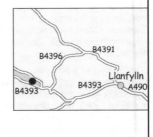

The lake is seven miles S of Bala. From Bala village, take B4391 S past the NE end of Bala Lake (Llyn Tegid). The road bends to the left – just beyond this, turn right onto minor road signposted for Lake Vyrnwy.

Follow this narrow twisting road through the wooded Cwm Hirnanant valley onto heather moorland before dropping down steeply into the Vyrnwy valley. At 'T' junction at bottom of hill, turn right to follow the lake shore to Visitor Centre.

From Dolgellau take A470 SE for ten miles. Turn left onto A458 for Welshpool and follow for ten miles, then turn left onto B4395. After seven miles, you reach a 'T' junction. Turn left onto B4393, which leads to Lake Vyrnwy.

500m before descending into the upper River Dyfi valley and Dinas Mawddwy.

The northern road heads out of the Vyrnwy valley at SH 964 243, then drops through the conifer woods of Penllyn Forest on through Cwm Hirnank to the town of Bala.

This is a narrow mountain road and great care should be taken if birding and driving! It is worth taking plenty of time to stop and scan the moorland, using your vehicle as a hide, as the special birds are tough to find.

Having driven the mountain roads as early as possible, return to the dam area and visit the RSPB Visitor Centre, located 100m south of the dam in Llanwddyn, built to replace the original village of that name which disappeared under the water.

Here, you can learn more about the history of the massive stone-built dam, which was completed in 1888

90

to provide a guaranteed water source for Liverpool, discover the latest sightings and get advice on where to search for any missing species.

If time allows, take one or more of the nature trails around the lake to add woodland species. The Grwn Oer trail is one and a half miles long, the Rhiwargor Island trail, part of which is suitable for wheelchair users, is two miles, and the Craig Garth-Bwlch trail three miles long.

Each of the trails will provide a representative selection of key species to be found at Vyrnwy, including Redstart, Tree Pipit, Wood Warbler and Pied Flycatcher in spring and summer.

However, the reserve is wardened during regular opening hours and it is wise to start your visit at the visitor centre before embarking on one of the trails, as the staff will be able to advise you which trail is most likely to provide your particular required species.

The majority of trails are not suitable for wheelchair users but the Coed-y-Capel hide is. It lies just beyond the RSPB Visitor Centre in the car park by the café, and gives great views of common woodland species. The birds here often include Great Spotted Woodpeckers, Nuthatches, Siskins and Coal Tits.

Some of the picnic areas allow for disabled access. For more information telephone the warden on 01691 870 278.

The reservoir itself, which can hold 13 million gallons of water when full, is extremely deep and the birdlife on its surface is limited – check for breeding Goosanders and Great Crested Grebes and the occasional Common Sandpiper at the margins. In winter small numbers of Teal, Tufted Ducks and Pochards can be seen.

Key points

- **Open access at all times.**
- **Penrhyn Bay side suitable for wheelchair users.**
- **Some steep paths to reach top.**
- **Parking is free on nearby roads and Penrhyn Bay Beach East housing estate.**
- **All facilities close by. Nearest public toilets on promenade opposite golf course heading E towards Rhos-on-Sea. More toilets on promenade heading W to Llandudno.**
- **Dangerous cliffs – care needed.**

Contacts

Llandudno Tourist Information – 01492 876 413.

North Wales WT (Neil Griffiths) – 01248 351 541.

THIS SMALLER VERSION of the Great Orme headland produces the same breeding species but is more compact and easier to cover. With magnificent cliffs and disused quarries, it has an impressive number of breeding birds, as well as good numbers of migrants in the spring and autumn. Seawatching can be excellent in the autumn.

Target birds
All year – Peregrine (70%), Little Owl (70%), Chough (50%). *Spring/summer* – Fulmar (100%), Kittiwake (100%), Guillemot (100%), Razorbill (100%), Lesser Whitethroat (50%). *Winter* – Black Redstart (70%).

Other possible bird species

All year		
Cormorant	Grey Plover	Gannet
Shag	Whimbrel	Shelduck
Sparrowhawk	Little Gull	Eider
Buzzard	Kittiwake	Common Scoter
Oystercatcher	Guillemot	Red-breasted Merganser
Curlew	Razorbill	Turnstone
Rock Pipit	Wheatear	Whimbrel
Stonechat	Hirundines	Common gulls and terns
Common thrushes		
Raven	*Summer*	*Winter*
	Manx Shearwater	Red-throated Diver
Spring	Gannet	Wigeon
Red-throated Diver	Sandwich Tern	Common Scoter
Manx Shearwater	Guillemot	Red-breasted Merganser
Gannet	Razorbill	Ringed Plover
Shelduck		Grey Plover
Common Scoter	*Autumn*	Turnstone
Red-breasted Merganser	Red-throated Diver	Commoner gulls
	Manx Shearwater	

Background information and birding tips

THE LITTLE ORME, a small headland just to the east of the Great Orme, is gaining a reputation for being one of the best seawatching vantage points along the North Wales coast. Given strong north-westerly winds between August and November, many birds blown into Liverpool Bay have to make their way back out into the Irish Sea by following the North Wales coast past this point.

All four skua species are regular, while Leach's Petrels can be seen in large numbers during really big blows. Sabine's Gull, Storm Petrel, Sooty and Balearic Shearwaters are recorded most years, and even if the rarer species are absent, there are often good offshore movements of auks, Kittiwakes, Fulmars, Gannets and Manx Shearwaters.

The most sheltered seawatching point involves a five-minute walk. Park in the Penrhyn Bay Beach East housing estate, located on the eastern side of the Little Orme and then head for the two gates that lead onto the headland. Walk along the path towards the sea, making your way to the large protruding rock at the end of the lower area of the headland.

On the right of this rock is Angel Bay, while on the left you can take shelter and view the Bay for seabirds. The sea here is also good for birds during the winter months, with Great Northern and Red-throated Divers being regular, as well as Great Crested Grebes and Common Scoters. Occasional Eiders, Slavonian Grebes and Black-throated Divers occur from time to time.

The entire area can be covered easily in a couple of hours, with a circular walk that takes in all the various habitats. There is interest throughout the year with seabirds breeding on the cliffs during spring and early summer, migrants in spring and autumn, some good seawatching in the right conditions during the autumn, and regular Little Owls and Black Redstarts in the winter.

A good route that takes about 90 minutes to walk, starts next to the Somerfield mini-supermarket located on the Little Orme side of the large roundabout in Penrhyn Bay – please use the nearby road for parking. Park here and walk up the hill towards Llandudno with the short stretch of dual-carriageway on the left.

After about 50 metres there is a small electricity sub-station, where you should turn left along a dirt track. A small wooded area to the left attracts roving flocks of Long-tailed Tits, often with Chiffchaffs among them. In spring and autumn there will be good numbers of Goldcrests

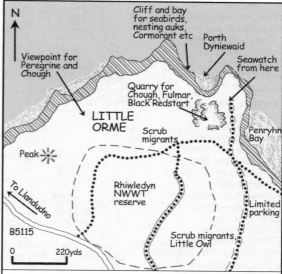

Access details

(One mile E of Llandudno).

From A55 Expressway follow signs to the promenade at Colwyn Bay. Proceed along the prom, past Rhos-on-Sea towards Penrhyn Bay. Half a mile beyond the golf course on your left, you will see a garage on the right. Immediately before this turn right into Penrhyn Beach. Turn first left, and left again just before the first right

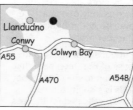

hand bend, and park in the road near the Somerfield supermarket.

and Willow Warblers, while Nuthatches, Treecreepers, Great Spotted Woodpeckers and Jays are resident.

Continue along the track until you can go no further. Walk through the gate and this will take you through to the lower level of the Little Orme. The path splits in two and though both routes lead to the same place, the

left hand one passes closer to the cliffs, so breeding Fulmars can be watched at close quarters.

Little Owls are often to be seen in the crevices.

Other nearby sites

RSPB Conwy, Great Orme, Rhos Point.

93

Good numbers of Goldfinches, Greenfinches and Linnets frequent this area and the flocks are worth checking in autumn for something more unusual.

Continue to the very end of the headland to overlook Angel Bay. Breeding Cormorants, Shags, Kittiwakes and auks make a cacophony of sounds here during the spring and early summer. Early morning is best, when the auks congregate on the sea just below the cliffs. Guillemots and Razorbills are abundant, while sightings of Puffins and Black Guillemots are becoming increasingly frequent. The area is good for Rock Pipits the year round.

Retrace your steps to the base of the steep path that leads up to the quarry above. This is a short, but very steep walk, and for the less energetic it would be wise to head back to the car park! If you continue on foot, keep an eye open for both Common and Lesser Whitethroats, Stonechats and Whinchats in the bracken to the left, as all are regular here outside winter.

On reaching a gate you are at the quarry, which is well known for it's wintering Black Redstarts, with three or four present in good years. Little Owls, Fulmars and Rock Pipits also use this area, and Peregrine Falcons use the

Pay a visit to Little Orme in winter and you'll get the chance to see Little Owl.

ridge as a look-out post.

The path to the left of the quarry will take you to the summit, where the bushes needed to checked during migration times. Warblers, especially Blackcaps and Garden Warblers, favour the area, while unusual birds have included recent Pallas's Warbler and Richard's Pipit.

As you climb towards the summit listen for Chough – their distinctive calls will lead to where they are feeding, usually on the grassy upper slopes of the quarry. Lesser Whitethroats breed in the gorse here and a Little Owl is often seen.

Head through the valley to the left hand peak marked by a concrete post and scan the limestone area for Wheatears,

Sky Larks, Meadow and Rock Pipits. The occasional Snow Bunting turns up here on passage or in winter. Don't forget to take in the amazing views from this summit point overlooking Llandudno and the North Wales coast.

Walk down the slope towards the gate landward of the summit. Go though it and down the path through the bushes. The fields to the left often have hunting Sparrowhawks and Buzzards. Again this area is good during migration times, especially in the early mornings before there is much disturbance. At the bottom of the path a gate takes you out to the main road leading out of Llandudno to Penrhyn Bay. Turn left and follow the pavement back to your starting point.

THE STRETCH of coast between Llanddulas and Pensarn provides great winter birding with regular Snow Buntings, sea-ducks and gulls. Easy access off the adjacent A55 North Wales Expressway makes it a popular birding area and though the beaches are heavily disturbed by dog walkers, the birds remain remarkably tolerant.

Target birds: *All year* – Fulmar (80%), Peregrine (50%), Dipper (70%). *Winter* – Common Scoter (100%), Velvet Scoter (30%), Red-breasted Merganser (100%), Scaup (40%), Snow Bunting (90%). *Spring* – Mediterranean Gull (70%).

Other possible bird species

All year	*Winter*	*Occasional*
Cormorant	Red-throated Diver	Surf Scoter
Ringed Plover	Great Crested Grebe	Iceland Gull
Grey Wagtail	Shag	Glaucous Gull
Dipper	Water Rail	Yellow-legged Gull
	Oystercatcher	
Spring	Sanderling	
Sandwich Tern	Turnstone	
Wheatear	Curlew	

Background information and birding tips

THIS IS principally a site to visit in winter when the main birding interest includes Snow Buntings, masses of Common Scoters and gulls. There are three main starting points for car drivers (see Access Details) and a cycle track gives access right along the coast.

If time allows, it is possible to walk the whole stretch – a distance of just over two miles, which will take you three hours to cover.

Starting at Llanddulas, park just west of the river mouth to scan the sea for flocks of Common Scoters. Check carefully for the small numbers of Velvet Scoter that are recorded every winter.

You can also expect to see Red-throated Divers (any other species of diver is a real rarity), Red-breasted Mergansers, Great Crested Grebes and Cormorants.

Walk east to the mouth of the river where large numbers of gulls gather to bathe and drink. It is worth spending some time looking for scarcer species because Iceland, Glaucous, Yellow-legged and Mediterranean Gulls have all been found, albeit rarely.

Scan the beach for Turnstones and the shingle ridge for a possible Snow Bunting. In spring, Wheatears are regular along the beach.

After checking the river for Grey Wagtails and occasional Goosander, if you have time and would like to see a Dipper, walk upstream to see if your luck is in. Walk at least as far as the minor road bridge over the river where riverside trees may add common passerines to your day list.

Drive east for one mile on the A547, then turn left into Beach Road to reach the next access

Key points

- **Open access all year.**

- **Free parking.**

- **No on-site facilities at Llanddulas.**

- **All facilities in Old Colwyn and Abergele.**

- **Toilets and summer season cafe in public car park at Pensarn.**

- **Suitable for all physical abilities — much can be done from the car.**

- **Telescope best for viewing gulls and seaduck.**

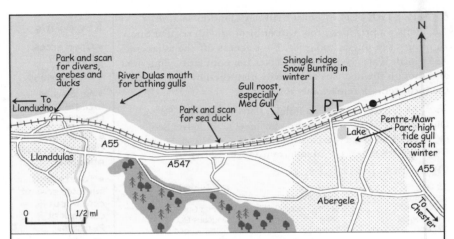

Access details

(Three miles from Colwyn Bay).

Leave A55 midway between Colwyn Bay and Abergele (junction 22), signposted Llanddulas. Follow signs to beach, go under the railway and onto a road running parallel to shingle beach.

Follow this road until it bends right, away from the beach. Turn left at this point onto the beach and park. You are now just west of the River Dulas mouth.

Retrace your route to the metalled road and turn left quickly, passing under A55. Take the first left, which follows River Dulas. Cross river to reach a 'T' junction with A547.

Turn left onto A547. After one mile, turn left at a minor

crossroads into Beach Road. Pass under A55 and railway line, then park on the gravel by the cycle track. Walk across the cycle track to view the beach.

Retrace your route and turn left onto A547. Follow this into the outskirts of Abergele. After one mile on A547, take left turn signposted for the beach, into a road with speed humps.

Continue north, passing Pentre Mawr Park on your right. Go over A55 and down to the car park on the other side by the seawall at the west end of Pensarn promenade.

Also check the beach to the east end of the promenade where you can drive onto the beach itself, handy on cold days!

Park at:
SH 905 786 (Llanddulas river mouth)
SH 928 783 (Beach Road)
SH 944 787 (Pensarn)

It is possible to drive west from Pensarn beach alongside the inland side of the seawall. Views are poor from a vehicle, but frequent stops to peer over the wall may be productive.

point. Again, scan offshore for sea-ducks, divers and grebes. The beach here, a mix of rocky foreshore and sand banks, may hold Oystercatchers, Curlews,

Redshanks and Turnstones.

In the early spring, this is a very good site for Mediterranean Gulls joining the huge roost of Common Gulls that builds up here in the

late afternoon. However, you will need a telescope to pick them out from the throng.

Continue further east along the A547 to Abergele and check the Pentre Mawr

Flocks of beautiful Snow Buntings are regular visitors to this stretch of the coast during the winter months.

Park, just south of the A55. The playing fields can often hold good numbers of gulls, particularly at high tide when they are pushed off the beach. Two small lakes in the park – the only fresh water for some miles around – can pull in quite a few ducks. Water Rails can be found in winter, around the reed beds of the largest pool.

Cross the A55 onto Pensarn Beach and park at the west end of the promenade. It is possible to walk over the sea-wall via several access ramps and head west along the shingle ridge. This is the most regular site for Snow Bunting in North Wales and up to 25 of these wonderful Arctic waifs can be found feeding here. The area is heavily disturbed by dog walkers that regularly flush the buntings.

The ridge is also good for Wheatears in spring and occasional White Wagtails join them. Scan offshore for huge numbers of Common Scoters, looking for Scaup among them. The beach can hold good numbers of gulls and small numbers of Ringed Plovers and Sanderlings.

You can also view from the east end of Pensarn Beach, where you drive onto the beach itself. The cycle track continues east if you have time to check further along the coast.

Other nearby sites

Rhos Point, River Clwyd.

Key points

- **Open access at all times.**

- **Toilets and two cafes on promenade — opening times erratic.**

- **Free parking by promenade.**

- **Easy walking on flat paths.**

- **Wheelchair access OK but no disabled toilet.**

- **Nearest disabled facilities at RSPB Conwy.**

- **Three hides at Morfa Madryn Local Nature Reserve.**

- **Telescope desirable.**

- **Snacks, hot drinks and bird information at RSPB Conwy (15 minutes drive).**

Contacts

Conwy CBC Countryside Warden, Alan Jones – 01492 575 200.

THE PROMENADE at Llanfairfechan gives great views across the shallow bay where many wintering birds feed at high tide, making this one of the best, and certainly the most accessible, sites in North Wales to observe divers, grebes and sea duck. A short walk to the west is an area of saltmarsh with a shingle spit, and beyond this lie the pools of the Morfa Madryn Nature Reserve. On the south side of the railway line, a sewage works is worth visiting. This mixture of habitats often makes for great birding, especially during the winter months.

Target birds

All year – Little Egret (100%), Red-breasted Merganser (100%), Peregrine (70%), Grey Wagtail (100%). *Spring/autumn* – Red-throated Diver (100%), Great Northern Diver (90%), Slavonian Grebe (90%), Common Scoter (100%). *Summer* – Mediterranean Gull (70%), Sandwich Tern (100%). *Autumn* – Red-breasted Merganser (100%). *Winter* – Great Northern Diver (90%), Red-throated Diver (100%), Slavonian Grebe (90%), Common Scoter (100%), Velvet Scoter (20%), Black Guillemot (40%), Dipper (80%), Firecrest (20%).

Other possible bird species

Spring/ summer
Manx Shearwater
Gannet
Kittiwake
Sandwich Tern
Swift
Hirundines
Common warblers

Spring
Wigeon
Teal
Pintail
Eider
Goosander
Grey Plover
Knot
Sanderling
Dunlin
Black-tailed Godwit
Bar-tailed Godwit
Whimbrel
Greenshank
Common Sandpiper
Turnstone

Common Gull
Other common gulls and terns
White Wagtail
Stonechat
Wheatear
Siskin
Lesser Redpoll

Autumn/ winter
Manx Shearwater
Gannet
Wigeon
Teal
Pintail
Eider
Goosander
Grey Plover
Knot
Sanderling
Dunlin
Snipe
Bar-tailed Godwit
Common Gull
Goldcrest

Siskin

Autumn
Little Stint
Curlew Sandpiper
Black-tailed Godwit
Whimbrel
Spotted Redshank
Greenshank
Arctic Skua
Hirundines
Common thrushes and warblers

All year
Grey Heron
Shelduck
Sparrowhawk
Buzzard
Oystercatcher
Curlew
Guillemot
Razorbill
Common tits, crows and finches

Background information and birding tips

WE FIND it is best to start a Llanfairfechan birding day at the promenade. To get the best out of this area, pick a day with a high tide close to the middle of the day and one that is relatively calm and sunny. Okay, so it's Wales, but try your best!

Aim to arrive a good two hours before high water. Park on the prom close to the Pavilion Cafe and scan the bay from the parking area. Should the day turn inclement, there is shelter round the back of the cafe.

Do not be disheartened if your first scan of the area reveals few birds — be patient, because there will be birds out there. As the tide begins to flood in, birds are carried west past the prom towards the Menai Straits, so the scene changes quickly.

Red-throated Divers should be seen between October and April, given a reasonably calm sea, and up to five Great Northern Divers overwinter, so you should pick out at least one.

A word of caution: Black-throated Diver, which is often claimed at this site, is an extremely rare occurrence. In a combined total of more than 30 years' watching the site, we can count their sightings on one hand, and these are usually spring passage birds.

Slavonian Grebes winter here, with double figure counts under ideal conditions, so again you would be unlucky not to score with at least one. Further out

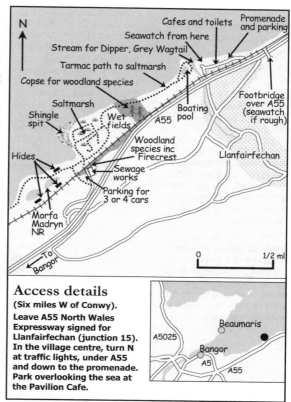

Access details

(Six miles W of Conwy).
Leave A55 North Wales Expressway signed for Llanfairfechan (junction 15). In the village centre, turn N at traffic lights, under A55 and down to the promenade. Park overlooking the sea at the Pavilion Cafe.

you should find Common Scoters.

The site has become famous (or infamous if you are one of the many who have visited and not seen the bird), as the winter home of a lone drake Black Scoter. It usually shuns the company of the commoner species, and once seen, it stands out, looking rather like a yellow-billed Coot! Good light, a top

telescope, and lots of luck are required to nail this bird though. Easier to find are Black Guillemots, which are increasing in North Wales. Birds regularly winter offshore here.

By scanning the skyline above the obvious quarry face to the south-east, you

Other nearby sites

Aber Ogwen, RSPB Conwy, Great Orme.

99

could add Peregrine and Raven to your day list, and, with luck, Chough.

By now the tide will be rushing in and it's time to set off west.

Check the stream at the west end of the prom, where it flows out to the sea. Look inland from the bridge to see if Dippers and Grey Wagtails are present. Then follow the flat coastal footpath, that is even tarmacadamed in its early stages, until you reach a small copse on your left, which is worth a quick scan for passerines.

Continuing west you will reach the saltmarsh, which should be checked for wildfowl and waders. Also in winter, and especially in early spring, check the Linnet flock carefully for Twite, which are sometimes present.

Keep on the south side of the saltmarsh, and look across the channel at the far end for roosting waders on the shingle spit. Cross the stream and you soon reach Morfa Madryn LNR, managed by Conwy County Borough Council, where three hides give good views over the two lagoons, which should have a number of the commoner wildfowl and waders.

Little Egrets and Kingfishers are both regular here and in the adjacent saltmarsh creeks. Ruff have overwintered.

Retrace your steps to the stream but do not cross it – instead continue straight on, taking great care when crossing the busy railway line, and bird the woodland on the far side.

There is a sewage works to your left a little way down the lane, where the filter beds attract wintering Chiffchaffs and Grey Wagtails. The low brambles in the area are the best place to search for a Firecrest, with one present, but often elusive, most winters.

Ringed Plover is a species that can be found at many coastal sites in Gwynedd and Clwyd.

THE LARGEST inland body of water on Anglesey, this reservoir attracts large numbers of wintering wildfowl, including Whooper Swans and occasionally Pink-footed and White-fronted Geese. The northern end attracts a good variety of waders in autumn, if the water levels are low.

Target birds *Winter* – Whooper Swan (50%), Hen Harrier (30%), Barn Owl (40%).

Other possible bird species

Summer	Curlew	*All year*
Grasshopper Warbler		Little Grebe
Sedge Warbler	*Winter*	Great Crested Grebe
Whitethroat	Wigeon	Mute Swan
Lesser Redpoll	Teal	Greylag Goose
	Gadwall	Canada Goose
Autumn	Pochard	Black-headed Gull
Peregrine	Tufted Duck	Herring Gull
Common Sandpiper	Goldeneye,	Goldcrest
Snipe	Ruddy Duck	

Background information and birding tips

A VISIT here in winter will certainly provide you with a wealth of wildfowl, but a telescope is essential for use from the hides.

Llyn Alaw is owned and managed by Welsh Water, and while the hides are permanently open, the paths leading to them are poorly maintained, making access difficult, particularly on the southern shore.

It is advisable to wear Wellington boots as the tracks are often muddy, while fallen trees blocking the path are more obstacles to overcome.

You approach the hide alongside a belt of conifers, which holds Goldcrests and sometimes Lesser Redpolls and Crossbills. Raptors are often seen with Sparrowhawks, Hen Harriers and Barn Owls all showing in winter. In autumn, especially if water levels are low, a Peregrine may be sitting out on the mud.

Whooper Swans are usually present from November through to March but are often feeding out in the surrounding fields. Greylag and Canada Geese are occasionally joined by Pink-footed and White-fronted Geese during cold spells. They are usually found in the fields opposite the hide.

Little and Great Crested Grebes are resident, while Black-necked and Red-necked Grebes both occur infrequently.

Wigeon, Teal, Tufted Duck and Pochard make up the bulk of wildfowl on the water, but more than 100 Ruddy Ducks have been recorded (in the days before the DEFRA-funded culling campaign), with smaller numbers of Goldeneyes and Gadwall. Long-tailed Ducks are scarce visitors.

In autumn, with the right conditions, i.e. plenty of mud, a good variety of wader species can be seen from the hide: Common,

Key points

- Open access at all times.

- Bird hides often difficult to access.

- Tracks get muddy in winter.

- Wheelchair users can get views from car park at dam end.

- Paths not suitable for less able birdwatchers.

- Telescope essential.

- Car park at southern end always open but toilets not always open.

Contacts

Welsh Water – 01407 730 762

Green and Wood Sandpipers, Snipe, Curlew, Whimbrel, Greenshank, Spotted Redshank, Ruff, Little Stint and Curlew Sandpiper all occur.

This is also the best site on Anglesey for vagrant Pectoral Sandpipers and it has produced records of Long-billed Dowitcher and Baird's Sandpiper.

At the southern end of the reservoir, there is a car park which is always open, but we have found that the toilets there are very erratic in their opening times.

From this car park you can walk around the edge of the water, or you can drive on down the hill below the dam (passing the toilets on your left) and continue towards the waterworks. Turn right just before the entrance gate and this track will take you down to the fisherman's car park.

The area below the dam is well worth checking for warblers and other migrants, including Grasshopper Warblers. This spot once famously held a Rock Thrush, so you never know what you might discover...

Walk east from here along the access road to check the scrub to the right of the path for more warblers and Reed Buntings.

Looking south from here, you

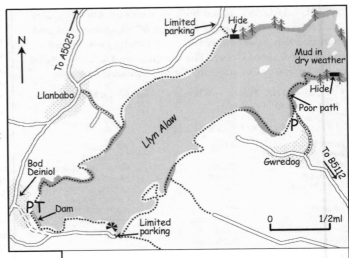

Access details

(Approx five miles SW of Amlwch).

Llyn Alaw is well sign-posted from all directions. From Holyhead, leave A55 at junction 3 onto A5025 and approach Llanddeusant and Llannerchymedd via Llanfachraeth. Alternatively leave A5025 and head for Llannerchymedd, S of reservoir.

For the southern hide, leave the village, taking first left and then the right fork. This will take you down to a farm (Gwredog) about two miles from the village. Park on left and continue on foot down to the lakeside, and walk

right along the conifer belt to the hide.

For the northern hide, approach on minor road from Llanddeusant, signed Amlwch, through Llanbabo. Hide is on right after one mile. Limited parking but road not busy.

will see a marshy area. Scan this for Barn Owl, Hen Harrier, Buzzard and Marsh Harrier. Black Terns occasionally visit the reservoir in spring and autumn, and once a summer-plumaged White-winged Black Tern was found here.

Other rare bird records here include Cattle Egret, Great White Egret and Rock Thrush.

Other nearby sites

Point Lynas.

HEATHER moorland bordering this huge man-made reservoir holds the promise of seeing both Black and Red Grouse – if you arrive early in the day. This is also an excellent area for raptors, including the majestic Hen Harrier. An island in the lake holds a colony of breeding Black-headed Gulls but the deep waters themselves have little bird interest.

Target birds *Spring* – Goldeneye (50%), Goosander (75%), Hen Harrier (50%), Goshawk (20%), Merlin (20%), Red Grouse (80%), Black Grouse (20%), Common Sandpiper (80%), Black-headed Gull (100%), Cuckoo (80%), Tree Pipit (90%), Grey Wagtail (100%), Dipper (60%), Whinchat (90%), Stonechat (100%), Wheatear (100%), Siskin (100%), Lesser Redpoll (70%).

Other possible bird species

Spring	Sand Martin	*Occasional species – spring*
Sparrowhawk	Meadow Pipit	Osprey
Buzzard	Grey Wagtail	Mediterranean Gull
Kestrel	Coal Tit	Crossbill
Curlew	Raven	
Sky Lark	Reed Bunting	

Background information and birding tips

WITHOUT doubt the best time to visit is spring, when breeding birds are displaying and at their most visible. Very few birds spend the winter in this tough upland habitat (around 1,200 ft) and you should also go prepared for chilly conditions, even in spring.

Dawn should see you on the B4501 at the north end of Llyn Brenig driving east from the junction at SH 963 577. Drive very slowly along the B-road with windows down and listen for the bizarre and distinctive bubbling and cooing of displaying Black Grouse.

Very few Black Grouse inhabit this area, so your luck will be definitely in if you come across any of these stunning birds. Take the utmost care not to disturb these rare breeding birds and view only from inside your vehicle. Carefully check the heather moorland for hunting raptors – Buzzard and Kestrel should be seen easily while sightings of a Hen Harrier or dashing Merlin will be rarer.

Fence posts may provide a handy perch for a calling Cuckoo. Meadow Pipit song fills the air and Stonechats should be perched up on the heather; check them all for Whinchat.

After one and a quarter miles, turn right onto a narrow minor road. Stop soon after making the turn and scan the small conifer plantation. These trees may hold Cuckoos, Lesser Redpolls and Tree Pipits.

From here, continue to the brow of the hill and park in the pull-off on the right. Scan the moorland to the west. This is your best chance

Key points

- **Be prepared with warm, waterproof clothing.**
- **Early morning, just after dawn, is best.**
- **Limited parking at moorland sites.**
- **Visitor centre with toilets (9am-5pm) and café (10am-4.30pm) open between March 12 and October 31 on W shore of Llyn Brenig near dam.**
- **Most birds can be viewed from your vehicle.**
- **Telescope very useful.**
- **Ten mile mountain bike trail is not productive from a birding point of view.**

Contacts

Welsh Water visitor centre at Llyn Brenig: 01490 420 463

of seeing a Hen Harrier. Given patience, you should see one of these majestic raptors quartering the heather hillside beyond the lake. The water below you is the northern arm of Llyn Brenig, but due to its depth, it is unlikely to hold many birds. However, always scan the water for the chance of Goosander or a lingering Goldeneye.

As you scan for Hen Harrier, you should hear and see Red Grouse among the heather – their 'Go Back, Go Back' calls echo across the water. Keep a look out for raptors all around. Most likely are Buzzards and Kestrels, but Merlin and Goshawk are both possible. Ospreys have been seen here on spring passage, occasionally lingering for several days, but they remain a rarity here.

Once satisfied that you have given this area a thorough scrutiny, continue to the parking area 300 yards further on. Park here and walk down to the edge of Llyn Brenig, a water created in 1976. It is one of the biggest lakes in Wales and hosts sailing and fishing as well as walks around its two nature trails.

From here you can enjoy a good view of the busy Black-headed Gull colony on the island in the lake. Check carefully for a Mediterranean Gull, as these scarce gulls have occurred on several

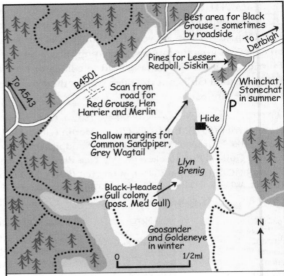

Access details

(Approx five miles N of Cerrigydrudion on A5).

From Llangollen drive W on A5 for 18 miles to Cerrigydrudion, then head N on B4501 signposted Llyn Brenig. After six miles, having passed signs to the visitor centre (located S of our map area) and the main body of the lake off to your right, take a right turn, still on B4501. After a further one and a quarter miles,

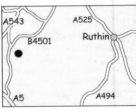

turn right onto a minor road. Park after half a mile at the brow of the hill, SH 984 577.

Other nearby sites

Clocaenog Forest.

occasions. A few Herring and Lesser Black-backed Gulls breed among the Black-headed Gulls.

Small numbers of Sand Martins are usually feeding over the lake and it is worth checking the shoreline carefully for Common Sandpipers. Wheatears are likely to be feeding on grass

areas around the parking area. Retrace your steps, checking for any species you may have missed.

When you reach the B4501, turn left and continue to the junction. Turn left again, still on the B4501. After one and a half miles turn left onto a narrow lane signposted for the visitor centre. Follow this

104

lane for half a mile until you reach the car park, where you can enjoy a well-earned drink and perhaps some food in the café here.

You can scan the huge lake, though few birds are likely. The area around the visitor centre car park is a great place to see Siskins close up. They are obviously well used to seeing people. The taller pines at the back of the parking area are worth checking for Coal Tit and possible Crossbill.

A good site for Dipper lies nearby. Just over one mile south of the visitor centre on the B4501, turn left onto a minor road. Check the stream from the road junction east to the small village of Pentre

Llyn Cymmer. The stream in the village often holds Grey Wagtails in addition to Dippers.

If time allows, retrace your route north past Llyn Brenig on the B4501 until you reach the A543. Turn left towards Pentrefoelas. The road soon crosses open heather moorland. Soon after you pass the Sportsman's Arms pub on your right, look for a lay-by on your left. Park here and scan the moorland and conifer edge.

This spot has produced sightings of Hen Harrier, Merlin, Goshawk, Black and Red Grouse. Much more likely are Buzzard, Kestrel and Sparrowhawk. Other species here include Wheatear,

Meadow Pipit, Reed Bunting, Whinchat and Stonechat.

Continue across the moor on the A543 for just under two miles, then turn right onto a minor road and drive slowly, scanning the open country for raptors including possible Hen Harrier. Wheatears, Stonechats and Meadow Pipits should all be easily seen.

It is worth driving past the lake of Llyn Aled to the far end of the next lake, Llyn Aled Isaf Reservoir, then retracing your steps back to the A543. By turning right here, you rejoin the A5 after five miles, some five and a half miles west of Cerrigydrudion. By starting at dawn, a good half-day should be sufficient to cover this whole area.

Key points

- **Open access all year.**
- **Free parking.**
- **Paths not suitable for wheelchairs.**
- **No facilities at lake.**
- **Aberffraw's public toilets and café open only erratically! Rhosneigr has more to offer. Malltraeth has a general store, pub and chip shop.**
- **Wellington boots recommended in winter.**
- **Telescope useful.**

A SHALLOW freshwater lake on the edge of Anglesey's Aberffraw dunes, Llyn Coron attracts substantial numbers of wildfowl in winter and can also hold good gull flocks. The lake, which is just a short but muddy walk from the parking area, is easily viewed and the surrounding fields and dunes also hold good birds. Sadly, shooting can occasionally disrupt birding trips.

Target birds

All year – Goosander (80%), Ruddy Duck (100% but this may change)! *Winter* – Wigeon (100%), Teal (100%), Shoveler (100%), Pochard (100%), Tufted Duck (100%), Goldeneye (100%), Water Rail (50%), Merlin (50%), Golden Plover (80%), Gulls (100%), Stonechat (100%), Chough (50%).

Other possible bird species

All year	Fieldfare	Glaucous Gull
Buzzard	Redwing	Mediterranean Gull
Kestrel		Yellow-legged Gull
Reed Bunting	*Occasional*	
	Scarce geese	
Winter	Smew	
Snipe	Iceland Gull	

Background information and birding tips

BEGIN birding as soon as you turn off the A4080 onto the minor road, a single track with passing places that runs along the border of Aberffraw sand dunes and adjacent farmland. Stonechats are resident and should be encountered along the fence lines.

Buzzards and Kestrels are usually seen hunting the dunes; in winter, if your luck is in, a Merlin or a Hen Harrier may join them. Also in winter, check any stubble fields for finch flocks, as they may well hold Bramblings and Reed Buntings.

Just after the road crosses a small stream and passes a farmstead, the field on the left holds large flocks of Golden Plovers and Lapwings in winter.

In spring, Sky Larks should be singing over the dunes. Ravens are easy to see here and it pays to check all flocks of corvids for Choughs, which often feed alongside the road.

The stream, which follows the road, holds Water Rail in winter and Reed Buntings throughout the year. Wheatears and Whinchats can be found on passage, while flocks of Redwings and Fieldfares are regular from October to March.

After driving a mile-and-a-quarter from the A4080, park opposite a house on the left-hand side of the road. Check the willows near the parking area for passerines, which in spring should include Reed Buntings, Sedge Warblers and Willow Warblers.

In winter, the stream often holds a Water Rail, though it is usually easier to hear than to see. Take the footpath over the stream to reach the lake shore where you will find a telescope is very useful to scan the large body of water and shoreline. Though good numbers of wildfowl are usually present throughout the year, occasional shooting parties will empty the lake of birds!

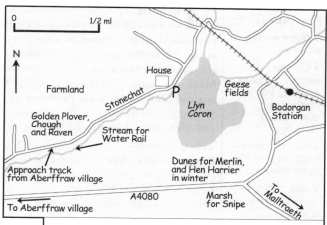

Species which can be found throughout the year still include Ruddy Duck (though the DEFRA-sponsored cull of this alien species from North America is reducing numbers all the time), plus Gadwall, Tufted Ducks and Pochards.

In winter, they are joined by Goldeneyes, Wigeon, Teal, Goosanders and occasional Smew. Both Great Crested and Little Grebes are resident, and Cormorants are daily visitors.

Gulls often bathe here, sometimes in their hundreds: if you have the patience to check them carefully, you may strike lucky as Glaucous, Iceland, Yellow-legged and Mediterranean Gulls have all been recorded in the past.

The fields on the far side of the lake hold Greylag and Canada Geese; in the winter, check for more unusual species among them. The marshy vegetation on the near shore holds wintering Snipe, sometimes joined by Jack Snipe. Peregrines hunt the area and you may be fortunate enough to witness an attack.

It is possible to walk south along the west side of the lake but the path is usually wet and muddy, so don't risk it without wearing Wellingtons.

Access details

(Two miles NW of Malltraeth).

From Malltraeth, take A4080 NW. After 0.75 mile turn left, signposted Aberffraw, still on A4080. This road crosses Aberffraw dunes.

At the far side of the dunes, just before the bridge and Aberffraw village, turn right onto a minor road. This narrow road with passing places runs along with the edge of the dunes on your right.

After 1.25 miles, you reach a house on your left. Park carefully on the grass opposite, not in the fishermen's car park.

Take the footpath over the

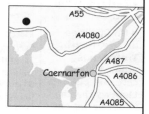

stream to view the lake. It is possible to follow the shore of the lake for further views but Wellingtons may be necessary!

From Rhosneigr, take A4080 S for 3.5 miles to Aberffraw. Cross the bridge, still on A4080, and turn left almost immediately onto the minor road.

Other nearby sites

Braint Estuary, Malltraeth, RSPB Valley Lakes.

Key points

- **Open access all year.**

- **Upland terrain, so take walking boots and warm waterproof clothing.**

- **Steep access road, not for the faint-hearted.**

- **Not suitable for wheelchair users.**

- **Early morning best.**

- **No facilities on site. Nearby Trefriw has public toilets, café and pubs. Llanrwst has a wider variety of places to eat.**

- **A café at nearby Llyn Crafnant is not always open in winter.**

- **For overnight accommodation and excellent food, try The Princes Arms Hotel, N of Trefriw on B5106.**

MANY OF THE Snowdonia National Park's upland species can be found in this area of rugged heather moorland and sheep-walk at an altitude of 350m above the village of Trefriw in the Conwy Valley. The weather can be changeable at this altitude, so go prepared with walking boots and warm, waterproof clothing. The scenery is beautiful but the birds are hard to find, so don't expect to be 'in and out' at this site. Arrive as early as possible to connect with singing and displaying species.

Target birds

Spring/summer – Hen Harrier (50%), Peregrine (70%), Merlin (50%), Red Grouse (50%), Dipper (60%), Grey Wagtail (80%), Cuckoo (80%), Whinchat (80%), Ring Ouzel (70%).

Other possible bird species

Spring/summer		
Goosander	Kestrel	Meadow Pipit
Buzzard	Common Sandpiper	Stonechat
	Wheatear	Raven

Background information and birding tips

TO COPE with the upland terrain at this site, stout walking boots, waterproofs and warm clothing are all essential, no matter how nice the weather may be in the valley floor. There are no facilities up here, so ensure you have sufficient supplies of food and drink.

Your birding can begin in the village of Trefriw. Check the fast-flowing stream by the woollen mill for Dippers and Grey Wagtails and look up for soaring Buzzards and the occasional Sparrowhawk.

From here, drive out of the village and turn right for Llyn Cowlyd Reservoir. The woodland alongside the road holds typical Welsh specialities, so keep a sharp look out for Pied Flycatchers, Redstarts and Wood Warblers.

Other regular birds encountered here include Great Spotted Woodpeckers, Treecreepers, Nuthatches, Goldcrests and Mistle Thrushes. Stop where you can, and listen for calls and songs – much the best way to locate woodland species.

As the road leaves the woodland behind, keep an eye open for birds of open habitats. Tree Pipits may well be found giving their parachuting song flights, while both Whinchats and Stonechats can be found on top of gorse and bracken.

Stop at the brow of the hill to admire the stunning view of the Conwy Valley far below and while you are there, check carefully for soaring raptors: most likely is a Buzzard but you might be lucky enough to encounter a Peregrine.

Continue a short distance to a cattle grid and park just before it. This is a great vantage point to scan the heather moorland. Your targets here are Hen Harriers, Merlins and Red Grouse, which need patience to find.

Driving slowly, check every bird before parking carefully at the

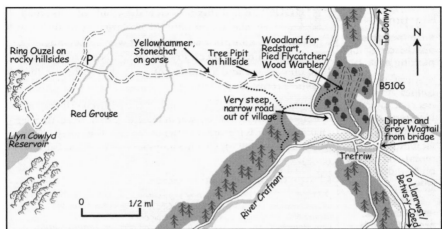

Access details

(12 miles S of Conwy).

From Conwy, take B5106 S down Conwy Valley for approximately nine miles to Trefriw. In village centre turn right onto minor road signposted for Llyn Crafnant. Climb through village and take third left turn for Llyn Cowlyd.

This winding minor road skirts the edge of deciduous woodland, then climbs steeply up onto the moorland. Note that this is an exceptionally steep road with sharp bends.

After just over a mile of steep climbing the road levels out. Pause here for breathtaking views of the Conwy Valley far below. Continue on this minor single-track road to the dead end. Park carefully and explore the whole area on foot.

A cart track leads SW from the left of the road to the dam wall. At the wall turn right, and then at the end of the dam turn left to view the open crater. You can follow the shoreline for half a mile before meeting a path

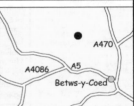

coming in from your right. Take this path, contouring the hillside, to meet another track above the road end. Turn right here to reach the road end and your vehicle.

---

dead end, ensuring you do not block any gateways or obstruct farm vehicles.

To explore the terrain around the lake from this point is likely to take between three and five hours. Take the track from the end of the road to the dam wall and keep scanning the ridges for raptors.

Listen for the distinctive calls of a male Cuckoo usually to be found here. Any grassy areas will hold Wheatears and with luck a

Ring Ouzel on the hunt for worms. Ravens should be seen, or very likely heard, overhead.

Scan the water of Llyn Cowlyd for Goosanders and/or a Red-breasted Merganser and check the shoreline for Common Sandpipers.

Follow the path along the shoreline for half a mile before taking the path to your right which contours back towards the car.

This section is often the most productive for Ring Ouzels, so search the rocky areas carefully for a singing male and the grassy areas for feeding birds.

Back at your vehicle, take a short walk along the stream, Afon Ddu, to look for Dippers and Grey Wagtails.

Other nearby sites

Coed Hafod, RSPB Conwy, Gwydyr Forest.

109

Key points

- No facilities, apart from small parking area.

- Shops, toilets etc in nearest town of Llangefni.

- Very limited viewing for less mobile birders on N and W sides.

- Park at N end and walk around road to view.

THOUGH it is difficult to view the whole of this small Anglesey lake, the possibility of Garganey in spring and a selection of autumn waders make it worth checking. Marsh Harrier, an unusual species on Anglesey, is occasionally seen here on passage and a number of rarer species have added to the site's reputation.

Target birds

All year – Great Crested Grebe (100%). *Spring* – Garganey (20%), Marsh Harrier (30%), Reed Warbler (100%), Lesser Whiethroat (70%). *Autumn* – Garganey (20%), Marsh Harrier (30%), Green Sandpiper (50%), Wood Sandpiper (20%).

Other possible bird species

All year	*Spring/ summer*	Willow Warbler
Little Grebe	Black-tailed Godwit	Lesser Redpoll
Cormorant	Common Sandpiper	
Grey Heron	Lesser Black-backed Gull	*Autumn / winter*
Mute Swan	Swift	Wigeon
Greylag Goose	Hirundines	Teal
Canada Goose	Sedge Warbler	Pintail
Gadwall	Whitethroat	Snipe
Mallard	Chiffchaff	Curlew
Shoveler	Willow Warbler	Redshank
Pochard		Common Gull
Tufted Duck		Lesser Black-backed Gull
Sparrowhawk	*Spring*	Meadow Pipit
Buzzard	Shelduck	
Kestrel	Wigeon	*Autumn*
Pheasant	Teal	Common Sandpiper
Lapwing	Snipe	Swift
Common gulls	Curlew	Hirundines
Pied Wagtail	Redshank	Common warblers
Common thrushes	Common Gull	Goldcrest
Raven	Cuckoo	
Other crows	Meadow Pipit	*Winter*
Starling	White Wagtail	Peregrine
House Sparrow	Linnet	Fieldfare
Common finches		Redwing
Lesser Redpoll	*Summer*	Linnet
Reed Bunting	Black-headed Gull	
	Sedge Warbler	

Background information and birding tips

THE BEST VIEWING point is at the north end of the medium-sized shallow lake, where there is a small parking area. A one-hour visit will ensure you see all the commoner species on offer.

From here you can view a good proportion of the water. In the winter, you will see a typical mixture of wildfowl: Greylag and Canada Geese, Mallards, Teal, Pochards, Tufted and Ruddy Ducks and one or two Goldeneyes. Lapwings are often found in the surrounding fields.

From this point, if you walk west and take the first turning on your left, the road runs alongside the water and from an elevated position you can get to see various areas of the lake. A Marsh Harrier is sometimes seen quartering the reed-bed and surrounding farmland.

One particular area worth checking is where the lake comes closest to the road, about 200 metres beyond the houses on your right. In the shallow weedy bay below, you may find a passage Garganey hiding among the vegetation in both spring and autumn.

In spring and summer, warblers can be found in the reedbeds and surrounding scrub. Both Reed and Sedge Warblers will be easy to hear but it is trickier to get decent views.

The hawthorn bushes midway up the western edge often hold a singing Lesser Whitethroat, so listen for its distinctive rattling call.

This is also an area in which to find a passing wader in autumn. Common, Green and Wood Sandpipers plus Black-tailed Godwits are the most likely. If the water level is low, Little Stints and Curlew Sandpipers will occur, along with Ruff.

There is always the chance of something better and Great White Egret, Spoonbill, Crane, Water Rail, Spotted Crake and Red-necked Phalarope have been found, plus Black Kite and Rough-legged Buzzard.

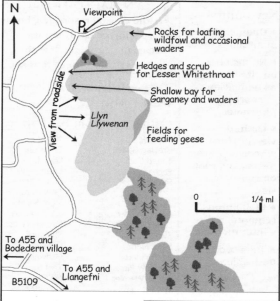

Access details

(Approx 5.5 miles E of Holyhead).

Leave A55 at junction 3 to RAF Valley and turn right towards Bodedern. Continue through village to 'T' junction.

Turn right out of the village and after about 300m, turn left onto a narrow winding lane. You will see the lake on your right. Drive on to the

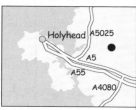

'T' junction and turn right. The parking space is a small pull-in alongside the lake.

Other nearby sites

Cefni Reservoir, Llyn Alaw.

Key points

- **Open access at all times.**
- **No facilities on site but all amenities in nearby Rhosneigr.**
- **Limited viewing for wheelchair users from road on southern side.**
- **Wellingtons required in winter months.**
- **Telescope desirable.**

L LYN MAELOG is a freshwater lake lying to the east of the coastal resort of Rhosneigr on Anglesey's south-west-facing coast. It holds a variety of wildfowl and reedbed species in summer, while the patient watcher may catch a glimpse of the Bittern that skulks in the reeds most winters.

Target birds *Summer* – Reed Warbler (75%), Grasshopper Warbler (40%).

Other possible bird species

All year	*Winter*	
Greylag Goose	Great Crested Grebe	Buzzard
Tufted Duck	Little Grebe	Water Rail
Pochard	Cormorant	Moorhen
Stonechat	Bittern (rare)	Coot
	Grey Heron	Snipe
Summer	Mute Swan	Black-headed Gull
Great Crested Grebe	Greylag Goose	Common Gull
Little Grebe	Canada Goose	Great Black-backed Gull
Swift	Shelduck	Herring Gull
Sand Martin	Wigeon	Sky Lark
House Martin	Gadwall	Meadow Pipit
Meadow Pipit	Teal	Raven
Sedge Warbler	Mallard	Reed Bunting
Whitethroat	Shoveler	
Blackcap	Pochard	*Passage periods*
Willow Warbler	Tufted Duck	Lapwing
Reed Bunting	Goldeneye	Golden Plover
	Sparrowhawk	Whimbrel
		Common Sandpiper

Background information and birding tips

DURING the summer months the reedbed around Llyn Maelog is alive with the songs of Reed and Sedge Warblers, with Reed Buntings delivering their simple ditties from atop the scrubby bushes that abound in the area.

Away from the reedbed area Whitethroats, Blackcaps and Willow Warblers prosper in the hedgerows and scrub that border the lake.

You can walk by the lake along a public footpath running from the southeast corner via the eastern shore to the southwest corner. The southern shore has impenetrable reedbed along its entire length.

During spring and summer there will be Little and Great Crested Grebes, Pochards and Tufted Ducks on the open water, while in the air you'll see masses of Swifts, House Martins, Sand Martins and Swallows feeding on the insect multitudes.

Once you reach the northern edge look out for Meadow Pipits and wagtails, and possibly a Common Sandpiper.

A small colony of Black-headed Gulls occupy the islets along the western shore, and a pair of Mediterranean Gulls spent part of the summer with them recently.

The area between the road and reedbed along the southern shore should have several Stonechats, and this is the best area to see the elusive Grasshopper Warbler as it 'reels' from the dense patches of brambles.

Scarce migrants seen in recent years during spring/early summer have been White-winged Black and Whiskered Terns, Cetti's Warbler and Red-backed Shrike.

Autumn passage sees Lapwings and Golden Plovers in the surrounding fields, Common Sandpipers frequenting the margins of the lake, and fly-over Whimbrels uttering their 'tittering' calls.

A visit in winter is well worth making as the regular wildfowl are joined by a few Goldeneyes and more occasional Red-breasted Mergansers and Scaup.

Single Red-throated Divers and Red-necked Grebes have both been reported, and a Bittern haunts the reedbed most winters, though it is rarely seen in the dense cover.

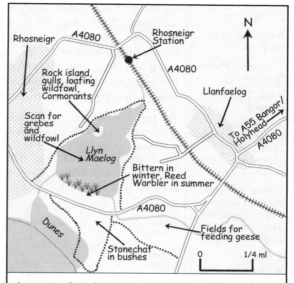

Access details.

(Approx 6 miles SE of Holyhead).

From A55 Expressway take the well signposted A4080 to Rhosneigr (junction 5). After crossing the railway line turn right.

The lake will be seen on right hand side of the road just before reaching Rhosneigr. Park safely anywhere along roadside and join the footpath at either the SW or SE corner of the lake.

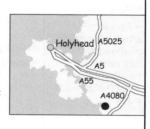

Other nearby sites

Inland Sea, Malltraeth.

113

Key points

- **Open access all year.**
- **Easy roadside birding.**
- **No facilities on site.**
- **Limited facilities in nearby Malltraeth and Newborough.**
- **Free parking by road bridge over Afon Cefni at north end of pool.**
- **Best for waders on incoming or falling tides.**
- **An excellent site for disabled birdwatchers, but park with care on busy A4080 alongside pool.**

Contacts

Countryside Council for Wales – 01248 385 500

THIS VERY accessible site was made famous by bird artist Charles Tunnicliffe and Shorelands, his long-time home, lies to the north of the pool. The Pintail flock that featured in so many of his paintings is still loyal to the pool and it is probably the best place in Wales to see this elegant species. The site holds good birds year round, particularly waders during passage periods and wildfowl in the winter.

Target birds

All year – Little Egret (90%), Black-tailed Godwit (80%). *Spring* – Passage waders (100%). *Summer* – Stonechat (100%). *Autumn* – Curlew Sandpiper (70%). *Winter* – Pintail (100%), Hen Harrier (80%), Merlin (80%), Peregrine (90%), Spotted Redshank (50%), Greenshank (30%), Short-eared Owl (30%), Kingfisher (70%).

Other possible bird species

All year	Sparrowhawk	*Recent rare and scarce birds*
Shelduck		
Mallard	*Winter*	Green-winged Teal
Oystercatcher	Golden Plover	Blue-winged Teal
Curlew	Common Sandpiper	Smew
Redshank	Woodcock	Pectoral Sandpiper
	Kingfisher	Osprey
Autumn		Hoopoe
Buzzard		Firecrest

Background information and birding tips

IMMORTALISED in the paintings of Charles Tunnicliffe, Malltraeth Cob Pool is a large body of brackish water on your left, when coming from Newborough. The site is a couple of miles in length, but no wider than a quarter-mile at any point – if you don't count the huge expanse of the Cefni estuary or the Newborough Forest conifers on the southern boundary.

Malltraeth can be covered from the roadside in ten minutes if all you want is a quick look at areas of open water and visible mud. However, the road grows increasingly busy and we now feel that we risk obstructing the flow of traffic by parking on the grass verge.

It is better, and of course safer, to use the car park at the north end – there you will find a path for a pleasant walk on top of an embankment, with views over the estuary and the Cob Pool. Sadly this is not accessible to wheelchair users.

By walking, you will ensure you don't miss any birds hidden in the sedges and grasses by the pool. It takes around two hours for the return trip, walking at a leisurely pace.

Park on the left and the house more or less immediately in front of you is Tunnicliffe's former domicile, so familiar to birdwatchers from his *Shorelands Winter Diary* and *Shorelands Summer Diary* books.

Start birding straightaway by scanning the Cefni estuary mudflats for waders: look especially for a Spotted Redshank or two which are usually found by the edges of the main channel in winter.

Cross over the road to view the three channels between it and the viaduct. These can hold godwits, Little Egrets, Greenshanks, Common Sandpipers, Goosanders, Kingfishers and, more rarely, Smew.

Crossing back over the road, go through the gate to follow the mile-long linear path on the west side of the pool. From here it is easy to obtain excellent views of the many wildfowl and waders usually present but also check the surrounding bushes for passerines.

Water levels fluctuate widely but ideally they will be low enough for waders to feed. Incoming or falling tides are best, as at low tide the waders can be very distant out on the Cefni estuary.

Waders will roost on the pool if the high tide water is not too high, or on the rocky spit near the bridge if undisturbed. An alternative high tide roost forms on the banks of the River Cefni to the landward side of the bridge.

In winter the saltmarsh to your right, beyond the estuary, is excellent for raptors, especially towards dusk, when Hen Harriers, and more occasionally Short-eared Owls come in to roost.

Look out for Woodcock along the forest edge at dusk in winter. At the end of the pool, either return the way you came or continue into Newborough Forest.

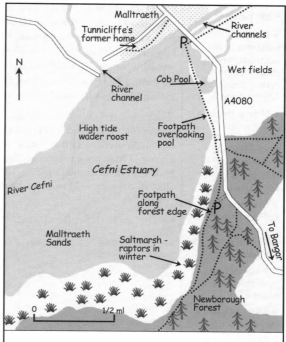

Access details

(Approx four miles SW of Llangefni).

Cross onto Anglesey on A55 Expressway and turn left as soon as you have crossed over the Britannia Bridge, then left again towards LlanfairPG (the village with the longest name in Britain!).

As you enter the village turn left on A4080, signposted to Newborough. Stay on A4080 through Newborough village heading towards Malltraeth.

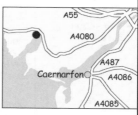

The pool is on the left, just after passing through Newborough Forest.

Other nearby sites

Braint Estuary, Llyn Parc Mawr (SH413671), Newborough Forest.

115

Key points

- **Do not confuse with popular beach of the same name south of Aberystwyth.**

- **Morfa Bychan village Spar shop has basic supplies. Porthmadog has plenty of facilities.**

- **Nearest public toilets behind dunes at SH 545 365 (turn left at village shop).**

- **Easy access, possible to view from car.**

- **Calm overcast days give best viewing of sea ducks.**

- **Telescope desirable.**

THIS SHALLOW BAY close to Porthmadog provides good feeding for wintering seaduck and it is possible to find Velvet Scoters, Long-tailed Ducks and Scaup among the large numbers of Common Scoters. The area has gained an amazing reputation for turning up rarities in recent times, including Elegant Tern, Ivory Gull, Ross's Gull and King Eider, but bear in mind it can be busy at weekends.

Target birds

Winter – Common Scoter (100%), Velvet Scoter (60%), Long-tailed Duck (70%), Scaup (70%), Eider (70%), Sanderling (60%), Little Gull (50%), Chough (50%). *Spring* – Manx Shearwater (80%), Pomarine Skua (40%), Arctic Skua (50%), Great Skua (40%), Little Gull (50%), Sandwich Tern (100%). *Summer* – Manx Shearwater (80%), Sandwich Tern (100%).

Other possible bird species

Winter	Rock Pipit	*Summer*
Red-throated Diver	Stonechat	Buzzard
Great Crested Grebe		Stonechat
Cormorant	*Spring*	
Shag	Buzzard	*Occasional*
Goldeneye	White Wagtail	Surf Scoter
Red-breasted Merganser	Rock Pipit	Mediterranean Gull
Buzzard	Stonechat	Glaucous Gull

Background information and birding tips

TO GET THE BEST from a winter's day at Morfa Bychan, try to visit when the sea is calm enough to show the birds well. Overcast days are best, as on sunny days you will find the birds are silhouetted on bright water.

The beach itself is beautiful, though it can be very busy, especially at weekends when jet skiers disturb the birds constantly.

Your birding can begin before you reach Morfa Bychan at a small lake on your left, one mile after leaving Porthmadog. A quick scan may boost your day list a little.

After passing through Morfa Bychan village, drive slowly, keeping a lookout for Stonechats

on fences and roadside bushes.

At Black Rock beach, park and scan the bay for sea duck. Common Scoters should be easy to see, relatively close into land. With a telescope, great views should be possible.

By scanning carefully, you should be able to pick out scarcer species. Remember the ducks feed beneath the waves, so it is easy to overlook individuals but patience and persistence will be rewarded!

Drive east along the beach for a mile, stopping to scan regularly. If the sea is choppy, climb up onto the dunes to gain height to look down onto the sea. Look for Long-tailed Ducks, one of the key

Access details

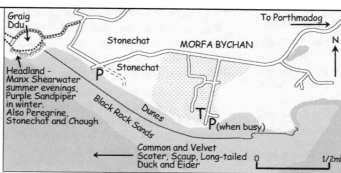

(Two miles S of Porthmadog).

In Porthmadog town centre, take minor road SW, signposted for Morfa Bychan.

Continue through Morfa Bychan and after just under one mile, the tarmacadamed road runs onto the open beach.

Driving with care, turn left and continue along sands for about one mile. Keep near the top of the beach – cars regularly become stuck by venturing too far out onto the wet sand.

On the highest tides it may not be possible to drive along the beach. In this case, park carefully at the road end, taking care not to block access.

Having driven the length of the beach, return to the metalled road and take the first left after only 50 metres for Black Rock Sands. Continue past a sharp right bend, park carefully and continue on foot.

Take the dirt track on your left just before the crest of the hill. Follow the track past a building on your left. Take the footpath into the field on your left and out onto the

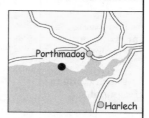

headland. Retrace your steps to the car.

target species, just beyond the breakers. Once found, they can give great views.

Check any gulls and waders along the beach. Anything can, and does, turn up here!

Work your way back along the beach, checking for missing species. Check the cliffs at the west end of the beach for Rock Pipits.

Leave the beach by the tarmacadamed road towards Morfa Bychan. After just 50 metres take the first left turn and start to look for Stonechats on either side of the road and Buzzards over the ridge to your right.

After a sharp right bend, park carefully and continue uphill on foot. At the brow of the hill, turn left onto a dirt track, walk past an old building on your left and then take the footpath on your left onto the headland. Walk to the point overlooking Black Rock beach to the east and across to Criccieth in the west.

This headland gives a panoramic view of the bay and you also have the chance of Choughs here, plus Rock Pipits on the cliffs at the end.

In spring, follow the same route. Given strong onshore, south-westerly winds, it is worth looking for skuas and Little Gulls offshore.

In recent years, Pomarine Skuas have been seen annually, particularly in May. Given the right conditions and luck you may see a flock lingering offshore.

These same conditions can produce Little Gulls over the breakers, plus Manx Shearwaters. Sandwich Terns often rest on the beach as they move north. Check the headland and any cover for migrants.

In summer, expect views of Manx Shearwaters, especially in the evening.

Other nearby sites

Borth-y-Gest, Criccieth, Pont Croeso, Porthmadog.

Key points

- **Open access all year.**
- **Public toilets at car park.**
- **Cafes and pubs in Harlech.**
- **Calm, overcast viewing conditions best.**
- **Telescope very desirable.**
- **Long walk on sand, not suitable for less able.**
- **Warm clothing essential.**

MORFA HARLECH beach stretches north from Harlech town and is a truly spectacular site thanks to the extensive, and still growing, sand dune scenery behind it. For birdwatchers the chief attraction is the large numbers of seaduck that spend winter close offshore in Tremadog Bay.

Target birds

Winter – Common Scoter (100%), Velvet Scoter (80%), Scaup (80%), Red-throated Diver (100%), Great Northern Diver (50%), Great Crested Grebe (100%), Slavonian Grebe (80%), Eider (60%), Sanderling (100%).

Other possible bird species

Winter	Kestrel	Razorbill
Cormorant	Merlin	Sky Lark
Shag	Peregrine	Meadow Pipit
Shelduck	Oystercatcher	Rock Pipit
Wigeon	Ringed Plover	Pied Wagtail
Long-tailed Duck (rare)	Grey Plover	Stonechat
Goldeneye	Knot	Raven
Red-breasted Merganser	Dunlin	Linnet
Hen Harrier	Bar-tailed Godwit	
Buzzard	Curlew	*Occasional*
	Common gull species	Surf Scoter
	Guillemot	Black-necked Grebe

Background information and birding tips

THE NATIONAL NATURE RESERVE of Morfa Harlech covers 1,080 ha of sand dunes and beautiful beach and is overlooked by the spectacular Harlech Castle. The walk north along the beach from the town is worthwhile in its own right, but it also provides great winter birding.

Huge rafts of Common Scoters loaf just offshore, making this an amazing place to get great views of an often-distant species.

Check the sea regularly for parties of Common Scoters – they are present for most of the winter.

Contacts

Countryside Council for Wales – 01248 385 500.

Patient scanning through the flocks will reveal other sought-after species, such as Velvet Scoter.

Small numbers of Velvet Scoter are present each winter and should be found easily enough as they are a little larger than the Commons, sit higher in the water, have larger bills and open their wings just before diving, revealing their best ID feature: white secondaries!

The Scoter flocks have occasionally attracted Surf Scoters, a vagrant from North America, and memorably, three of these striking Yanks were here together one winter!

Scaup and Eiders should also be picked out. Red-throated Divers are present throughout the winter and are occasionally joined by one or two Great Northern Divers.

Great Crested Grebes are common and Slavonian Grebes are a regular feature, numbers often reaching double figures. Sharp eyes have also detected a Black-necked Grebe among the wintering Slavonians on more than one occasion.

Small numbers of Guillemots and Razorbills can be found feeding offshore and in winter you may spy a Long-tailed Duck in the breakers.

It is probable that wintering species such as the divers and grebes may linger until April – this is the case at other North Wales sites such as Llanfairfechan.

Manx Shearwaters are a distinct possibility in spring and summer, while the Warren area, north of

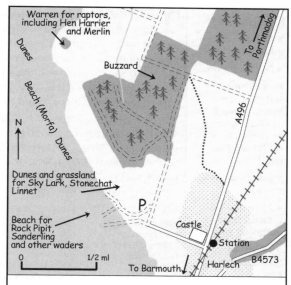

Access details.

To reach Harlech from E take A496, which runs SW from Blaenau Ffestiniog for approximately 17 miles. As you enter the town, you will have the railway station on your left and a large school on your right. Turn right into a narrow road, which leads straight out towards the sand dunes, and a public car park after approximately half a mile.

From S, follow A496 into the centre of Harlech, ignoring B4573, which forks off to your right. Immediately after

the railway bridge crosses the road and before you reach the railway station on your right, take the small road off to your left, which leads as above to the car park.

the conifers, attracts raptors such as Peregrine and Buzzard.

The area is very under-watched, so who knows what you might find here? A rare gull, perhaps, or a Shore Lark along the

tideline? The habitat certainly looks good for either or both!

Other nearby sites

Criccieth, Porthmadog.

119

Key points

- Open access all year.
- Free parking.
- Café and toilets near Youth Hostel at south end of valley, or in Bethesda at north end.
- Spectacular scenery.
- Area can be viewed from metalled road.
- Ideal for all physical abilities.
- Warm clothes needed if you explore on foot.

THE CLASSIC glacial valley of Nant Ffrancon runs south from Bethesda to Llyn Ogwen and a single-track tarmacadamed road on the western side gives easy access to its mountain birds. Famous for Twite and Ring Ouzels, the valley has plenty more to offer, so be prepared to spend at least half a day to do it justice. Spring is the time to visit – in winter, any bird you see would be a bonus!

Target birds:
All year – Peregrine (60%), Grey Wagtail (80%), Dipper (80%), Chough (50%), Raven (100%). *Spring* – Goosander (70%), Common Sandpiper (80%), Tree Pipit (100%), Redstart (100%), Wheatear (100%), Stonechat (100%), Ring Ouzel (70%), Twite (80%). *Summer* – Wheatear (100%), Stonechat (100%), Twite (80%).

Other possible bird species

Spring/summer

Grey Heron	Sky Lark	Willow Warbler
Red-breasted Merganser	Meadow Pipit	Pied Flycatcher
Sparrowhawk	Pied Wagtail	Jay
Buzzard	Whinchat	Siskin
Kestrel	Grasshopper Warbler	Lesser Redpoll
Cuckoo	Sedge Warbler	Reed Bunting

Background information and birding tips

DESPITE being the route of the busy A5 trunk road, there is plenty of birdwatching potential in this glacial valley – as long as you keep to the minor road on the western side. Approaching from Bethesda, turn off the A5 and park carefully on the left just beyond a stone bridge.

Walk back to the bridge to scan the fast-flowing River Ogwen for Dippers, Grey Wagtails and Goosanders. The scattered trees here should produce Redstarts and a chance of a Tree Pipit.

Keep scanning the ridges either side of the valley for soaring raptors and Ravens. Walk a little further along the road to get good views along the river.

Keep a lookout for a Common Sandpiper whirring over the waters. You will soon reach a birch

wood where it is worth looking for Lesser Redpolls, Redstarts and Tree Pipits.

Return to the car and continue along the road past the birch wood. As vegetation becomes scarcer and the terrain rockier, look out for Wheatears and Meadow Pipits. Stonechats are regularly seen on roadside fences and walls and it is worth carefully checking all corvids in case one is a Chough.

After about one-and-a-quarter miles, you reach the farm of Pentre, where the road passes right through the farmyard! The area either side of the homestead can be good for Twite. These scarce finches are sometimes found along the fence lines.

A little beyond the farm, the road crosses a flat unfenced grassy area, a favourite spot for feeding

Access details

(1.5 miles S of Bethesda on A5).

For birding, there is great access along the old single-track road on W side of the valley.

From Bethesda, take A5 S from town for just over one mile. Turn right into the narrow minor road — be warned it is easy to miss. If you see a complex of buildings on your left, you have gone too far!

Once on the right road, continue for 200m and cross a narrow stone bridge and park carefully on the left. Continue to drive and stop frequently along this road until you rejoin A5 at Llyn Ogwen, by the Ogwen Cottage Youth Hostel.

From Betws-y-Coed, take A5 W for approximately ten miles. At the far end of Llyn Ogwen, turn left, signposted Youth Hostel.

Continue past the hostel and bird the minor road down the valley until you rejoin the A5 just south of Bethesda.

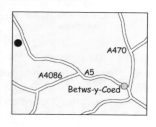

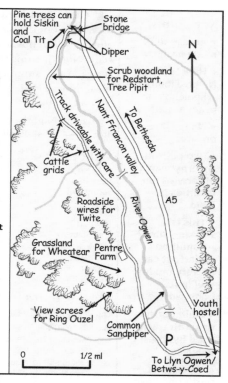

Wheatears and occasional Ring Ouzels.

Further on you reach a cattle grid, not long after a farm track off to the left. Park on the right immediately before the cattle grid at SH 641 610. This is the best place in the valley to look for Ring Ouzels. Scan the scree slopes to your right and listen for the rather monotonous song and 'chack-chack' calls. The males can sit very high on the crags when singing, so scan very carefully and be patient.

Wheatears should be easily seen here and perhaps a Redstart in the hawthorns clinging to the cliffs. Look for Peregrine and Raven overhead. Scan the river below for Dippers, Grey Wagtails and Common Sandpipers. Birds can be elusive but the patient watcher may discover a Twite or two on the stone walls.

From this point the road climbs steadily up to the Youth Hostel by Llyn Ogwen. Check out the plantation around the Hostel for Siskins and perhaps a Pied Flycatcher. The stream between the Hostel and the A5 can hold Dipper.

Llyn Ogwen is generally fairly bird-less, though in summer a pair of Great Crested Grebes may be present. A few Pochards are likely in winter and Goosanders are possible throughout the year.

If approaching from Betws-y-Coed, simply follow the route in reverse.

Other nearby sites

Aber Ogwen, Llanfairfechan.

121

Key points

• **Access to many paths.**

• **Hilly terrain. No possibility of wheelchair or pram access.**

• **No facilities on site.**

• **Two pubs in Gwernymynydd, otherwise full facilities in Mold.**

• **This is a working site – conditions underfoot can be very muddy. Wellington boots advised.**

• **Main north to south track used by forest vehicles.**

• **Vehicles at north end have been subject to sporadic vandalism.**

• **Expect cold conditions – site is above 350 metres.**

Contacts

Forest Enterprise – 01341 440 666.

A GROUP of hard-to-see species live at this site south of Mold but the birds can sometimes remain frustratingly elusive within this man-made forest. However, if you want to see a Nightjar, this remains one of the leading sites in North Wales. A fine summer evening towards the end of May is the ideal time to visit.

Target birds

All year – Woodcock (70%), Firecrest (20%). *Summer* – Nightjar (80%), Long-eared Owl (20%). *Winter* – Crossbill (80%).

Other possible bird species

All year	Redstart	Moorhen
Buzzard	Sedge Warbler	Linnet
Tawny Owl	Whitethroat	Brambling
Raven	Blackcap	Siskin
Goldcrest	Willow Warbler	
Bullfinch		*Spring/autumn*
Tree Sparrow	*Winter*	Mallard
	Mallard	Green Sandpiper
Summer	Teal	Common Sandpiper
Cuckoo	Tufted Duck	Greenshank
Tree Pipit	Coot	

Background information and birding tips

IF YOU LIKE to birdwatch away from the crowds, then this extensive area of conifer plantations and mixed woodland is the ideal site for you. Basically there are two sets of birds – those viewable during the day, and those that only put in an appearance at dusk.

During daylight hours in winter, wander up the central path looking for finches — especially Bullfinches, as the mature mixed woodland is excellent for this species.

Watch also for Crossbills as flocks of up to 40 are regularly seen. Goldcrests can be seen in all the clear-fell areas, where new stock has been replanted.

Nearing the northern end at SJ 218 589, turn left. Firecrests are infrequently seen along this path at all times of year, but most often in winter. Woodcock are often flushed here, too.

Continue along to a stile and cross it to view a small reservoir, where winter wildfowl, such as Mallard, Teal, Tufted Ducks, Coots and Moorhens may be present to boost the day list. During passage, Green and Common Sandpipers and Greenshanks are recorded here.

Around dusk in early January is a good time for seeing and hearing Tawny Owls as they stake their claims to territory.

From mid-March, Woodcock can be seen roding and they will continue to make these display flights into July, but the prize at dusk in summer is Nightjar, with usually at least two pairs present.

They can best be heard and seen at the south end of the site, and are at their most obvious at the end of May and in early June.

Calm, still evenings usually produce the best viewing. Sometimes the birds hunt over adjacent fields, and can be missed by the uninitiated observer.

The same walk is possible during daylight in summer with good numbers of Willow Warblers, Chiffchaffs and Whitethroats always present. Small numbers of Tree Pipits breed, and Redstarts may be seen on the outer fringes of the woods.

Migrant Hobbies are increasing across the country and this exciting summer visitor is now regularly seen at this site during the month of July – an indication that the species is breeding perhaps?

With luck, July evenings can produce excellent views of Long-eared Owls in a family group, with young birds practising their flying skills in the more open areas surrounding the forested areas.

A word of warning concerning the car parks – the main site at the north end has been subject to sporadic vandalism in the past, so it is a good idea not to leave any valuables in your vehicle when it is left unattended.

During holiday periods, when trouble is most likely to occur, it may pay to use the smaller parking area at the southern end of the site

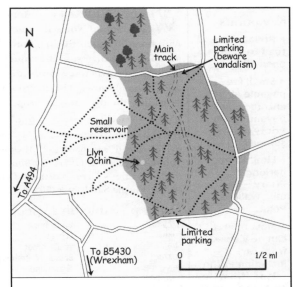

Access details

(Approx 1.5 mile S of Mold).

From A55 Expressway at Ewloe (junction 34) take A494, signposted Mold/Yr Wyddgrug.

On reaching the village of Gwernymyndd turn left at top of hill just before the Rainbow pub into Owain Glyndwyr Lane, which has a very steep gradient.

Continue past the Owain Glyndwyr pub, straight over the crossroads and continue until a T junction is reached. Turn right and after a quarter of a mile park on the right at the entrance to Nercwys Mountain. There is room for

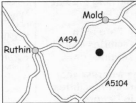

at least six vehicles to park at this northern car park. The southern parking area, reached via a minor road E of the B5430 is even smaller but may provide more security.

Key points

- Private access road to Point open all year.

- Small fee payable at entrance, just beyond Penmon Priory, during summer.

- Limited free parking at Priory – one mile walk to Point.

- Most of area can be viewed from car, including Puffin Island (from the parking area at the Point).

- Cafe with facilities open in summer only.

- Nearest year-round facilities in Beaumaris. Public toilets on west side of castle.

Contacts

Puffin Island Cruises: Adults £6, OAP £5.50, Child £4.50. Dogs free. Group discounts. Leaves every hour from Beaumaris, weather permitting. Call 01248 810 251.

WHENEVER you visit Anglesey's most easterly watchpoint, you will almost certainly see good birds, with breeding seabirds in summer, migrants in spring and autumn, plus divers, grebes, ducks and auks in winter. On the rare days when few birds are in evidence, the coastal scenery is glorious, with the mountains of Snowdonia providing the distant backdrop.

Target birds

All year – Eider (90%), Black Guillemot (90%), Green Woodpecker (20%), Stonechat (95%), Chough (60%). *Spring* – Cuckoo (40%), Grasshopper Warbler (70%), Spotted Flycatcher (70%). *Summer* – Gannet (90%), Puffin (80%). *Winter* – Great Northern Diver (30%) Red-throated Diver (80%), Purple Sandpiper (70%).

Other possible bird species

All year	Whinchat	Blackcap
Fulmar	Wheatear	Chiffchaff
Shag	Whitethroat	Goldcrest
Buzzard	Lesser Whitethroat	
Peregrine	Grasshopper Warbler	*Winter*
Razorbill		Common Scoter
Guillemot	*Summer*	Turnstone
Kittiwake	Sandwich Tern	
Rock Pipit	Arctic Tern	*Recent rare and*
Raven	Common Tern	*scarce birds*
		Red-necked Phalarope
Spring	*Autumn*	Alpine Swift
Sandwich Tern	Meadow Pipit	Spoonbill
Swallow	Grey Wagtail	Bee-eater
House Martin	Wheatear	Golden Oriole
Meadow Pipit	Fieldfare	Red-backed Shrike
Grey Wagtail	Redwing	Pallas's Warbler
White Wagtail	Garden Warbler	Yellow-browed Warbler
		Firecrest

Background information and birding tips

ITS LOCATION at the most easterly point of Anglesey, overlooking Conwy Bay, means that Penmon is a good place for finding birds on migration and enjoying views of breeding seabirds on nearby Puffin Island.

On route to the Point you must pass Penmon Pool (SH629798), which has turned up some unusual species, such as a recent Red-necked Phalarope and Red-backed

Shrike. The Pool itself and the surrounding fields are good for wildfowl and waders at high tide times. Looking to the shoreward side of the road there is an excellent chance of divers in winter and terns in spring.

Between the Pool and Penmon Priory the shore is good for Ringed Plovers and Rock Pipits. You can park free at the Priory and bird around it and the nearby medieval dovecote — the surrounding woodland is the best place for the locally scarce Green Woodpecker. You'll see other more common woodland species, plus migrants in season, especially in autumn when Pallas's and Yellow-browed Warblers have been recorded.

You must now decide if you are going to walk the road to the Point, or drive (fee charged). Walking in spring and autumn will produce passage migrants including Chiffchaffs, Blackcaps, Willow and Sedge Warblers, Common and Lesser Whitethroats, and hirundines. The coastal fields to the west of the road regularly hold small numbers of Choughs.

In late autumn there are often good numbers of thrushes and finches, including Siskins and Bramblings, passing over and sometimes coming down into the numerous thickets.

At Penmon Point the gardens of the former coastguard cottages are worth checking for migrants in season, and Rock Pipits and Stonechats are common year round.

In winter it is worth 'scoping offshore for divers, grebes and auks, plus Eiders. At this time the rocky shore here usually has Turnstones and Purple Sandpipers.

Puffin Island lies just offshore and in spring and summer it, and the surrounding sea, can be 'scoped for Puffins, Razorbills, Guillemots, Black Guillemots, Cormorants, Shags, Fulmars, Kittiwakes, Sandwich Terns and passing Gannets and Manx Shearwaters.

Daily boat trips depart from

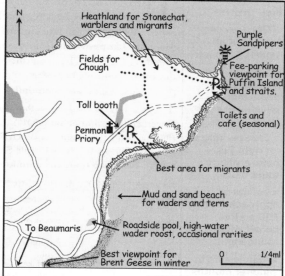

Heathland for Stonechat, warblers and migrants

Purple Sandpipers

Fields for Chough

Fee-parking viewpoint for Puffin Island and straits.

Toll booth

Penmon Priory

Toilets and cafe (seasonal)

Best area for migrants

Mud and sand beach for waders and terns

To Beaumaris

Roadside pool, high-water wader roost, occasional rarities

Best viewpoint for Brent Geese in winter

0   1/4ml

Access details.

(Three miles E of Beaumaris).

From Beaumaris (which boasts all facilities and a castle that looks like our childhood imaginings!) head out, along the main street, on B5109 towards Llangoed. Before reaching the village take a right turn clearly marked Penmon.

Follow this road past Penmon

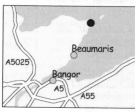

Beaumaris

A5025

Bangor

A5   A55

Pool to the Priory, and ultimately the Point itself.

Beaumaris and circle Puffin Island during the summer months (see opposite).

No landings are possible but you will be able to observe birds from the boat.

The Island's shingle beach will have loafing Eiders and Red-breasted Mergansers at this time. Peregrines are frequently seen overhead from the Point.

Other nearby sites

Fedr Fawr, Friar's shoreline (SH 609 773) for wintering Pale-bellied Brent Geese and waders, Llangoed river walk (SH 610 797) for wintering Chiffchaffs and Firecrests, Puffin Island.

Key points

- **Open access on foot at all times.**

- **Limited parking on headland. Fee payable at peak times.**

- **Free parking on right just before village toilet block.**

- **Toilets on approach road 100 metres before mini-roundabout.**

- **Mobile cafe in summer months only.**

- **Full facilities in nearby Amlwch.**

- **No facilities for disabled – access to headland is difficult.**

- **Please keep to paths – the site is privately owned with public access at discretion of owners.**

T HIS SMALL peninsula at the north-east tip of **Anglesey** is probably the best seawatching site in **North Wales**, especially during the late summer and autumn months when there are strong winds from the north-west. Interesting breeding birds can be seen during summer and it is without doubt the region's best site for cetaceans, especially harbour porpoises, which are seen daily.

Target birds
All year – Peregrine (70%), Chough (100%), Raven (100%), Stonechat (100%). *Summer* – Black Guillemot (90%). *Autumn* – seabirds, Black Redstart (50%), Lapland Bunting (40%). *Winter* – Purple Sandpiper (80%), Black Redstart (30%), Blackcap (gardens around toilet block 50%).

Other possible bird species

All year	Summer	Autumn
Fulmar	Manx Shearwater	Common Scoter
Gannet	Storm Petrel	Merlin
Cormorant	Guillemot	Arctic Skua
Shag	Razorbill	Great Skua
Rock Pipit	Puffin	Pomarine Skua
Linnet	Kittiwake	Turnstone
	Sandwich Tern	Sky Lark
	Common Tern	Blackbird
Spring	Arctic Tern	Song Thrush
Wheatear		Mistle Thrush
Common passerine migrants		Common finches

Background information and birding tips

L ATE SUMMER and autumn are the premium times to be at Point Lynas for a seabird spectacular, especially when winds are from the north-west. The majority of seabirds then pass east to west as they move out of Liverpool Bay.

July and early August produce regular sightings of Storm Petrels and big numbers of Manx Shearwaters. The occasional Balearic Shearwater is seen, and, very rarely, both Great and Cory's Shearwaters.

All the skuas – Arctic, Great, Pomarine and occasionally Long-tailed – are usually seen in September and October, with the two first mentioned making regular appearances in the right conditions.

North-west gales usually bring Leach's Petrels close to land during the same months, along with big numbers of Kittiwakes.

Sabine's Gulls and Sooty Shearwaters are seen most autumns, while other birds seen passing the Head in autumn include Sandwich, Common, Arctic and occasionally Little and Black Terns, wildfowl (especially Common Scoter) and waders.

Divers pass by in winter, and during early winter gales Little Auks may pass in small numbers.

For the most productive seawatching we advise you to arrive at Lynas just before dawn. This gives you time to get into position prior to the heaviest seabird passage, which is usually during the first few hours of daylight.

However, in the right conditions seabirds can pass at any time of the day and light conditions, which are so important for seawatching, tend to improve as the day progresses.

To reach the best seawatching place, walk to the lighthouse, follow the path to the right of it, and then head down to the Point, passing the fog horn on your left. There is little, or no, shelter at this site so a set of good waterproofs is essential – remember it is usually wet and windy during the most productive birdwatching conditions.

A tip while seawatching here is to check both near and far distances, as birds sometimes pass over the Point itself. So don't miss good birds by constantly focussing on the horizon!

If the expected passage does not materialise, or you simply get fed up, a walk around the headland should produce good views of Choughs and Ravens, and, in winter, Purple Sandpipers are often present on the rocky shore.

In summer, Black Guillemots can usually be found in the sheltered bay to the west side of the headland, marked on the map as Porth Eilian. If you miss them there, try the area around the jetty on the east side of Lynas.

The bushes are likely to have

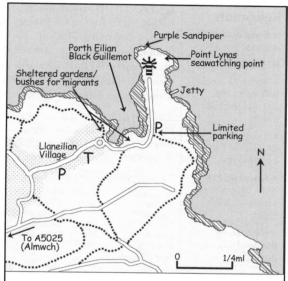

Access details.

(Three miles E of Amlwch).

From Menai Bridge head N on A5025 to Benllech, then continue towards Amlwch. After passing Pen-y-Sarn look out for signs for Cerrigman – soon after these, turn first right on B road to Llaneilian. Use car park in Llaneilian village, and walk to mini-roundabout at the end of road. Turn right, over the cattle grid, and

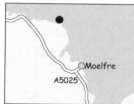

continue to the lighthouse. The walk takes about 15 minutes.

grounded migrants during both passage periods, but perhaps the best area to search for sheltering passerines is in the gardens and bushes in the vicinity of the mini-roundabout and nearby toilet block.

Little attention has been given to passage migrants so far but considering the site's position, it looks a good bet to turn up some great birds.

Other nearby sites

Cemlyn Lagoon, Llyn Alaw.

127

Key points

- **Easy open access.**
- **Good parking.**
- **Natural tracks not suitable for wheelchair users.**
- **Telescope desirable for best views.**
- **Good RSPB hide offers best views at high tide.**
- **Very busy during holiday periods.**

STRATEGICALLY placed at the western tip of the bird-rich River Dee estuary, the Point's mix of mud, sand, saltmarsh and scrub, liberally sprinkled with small fresh pools, has always attracted birds, with some that are scarce and even rare. The area suffers regular disturbance in summer, but in winter the RSPB reserve is an ideal place to witness huge numbers of waders.

Target birds

Winter – Pintail (100%), Hen Harrier (40%), Merlin (60%), Peregrine (90%), Mediterranean Gull (20%), Short-eared Owl (20%), Snow Bunting (60%). *Summer* – Storm Petrel (20%), Common, Little and Sandwich Terns (100%).

Other possible bird species

All year
Fulmar
Cormorant
Grey Heron
Little Egret
Shelduck
Sparrowhawk
Buzzard
Kestrel
Oystercatcher
Ringed Plover
Curlew
Redshank
Lapwing
Herring Gull
Great Black-backed Gull
Lesser Black-backed Gull
Sky Lark
Stonechat
Reed Bunting

Spring
Red-throated Diver
Manx Shearwater
Black-tailed Godwit
Whimbrel
Common Sandpiper
Hirundines
White Wagtail
Whinchat
Wheatear
Grasshopper Warbler
Sedge Warbler

Reed Warbler
Whitethroat
Lesser Whitethroat
Blackcap
Chiffchaff
Willow Warbler
Siskin
Lesser Redpoll

Summer
Gannet
Red-breasted Merganser
Swift
Hirundines
Common warblers

Autumn /winter
Red-throated Diver
Brent Goose
Wigeon
Teal
Common Scoter
Red-breasted Merganser
Golden Plover
Knot
Dunlin
Snipe
Black-tailed Godwit
Bar-tailed Godwit
Mediterranean Gull
Meadow Pipit
Grey Wagtail
Fieldfare

Redwing
Goldcrest
Linnet

Autumn
Manx Shearwater
Gannet
Grey Plover
Spotted Redshank
Greenshank
Arctic Skua
Great Skua
Sandwich Tern
Common Tern
Short-eared Owl
Hirundines
Wheatear
Common warblers
Brambling
Siskin

Winter
Great Crested Grebe
Goldeneye
Black-headed Gull
Common Gull
Guillemot
Kingfisher
Long-tailed Tit

Contacts

For information about RSPB reserve, call 0151 336 7681 or visit: www. rspb.org.uk

Access details

(Point of Ayr lies four miles E of Prestatyn).

From A548, that runs between Flint and Prestatyn, take the minor road signposted Talacre Beach from the roundabout at Tanlan. Continue over the railway bridge to the end of Station Road, where there is a car park on the right just before the seawall.

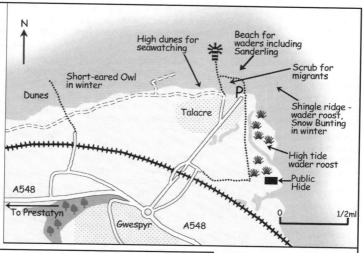

Background information and birding tips

VISITING BIRDWATCHERS can look forward to a variety of experiences at Point of Ayr. The site is very good for huge numbers of waders, plus wildfowl, gulls and terns that frequent the estuary.

However, it also provides a landfall for migrants either before or after crossing the estuary's vast expanse of mud and sand and, more surprisingly, Point of Ayr has proved a seawatching point for birds blown or drifted into the estuary from the adjacent Irish Sea.

In some books the site name is spelt Point of Air but we have chosen the version most commonly used.

The best place to view waders and wildfowl is the hide set up by the RSPB for this purpose – the Society's reserve comprises just the saltmarsh and seawall but

there will be no shortage of birding action.

From the car park at the end of Station Road walk up onto the seawall and take the path to the right for about half a mile, to reach the hide.

A visit here should be ideally timed for about two hours before high tide. Across the channel from the hide is a spit, which remains uncovered on even the highest of tides – thousands of waders can be forced onto it, especially on spring tides, when a visit here will make you a witness to one of nature's real spectacles.

All the common waders can be seen, together with Greenshanks, Spotted Redshanks, Curlew Sandpipers and Little Stints

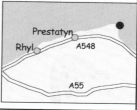

at passage times. Several rare waders have been discovered over the years including Marsh, White-rumped, Buff-breasted and Pectoral Sandpipers.

The rising tide brings wildfowl off the estuary and these should include Pintails with the more numerous Mallards, Teal and Shelducks. Peregrines, Merlins and Short-eared Owls are regularly seen hunting the

Other nearby sites

Connah's Quay, Flint Castle, Gronant.

129

marsh in autumn and winter.

Migrants are best looked for in the area known as The Warren, an extensive area of scrub grassland inland of the dunes. By heading across the beach from the lighthouse and climbing the dunes to the left you will see an area of damp grassland and drier scrub.

In autumn birds flying south cross the estuary, over the high dunes, and drop into these scrub areas. A good mix of the commoner migrants is usually to be found, with something unusual turning up on an almost annual basis.

Seawatching from the high dunes backing the beach has become ever more popular over the years, with periods of autumn gales yielding the best results.

Perfect conditions are when the strong south-westerlies, which push seabirds up the Irish Sea, are followed by westerly or north-westerlies that then force them across to the shores of north-west Britain.

Once birds have been blown into the estuary in this way they have to struggle back out, against the wind, into the Irish Sea. Kittiwakes, Gannets, auks and Manx Shearwaters are the species most frequently recorded, but autumn gales can bring Leach's Petrels, sometimes in large numbers, and all four species of skua.

In summer Storm Petrels and Little Gulls are sometimes seen along with a number of tern species.

The beach and sand flats should not be neglected as Snow Buntings and more occasionally Shore Larks and Twite can be found during the winter months.

In summer the sand flats hold a major concentration of roosting Common and Sandwich Terns, with usually a sprinkling of Little Terns among them. Arctic, Roseate and Black Terns are more occasional.

Pintails are attractive additions to the wildfowl gatherings in winter.

AFTER A PAIR of Ospreys nested in the Glaslyn Valley in 2004, the RSPB set up this very popular viewing scheme at Pont Croesor. You can view the distant nest through a telescope or enjoy amazing live pictures of life in the nest via a CCTV screen in the visitor centre. Pont Croesor lies on the west bank of the River Glaslyn and is a beautiful place to watch birds.

Target birds
Spring/summer – Goosander (70%), Red-breasted Merganser (60%), Osprey (100%), Peregrine (60%), Buzzard (100%), Grey Wagtail (100%), Common Sandpiper (80%), Raven (100%). *Winter* – Whooper Swan (100%), Goosander (90%), Goldeneye (100%).

Other possible bird species

Spring/summer	Sand Martin	Red Kite
Sparrowhawk	Siskin	Kingfisher
Kestrel	*Occasional*	
Great Spotted Woodpecker	Little Egret	

Background information and birding tips

THE OSPREY Viewing Scheme runs each year from April to September – providing of course the birds return to the nest. A large hide looks across the River Glaslyn to the distant trees, where the nest is located. The nest itself is under 24-hour protection by a team of wardens to prevent disturbance.

Telescopes are available for visitors to use and staff and volunteers are to hand to help you see the birds and provide information. CCTV pictures are beamed live to the visitor centre on a large screen, giving an intimate view of the family life of Ospreys.

Be aware that there can be long periods of inactivity early in the season, when the birds are incubating the eggs and much of the feeding takes place in upland lakes north of the nest.

Once the eggs have hatched at the end of April, the birds are much more active around the nest and most of the fishing takes place on the nearby Glaslyn Estuary for grey mullet. The birds pass over the viewpoint on each fishing trip to and from the estuary.

Early mornings or late afternoons are good times to visit, as heat haze can hamper midday viewing on warm days. Avoid wet and windy days because the level of activity is greatly reduced.

As the young develop they can be seen exercising their wings on the nest, and the frequency of feeding by the adults increases greatly.

As you wait for activity at the nest, you can take in the stunning scenery of Snowdonia. It is worth scanning the surrounding ridges for other raptors, as in fine weather Buzzards should be easy to see, often sparring with Ravens.

Peregrines are resident in the

Key points
- Open access for all abilities between April to mid September.
- Osprey viewing scheme operated by RSPB.
- Free parking.
- Public toilet at visitor centre.
- Nearest cafe on A498, one mile SW of junction with B4410.
- Live CCTV footage of nest.
- Hide equipped with free-to-use telescopes.
- Beautiful location with stunning scenery.

Contacts
RSPB Bangor Office – 01248 363 800.

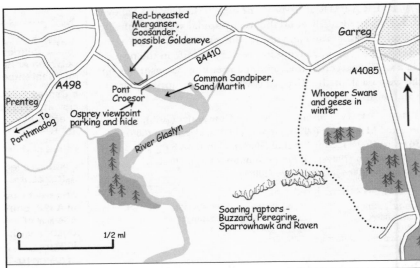

Red-breasted Merganser, Goosander, possible Goldeneye

Garreg

B4410

A4085

A498

Pont Croesor

Common Sandpiper, Sand Martin

Whooper Swans and geese in winter

N

Prenteg

To Porthmadog

Osprey viewpoint parking and hide

River Glaslyn

Soaring raptors - Buzzard, Peregrine, Sparrowhawk and Raven

0   1/2 ml

Access details

(Four miles NE of Porthmadog).

Leave Porthmadog heading N on A487 (the main street). After a mile you reach a 'T' junction in Tremadog. Turn right onto A498 for Beddgelert.

After two miles, in the small hamlet of Prenteg, turn right onto B4410 for Garreg.

The Osprey Viewpoint is just under half a mile along B4410 on the right immediately before the road crosses the Glaslyn River bridge.

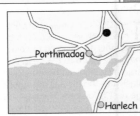

Porthmadog

Harlech

---

area and should be seen with patient scanning. Sparrowhawks and Kestrels are regular, and following good coverage since the Ospreys arrived, other species have been logged occasionally. These include Red Kite, Honey Buzzard, Goshawk, Hen Harrier, Merlin and Hobby, but you should count yourself very fortunate if you encounter any of these on a casual visit!

By keeping an eye on the river you should be rewarded with Goosander and Red-breasted Merganser sightings. Walk to the bridge to scan for Grey Wagtails and Common Sandpipers. The bird feeders near the hide often attract Great Spotted Woodpeckers and Siskins.

In winter a small herd of Whooper Swans feed on the fields one mile beyond Point Croesor bridge on the south side of the B4410. A flock of Greylag Geese here sometimes attracts stragglers such as Pink-footed or White-fronted Geese.

Check the river from the bridge at this time as Goosanders and Goldeneyes are regular, with Kingfishers seen more occasionally.

Other nearby sites

Borth y Gest, Criccieth, Morfa Bychan, Porthmadog.

THE TOWN has an amazing track record for producing rare birds. How many other sites can boast sightings of Elegant Tern, Ross's, Laughing and Ivory Gulls, Long-billed Dowitcher and American Wigeon in recent years? So, with this in mind, check the waders and wildfowl on the pools and estuary on each visit and you might discover the next mega-rarity yourself.

Target birds *All year* – Little Egret (90%), Red-breasted Merganser (100%). *Winter* – Whooper Swan (50%), Peregrine (70%), Black-tailed Godwit (90%), Kingfisher (60%), Water Pipit (50%). *Summer* – Osprey (60%), Mediterranean Gull (50%). *Autumn* – Curlew Sandpiper (30%), Mediterranean Gull (50%), waders and gulls (100%).

Other possible bird species

All year	*Winter*	
Little Grebe	Wigeon	Dunlin
Mute Swan	Teal	Snipe
Grey Heron	Pintail	Bar-tailed Godwit
Cormorant	Shoveler	Whimbrel
Shelduck	Goldeneye	Greenshank
Red-breasted	Hen Harrier	Common Sandpiper
Merganser	Golden Plover	Mediterranean Gull
Sparrowhawk	Grey Plover	Little Gull
Buzzard	Snipe	Sandwich Tern
Kestrel	Oystercatcher	Common Tern
Peregrine	Bar-tailed Godwit	Hirundines
Oystercatcher	Curlew	Wheatear
Ringed Plover	Redshank	Chiffchaff
Lapwing	Mediterranean Gull	
Black-tailed Godwit	Common Gull	*Summer*
Curlew	Rock Pipit	Lesser Black-backed Gull
Great Black-backed	Fieldfare	Swift
Gull	Redwing	Hirundines
Common gull species		Sedge Warbler
Sky Lark	*Spring/autumn*	Whitethroat
Grey Wagtail	Wigeon	
Pied Wagtail	Teal	
Common thrushes	Hen Harrier	
Raven	Golden Plover	
Common finches	Grey Plover	

Background information and birding tips

THE TOWN'S position acts as a catchment area for birds blown into Cardigan Bay by the prevailing south-westerly winds and over the years these have included a generous sprinkling of rarities, such as Laughing Gull, Ross's Gull, Elegant Tern and Long-billed Dowitcher.

By parking at the west side of

Key points

- **Open access all year.**

- **Town has a wide range of food and accommodation.**

- **Public toilets in town centre (see map).**

- **Spectacular views to Snowdonia and across the Glaslyn Estuary.**

- **Good level paths, suitable for wheelchair users.**

- **Close views of many species.**

- **Telescope useful for estuary.**

Contacts

Porthmadog Tourist Information, Stryd Fawr, Porthmadog LL49 9LD – 01766 512 981.

Llyn Bach (the tidal inner part of the harbour, at SH 571 387), you can explore the whole area on foot.

Llyn Bach itself is well worth a good look, for it is here that many of the area's rarities have been found, including the overwintering adult Laughing Gull of 2005/2006 which delighted thousands of observers from all parts of the country.

The mudflats will be exposed at low tide and there is a good chance of feeding Black-tailed Godwits, apart from mid-summer. Other waders may include Oystercatchers, Curlews and Redshanks with a good chance of Common Sandpiper in spring and autumn.

Check any gulls carefully, and keep an eye open for Kingfishers in winter. If the tide is in, fewer birds are present but a Little Grebe in winter is often joined by a few Wigeon and Teal. Cormorants can be seen year-round.

By walking north from the car park and then turning right you can follow the edge of Llyn Bach, scanning as you

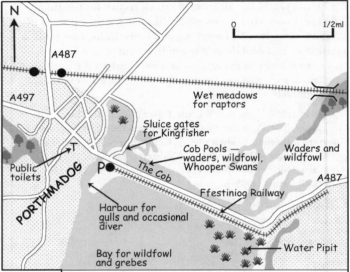

Other nearby sites

Borth-y-Gest, Morfa Bychan, RSPB Pont Croesor.

Access details

Approaching Porthmadog from N, continue on A487 through the high street to a petrol station on left. Turn left immediately before the garage and follow signs to car park. Park overlooking Llyn Bach and continue on foot around tidal pool onto the Cob embankment east of the town. A lay-by beyond the east end of the Cob embankment on A487 gives views over the pools on the inland side. Access is also possible, on foot,

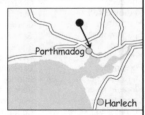

from here onto the east end of the Cob embankment to look for Water Pipits. A car park by the railway station gives access to the W end of embankment.

go. The path follows a raised embankment, giving views of fields on the left and the water on the right.

You reach the Glaslyn estuary pools on the left and a great view opens up. Spend time scanning the whole area as waders, wildfowl and gulls

gather here to feed and rest, and the scene is constantly changing.

Many of the birds have become accustomed to seeing people and are remarkably approachable. In winter, Wigeon, Teal and Goldeneyes should be easy to see, while

134

Little Egrets fish the shallow waters at all times of year.

Between June and August, look out for one of the local Ospreys (see Pont Croesor), fishing for grey mullet over the pools. This is also a good place to find a Mediterranean Gull loafing among the local Black-headed Gulls.

Continue across the sluice gates, checking for wintering Kingfishers either side, and follow the path to the right to reach the A487.

Cross the road and walk east across the Cob embankment, which gives great views of the estuary on the southern side, Glaslyn marshes and pools on the north side and stunning views of Snowdonia beyond. The Cob was built in the 19th Century by William Maddocks and now carries the A487 and the Ffestiniog light railway across the Glaslyn estuary.

Wildfowl and waders can be seen on both sides and a telescope is recommended to get the best from this viewpoint. Little Egrets should be found towards the east end of the Cob on the saltmarsh. In winter, at high tide, this saltmarsh can hold Water Pipits, though luck will be needed to secure good views.

Keep a look-out for raptors on the north side of the Cob, especially in winter when the local Peregrine and Buzzards may be joined by occasional Hen Harriers and Merlins. In the evenings, gulls roost on the estuary and, at times, on the pools, making this is one of the most reliable sites for Mediterranean Gull in North Wales.

In July and August the gulls are joined by Sandwich Terns and occasionally other tern species.

Strong south-westerly winds may push more pelagic species into the bay, with Little Gulls particularly likely in winter and early spring, and skuas possible in May.

Retrace your steps back to Porthmadog and check the outer harbour, beyond the railway station.

This area usually just holds a few gulls but Great Northern Divers and Black Guillemots have been recorded in winter.

Be prepared to work hard for views of Water Pipits from the Cob embankment – they are there but tend to be hard to spot.

Key points

- **Primarily a seawatching site.**

- **Free parking.**

- **Have warm and waterproof clothing available.**

- **No facilities on site.**

- **Nearest facilities, including public toilets, at Morfa Nefyn, three miles to NE.**

- **Limited viewing from car park for the less able.**

THIS SMALL rocky headland, which lies on the lower end of the north coast of the Lleyn Peninsula, is gaining a reputation as a good site from which to seawatch during north-westerly winds from late July to early November. The dramatic coastal scenery enhances the birding experience.

Target birds

Late summer – Storm Petrel (70%), Manx Shearwater (100%). *Autumn* – Manx Shearwater (100%), Balearic Shearwater (30%), Storm Petrel (50%), Leach's Petrel (40%), Arctic Skua (90%), Great Skua (50%), Pomarine Skua (10%).

Other possible bird species

All year	Raven	Kittiwake
Cormorant	Starling	Sandwich Tern
Shag		Common Tern
Sparrowhawk	*Autumn*	Arctic Tern
Buzzard	Red-throated Diver	Guillemot
Kestrel	Fulmar	Razorbill
Peregrine	Gannet	Meadow Pipit
Oystercatcher	Eider	Wheatear
Herring Gull	Common Scoter	
Great Black-backed Gull	Red-breasted Merganser	*Occasional*
Sky Lark	Ringed Plover	Great Northern Diver
Rock Pipit	Bar-tailed Godwit	Pomarine Skua
Pied Wagtail	Whimbrel	Little Gull
Stonechat	Curlew	Black Tern
Common thrushes	Turnstone	
Common crow species	Common gull species	

Background information and birding tips

IF YOU ARE a birdwatcher who prefers not to follow the crowd, there is still much to discover about this potentially excellent seawatching site, a small headland on the northern side of the Lleyn Peninsula.

Your target seabirds will generally be flying right to left, moving out of Caernarfon Bay towards the Irish Sea. Given a good onshore blow, preferably from the north-west, passage in late summer and autumn can be spectacular and often close inshore.

As late summer becomes autumn, keep a close watch on the weather forecasts. The ideal conditions are a south-westerly blow which rapidly switches to the north-west. Be on the headland at dawn – dressed for the occasion in good waterproofs – and you should witness a good passage of seabirds streaming west past your position.

The headland provides virtually no cover, apart from limited shelter by the gable end of a derelict building, so be prepared for exposure to the elements when the weather turns nasty.

There is no established point from which to watch, so pick the most comfortable viewpoint for you.

Patience is the watchword for success at Porth Ysgaden (pronounced Us-ga-den). You would be lucky indeed to chance upon a petrel or skua within a few minutes, but persistence should provide the target species within the percentage chances given above.

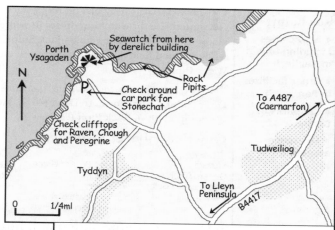

Large numbers of Manx Shearwaters may well be passing and it is worth examining them carefully to pick out the occasional Balearic Shearwater. These rare birds are slightly larger than Manx and have a pot-bellied appearance and a more direct flight action. Their plumage is browner above and crucially, the underparts are mottled brown, whereas Manx Shearwaters have clean white bellies.

Another possibility is the much larger Sooty Shearwater, which is dark brown all over, apart from silvery underwings.

In late summer, numbers of Manx Shearwaters can be amazing, particularly in the evenings when birds are returning to their Bardsey Island breeding colony. Late summer is also the best time to look for Storm Petrels, this being the most reliable site in North Wales for this elusive pelagic species.

Be prepared for a variety of skuas – Arctics are by far the most common, followed by bulky Great Skuas. Pomarine Skuas, slightly larger than Arctics, are

Access details

(12 miles west of Pwllheli).

From Caernarfon, head S on A487, then A499. After approximately eight miles, turn right onto B4417, signposted Morfa Nefyn.

Continue through village to Tudweiliog. Half a mile beyond the village, still on B4417, turn right onto a minor road and follow for three-quarters of a mile to a sharp left-hand bend.

Go straight on at this bend onto a narrow but surfaced track. Follow this to the dead

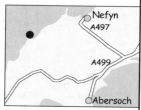

end where there is a small parking area.

From Porthmadog head W on A497 to Pwllheli, continuing on same road to Morfa Nefyn. Once there, follow instructions as above.

not so common and the lightweight Long-tailed Skuas are positively rare. Look out for an almost tern-like buoyant flight pattern as a key ID pointer for the latter species.

Rock Pipits can be found anywhere but east of the seawatching point is most reliable. For views of Ravens and Choughs, scan the clifftops south of the car park.

Other nearby sites

Porth Mendwy, Uchmynydd.

137

Key points

- **All facilities including toilets in Benllech.**
- **Other facilities in Pentraeth.**
- **Car parks in Benllech.**
- **Telescope essential.**

THIS HUGE sandy bay on Anglesey's east coast is a noted site for watching divers in winter. The saltmarsh along the landward edge holds Jack Snipe and Little Egrets, while flooded fields towards the eastern end regularly attract Water Pipits.

Target birds   *Spring, autumn and winter* – Red-throated Diver (80%), Great Northern Diver (40%), Jack Snipe (50%), Water Pipit (40%), Rock Pipit (90%).

Other possible bird species

All year	*Winter*	
Buzzard	Great Crested Grebe	Common Scoter
Oystercatcher	Shelduck	Snipe
Black-headed Gull	Wigeon	Redshank
Herring Gull	Red-breasted	Sky Lark
	Merganser	Linnet
		Reed Bunting

Background information and birding tips

IF YOU ARE keen to see good numbers of Red-throated Divers, head for the village of Benllech at the western end of the bay, where you can drive down to the sea-front and park alongside the sea wall.

In winter, using a telescope, you should see plenty of your target bird offshore, plus the odd Great Northern Diver. Great Crested Grebes, Red-breasted Mergansers, Cormorants and Shags are also present.

Common Scoters are often seen, usually as a long line of black dots along the horizon, though a few do come in closer at times. Velvet Scoters and Scaup are infrequent visitors.

A few gulls are always present and Mediterranean and Glaucous Gulls have been seen here.

From here, drive east to Pentraeth and take a narrow winding road down to the beach. Cross the small bridge and park on the beach. To the east, the area

of saltmarsh just alongside the parking area is the prime spot for Jack Snipe, along with many more Snipe.

The diminutive Jack Snipe is notoriously hard to find. The only sure way to find one is to walk slowly through the saltmarsh, so Wellingtons are essential. It is very likely that many Common Snipe will fly up from the vegetation, so be aware that they will invariably call as they fly off, whereas Jack Snipe never do.

Jack Snipe are far smaller and rarely fly far once on the wing. If you are exceptionally lucky and manage to see one on the ground, you'll notice the Jack Snipe's bill is proportionately much shorter than its larger relative. Jack Snipe also have the habit of bobbing up and down – the result of flexing their legs.

Check the small stream along the edge here for Kingfishers and on the fields inland for Wigeon, Teal and Little Egrets, which are often here.

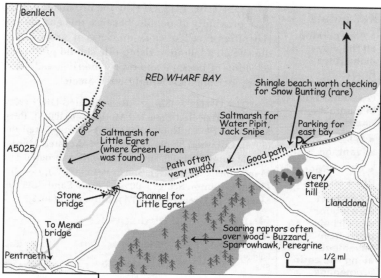

To find a Water Pipit, you will have to walk a mile or so to the east from here. As you go along, you will see plenty of Rock Pipits in the saltmarsh, plus Sky Larks, Linnets and Reed Buntings.

Though superficially similar to the familiar Rock Pipit, you should have no difficulty in identifying the much rarer Water Pipit, given good views.

In winter, Water Pipits are strikingly clean looking, with white underparts, wing bars, outer tail feathers and supercillium. On the Rock Pipit all these features look dirty.

Upperpart colouration on Water pipit is pale brown compared to the Rock Pipit's darkish grey hue. Leg colour is different too – Water Pipit has pale legs and Rock Pipit has black ones. There is an isolated chalet just inland of the path, and beyond here, in

Access details.

(Eight miles north of Menai Bridge).

Leave A55 at Menai Bridge onto A5025 towards Amlwch. In Pentraeth, take first right by the Panton Arms. Then filter left after about 200m and left again down to the beach.

For Benllech, continue along A5025, and in the village,

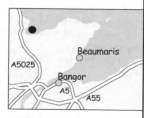

follow signs down to the beach.

the flooded fields just inland behind a long stone wall, you may find a Water Pipit waiting.

From the wall you can check the streams running into the fields. In October-November 2005, a Green Heron from America was found in the saltmarsh near to the car park. This 'first' for Wales attracted thousands

of admirers during its long stay.

To the east lies another access point below the village of Lladdona – from the car park you can scan for divers, grebes and seaduck.

Other nearby sites

Fedw Fawr, Penmon.

139

Key points

- **Free parking all the way along Rhos Promenade but busy at weekends and in summer months.**

- **Telescope an advantage.**

- **All facilities in Rhos-on-Sea.**

- **Excellent viewing for wheelchair users from pavement along the entire promenade.**

- **Public toilet (not disabled) on promenade by stone jetty, 200 yards from Point.**

Contacts

Colwyn Bay Tourist Information, Imperial Buildings, Station Square, Princes Drive LL29 8LF – 01492 530 478.

DON'T BE PUT OFF by the urbanised setting and the proximity of people, because this site close to Colwyn Bay offers excellent close-up views of waders. A visit to the site on a falling or rising tide should produce a good selection of passage and over-wintering waders, with Purple Sandpiper the most sought-after species.

Target birds

Winter – Red-throated Diver (90%), Common Scoter (100%), Red-breasted Merganser (100%), Purple Sandpiper (90%), Rock Pipit (90%). *Spring* – Red-throated Diver (50%), Common Scoter (100%), Red-breasted Merganser (100%), Purple Sandpiper (90%). *Autumn* – Red-throated Diver (50%), Manx Shearwater (70%), Storm Petrel (30%), Leach's Petrel (30%), Common Scoter (100%), Purple Sandpiper (90%), Arctic Skua (50%), Great Skua (50%), Little Gull (40%).

Other possible bird species

All year	Gannet	Gannet
Cormorant	Shelduck	Lesser Black-backed Gull
Fulmar	Eider	Kittiwake
Shag	Ringed Plover	Sandwich Tern
Kestrel	Grey Plover	Guillemot
Peregrine	Knot	Razorbill
Curlew	Sanderling	Swallow
Oystercatcher	Bar-tailed Godwit	House Martin
Pied Wagtail	Whimbrel	
Common farmland birds	Redshank	*Winter*
	Mediterranean Gull	Great Crested Grebe
Spring	Common gull species	Shelduck
Manx Shearwater	Passage terns	Eider
Whimbrel	Guillemot	Wigeon
Curlew	Razorbill	Ringed Plover
Little Gull	Hirundines	Grey Plover
Pied/White Wagtail	Rock Pipit	Bar-tailed Godwit
		Redshank
Spring/autumn	*Summer*	Guillemot
Great Crested Grebe	Manx Shearwater	Razorbill

Background information and birding tips

THIS IS the leading place to visit in North Wales in winter if you wish to see Purple Sandpipers.

Spend enough time here and you should be rewarded with excellent close views of this species, with up to 20 birds present on the rocky shore off the Point between late September and early May. At high tide, they roost along with other waders on the sea defences near the Point itself, or failing this, just to the east of the groyne opposite Rhos-on-Sea Golf Club — this is three-quarters of a mile west of the Point heading towards the Little Orme headland and Llandudno.

It is worth getting out at, or near,

Access details

(One mile NW of Colwyn Bay).

Travelling west, leave A55 North Wales Expressway at junction 20, signposted 'Rhos-on-Sea'. Turn right at traffic lights, then right again at the crossroads.

At mini roundabout turn right to another set of traffic lights. Go straight on to a large roundabout and turn right, signposted 'promenade'.

Follow road to T-junction with the promenade. Turn left and proceed for half a mile until you see a small café on right. Park anywhere in this area.

Travelling east on A55, take exit 20, marked Rhos-on-Sea. From the slip road, turn left at the lights, which brings you to the large roundabout referred to above.

Little Ormes Head

Shingle beach

Road along prom — parking along whole length

High tide roost waders inc. Purple Sandpiper

Look for Purple Sandpipers on rocks

Golf club house

Golf course

Pond

To Llandudno

Ramp for access to lower promenade

Rhôs Point

Café

High tide wader roost

B5115

College

Rhôs-on-Sea

N

To A55 Expressway

0   1/2ml

Take steps down from promenade to reach the obvious Rhos Point.

If unable to negotiate the steps, continue W for 300m to a tarmacadamed ramp down to the lower promenade.

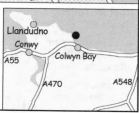

Llandudno

Conwy

A55

Colwyn Bay

A470

A548

Rhos Point, and walking west along the promenade checking the beach and sea.

A small shingle beach opposite the golf club occasionally holds Snow Buntings in winter. The same area has also produced more than one Grey Phalarope in rough weather.

The golf course itself often has a large high tide gull roost worth checking for Mediterranean and other scarce gull species.

In spring, the fairways are likely to have Wheatears and White Wagtails. Check the golf course pools for Little Egrets.

Rhos Point has the great advantage that seawatching can be carried out from the relative comfort of your vehicle.

North-westerly winds provide the best prospect of exciting birds between late July and November, especially when coincident with high tides.

A good selection of seabirds includes Storm Petrels in late summer and Leach's Petrels in October and early November.

Arctic Skuas are regular, harassing Sandwich Terns offshore in August and September, while in winter, scanning out to sea should produce sightings of Red-throated Divers, Red-breasted Mergansers and Common Scoters.

Other nearby sites

RSPB Conwy Reserve, Great Orme, Little Orme, Llandulas and Pensarn.

Key points

- **Open access all year.**

- **Footpaths run entire length of each bank of the river.**

- **Series of stiles to negotiate.**

- **Limited parking at both ends — do not leave valuables in vehicle.**

- **Area can be disturbed by wildfowling.**

- **No facilities on site — go to Rhyl for toilets, shops etc.**

- **Close views of wader, wildfowl and gulls.**

- **Telescope recommended.**

Contacts

Environment Agency – 08708 506 506.

THE STRETCH of the tidal River Clwyd between Rhyl and Rhuddlan provides great birdwatching, with close views of the mudflats and river channel from either bank. The site is best visited on a falling or rising tide, as at high tide the mud is covered and waders are less numerous. Spring and autumn visits are best for unusual birds, but the area is worth a look at any time.

Target birds *All year* – Goosander (90%), Shelduck (100%), Peregrine (70%). *Spring* – Whimbrel (80%), Common Sandpiper (100%), Mediterranean Gull (50%), Wheatear (90%), Yellow Wagtail (50%). *Summer* – Hobby (40%), Green Sandpiper (70%). *Autumn* – Curlew Sandpiper (50%), Black-tailed Godwit (100%), Greenshank (90%), Ruff (60%), Spotted Redshank (60%). *Winter* – Merlin (60%), Green Sandpiper (50%), Kingfisher (80%).

Other possible bird species

All year		*Occasional*
Little Grebe	Sky Lark	Whooper Swan
Red-breasted Merganser	*Winter*	Pink-footed Goose
Oystercatcher	Wigeon	Garganey
Lapwing	Teal	Osprey
Linnet	Dunlin	Little Stint
	Knot	Golden Plover
Spring	Bar-tailed Godwit	Short-eared Owl
Sand Martin	Ringed Plover	
White Wagtail	Redshank	

Background information and birding tips

IF YOU MAKE an early morning visit we recommend starting on the east bank at the south end so the sun will be at your back when facing the river. Walk north under the flyover, keeping a look out for Goosanders and Kingfishers.

A small water treatment works off to your right sometimes has a few gulls around it and the bushes and trees here hold common passerines.

Timing your visit to avoid a high tide will ensure a shingle and mud area beyond the treatment works should be exposed. This is a good area for waders and gulls. Scan carefully; small waders are easily overlooked among the stones on the mud. The mud can often hold a Green Sandpiper in winter and it is favoured by Common Sandpipers on passage, when numbers often reach double figures.

The wet grassland on the opposite bank can hold a gull roost, and it is worth checking carefully for Mediterranean Gulls among the commoner species. Any pools on the grassland can hold passage waders and wintering Snipe.

Continuing north, check any ditches and dykes that you cross for a Kingfisher or Green Sandpiper. Along the tideline you may spot Wheatears and possibly a Yellow Wagtail on passage.

As the river widens, more mudflats appear when the tide is low, and more waders and wildfowl should be encountered. In the autumn, look carefully for Curlew Sandpipers among Dunlin flocks and perhaps a Little Stint if you are lucky. Peregrines occasionally use the nearby pylons to perch, waiting a chance to attack, so keep an eye on the sky for hunting raptors.

Canada and Greylag Geese should be feeding on the marsh or in adjacent fields and we always scan them for scarcer species. Where the path turns inland, stop and scan the river, because the area below the railway bridge often hides good numbers of gulls.

Occasional sightings of Short-eared Owls are reported over the rough ground to the north, on the east side of the river. Having given the area a really good grilling, retrace your steps to the car.

On sunny afternoons, start at the north end and walk south on the west bank so the sun will be at your back. The area of small fields with hedges at the start of the path may hold passerines and migrants at appropriate seasons.

The birding will be very similar to the route described above. Fields on the west side of the path may well hold flocks of Lapwings in winter. The stream that runs under the path can hold Kingfishers and Green Sandpipers in winter.

Good number of wagtails can be found on the grassland between the path and river all year round, together with Wheatears in spring.

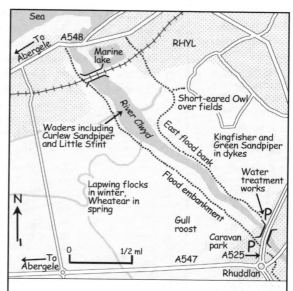

Access details

(Approx half-mile W of Rhyl).

For southern end, leave A55 at St Asaph (junction 27), heading N on A525 dual carriageway. After two miles, at a roundabout, turn right for Rhuddlan. Cross hump-backed bridge and turn first left after 100m. Follow narrow lane past church, then fork left and park almost immediately on left. Parking is very limited; do not block access. Walk N under flyover to follow E bank of river for just over a mile, then retrace your steps.

To access W bank of river, return to road. Cross river bridge, then first right. Continue past caravan park and park before gate, taking care not to block access. Footpath continues N for 1.75 miles. Retrace your steps.

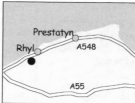

To reach northern end, leave Rhyl W on A548. Cross blue metal bridge over River Clwyd and turn first left into a small housing development. Follow road past houses to a small field on left. Park here and continue on foot under railway line. Emerging from the underpass, take footpath on left, over a metal gate with stile. Follow path S.

Key points

- **Open access at all times.**
- **RSPB visitor centre open April-September (10am–5pm)**
- **Free car park for RSPB members.**
- **Café (privately owned) and toilets open April-September. Café car park for customers only.**
- **Shops, toilets and all other facilities in Holyhead.**
- **Wheelchair access to cliffs but very limited viewing.**

SITUATED at the western extremity of Anglesey, this bustling, noisy seabird colony offers excellent viewing facilities and is a popular attraction for summertime visitors. It is also a good sea-watching site in both spring and autumn, and a migration hotspot, though generally birds move on quickly.

Target birds *All year* – Peregrine (60%), Chough (85%), Raven (80%), Stonechat (70%). *Summer* – Guillemot (100%), Razorbill (100%), Fulmar (100%), Kittiwake (100%), Puffin (60%), Manx Shearwater (50%).

Other possible bird species

All year	Sky Lark	Goldcrest
Shag	Whitethroat	Redpoll
Kestrel	Linnet	Spotted Flycatcher
Rock Pipit		Finches
	Passage	Thrushes (October-November)
Summer	Wheatear	
Herring Gull	Willow Warbler	
Lesser Black-backed Gull	Chiffchaff	

Background information and birding tips

THIS IS a superb area for birdwatching, with some spectacular coastal scenery. It is an RSPB reserve, created in 1976, and has a visitor centre in Ellins Tower, which overlooks the main buttresses of the seabird colony.

Approaching the area from Holyhead, you will notice a couple of small reservoirs on your left. It is worth a quick look here: Coots, Pochards and Tufted Ducks are often present and Ring-necked Duck and Red-rumped Swallow were both found here in May 2004.

Moving on, check the pasture fields on either side of the road; you will often find Choughs feeding here. Another place to stop is at the junction of the road leading up to South Stack.

This is a prime spot for finding grounded migrants in the early morning. Meadow Pipits, Wheatears, Whinchats and

Whitethroats are often here with the odd Ring Ouzel, while a Black-headed Bunting, which should have been to the east of the Black Sea, spent a few days here one May.

This is also a good vantage point for seeing the resident Hooded Crows, plus Choughs, as you can observe most of the pasture fields from here.

Driving up the hill, you will find the RSPB car park on your left, a familiar site for many of the pilgrims who made the journey in June 2003 when a vagrant Black Lark – a refugee from far-off Kazakhstan spent a glorious week here.

From the car park there is a level sealed wheelchair-friendly path to the visitor centre. You should see Stonechats on the top of the gorse bushes and will probably hear Choughs and Ravens calling. When you reach the tower, you will be looking down on the seabird colony. From here you will see Guillemots packed tightly on the ledges, with smaller numbers of Razorbills in the deeper crevices at the edges.

A few Puffins are usually to be seen on the sea below the tower, but they are best observed by descending a short way down the lighthouse steps, from where you can look across to see them under the boulders on the buttress opposite. Fulmars will be above the auks, and Kittiwakes will be seen flying in and out from their nests between the buttresses.

There is also a small colony of Kittiwakes on the lighthouse island, along with breeding Herring Gulls and Lesser Black-backed Gulls. A pair of Peregrines nest in the area and can often be seen flying over the cliffs or perched somewhere above the colony.

Leaving Ellins Tower, you can make the steep climb up to the road or return to your car and drive up to a small car park above the lighthouse steps. (There are guided tours of the lighthouse during the summer months, but it is a very strenuous climb back up some 400 steps!)

There are many paths over the heathland towards Holyhead Mountain, and migrants can drop down anywhere. One of the easiest areas to check is in the fields opposite the café. Though they have produced Bluethroat, Hoopoe, Wryneck, Bee-eater, Red-backed Shrike and Short-toed Lark, the usual fare consists of Meadow Pipits, Wheatears, Linnets and Stonechats, plus occasional Ring Ouzels and Black

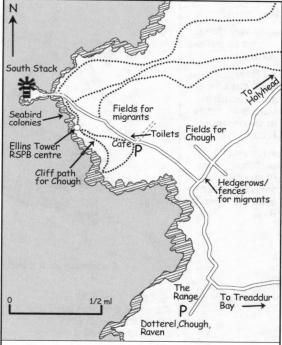

Access details

(Approx 4.5 miles from Holyhead).

In Holyhead drive through to the harbour, from where South Stack is well signposted. For The Range from South Stack, head towards Trearddur and take the first turning right after about a mile.

Redstarts in spring and autumn. It is also worth keeping an eye on the sky, as flyovers have included Black Kite, Alpine Swift and White Stork.

So far I have not mentioned sea-watching. You can obviously look out from Ellins Tower or from the lighthouse steps, but the best site is an area known locally as 'The Range'.

Other nearby sites

Holyhead Harbour, Soldiers Point, Trearddur Bay.

145

Key points

- **No wheelchair access to visitor centre.**
- **Terrain: a level path to visitor centre but steep paths in surrounding area.**
- **For sea-watching, visit in morning, sun could be a problem later in day.**

Guillemots pack tightly together on the ledges.

Still part of the RSPB reserve, The Range is situated about one mile south of South Stack. It is a large, gently sloping maritime heathland with heather and gorse, and though seemingly birdless, at times it produces some interesting species.

Dotterel stop here annually in May and September. From the car park, it is a 15-minute walk down to the headlands. On your way you should see Meadow Pipits, Sky Larks, Linnets and Stonechats. Rock Pipits nest along the low cliffs here, as do Choughs and Ravens.

Along with the regular auks, Kittiwakes, Fulmars, Gannets and Manx Shearwaters, there is a spring passage of Arctic and Great Skuas, often joined by Pomarine Skuas, mainly during May.

Red-throated Divers and Common Scoters are also regularly seen. During the summer months, terns can be seen passing on feeding trips from their nearby colonies — Common, Arctic and Sandwich are regulars, though sometimes Roseate Terns may be observed.

Autumn passage includes all the species seen in spring, plus the chance of seeing Balearic Shearwater, Sooty Shearwater, Storm and Leach's Petrels and possibly that once-in-a-lifetime Black-browed Albatross or Little Shearwater, both of which have occurred here.

In late autumn The Range is a regular site for Lapland Buntings. Merlins often accompany the hordes of Meadow Pipits passing through; Short-eared Owls and Jack Snipe are also visitors in this season.

Contacts

RSPB South Stack - call 01407 764 973 or visit: www.rspb.org.uk

THIS SANDY BEACH on the east coast of Anglesey can be viewed from your vehicle in the car park — very handy on a bitter winter's day! The area holds gulls, divers and auks but is heavily disturbed by dog-walkers, so aim to be there in early morning or late afternoon to avoid the majority of non-birding visitors.

Target birds   *Winter* – Red-throated Diver (90%), Great Northern Diver (50%), Black-throated Diver (10%), Black Guillemot (70%), Chough (60%).

Other possible bird species

Winter	Turnstone	*Occasional*
Great Crested Grebe	Dunlin	Purple Sandpiper
Guillemot	Sanderling	Sanderling
Razorbill	Ringed Plover	Mediterranean Gull
Cormorant	Gulls	Glaucous Gull
Shag	Red-legged Partridge	Iceland Gull
Oystercatcher	Yellowhammer	

Background information and birding tips

TRAETH LLIGWY is a lovely sandy beach with rocky headlands to either side. A small stream runs out across the sands to the sea. This freshwater outfall attracts gulls to wash and bathe and is always worth checking.

The gulls come and go throughout the day, so patience is a virtue — the longer you wait, the better the chances of finding something good!

Late winter (February-March) is often the best time to connect with a white-winged gull (Glaucous or Iceland), so it is worth using your telescope to check the roosting gulls on offshore rocks.

Scan the sea offshore for divers during the winter months. A calm sunny day will greatly increase your chances of success.

All three species of regularly-occurring diver have been seen here but the Red-throated is by far the most likely to be encountered. Great Northern Divers are seen every winter but the Black-throated is a rarity that is best looked for in early spring (March or early April) as the birds migrate northwards.

Black Guillemots winter along the coast here and with careful scanning you should be rewarded with a sighting of one of these charismatic auks.

They are usually close inshore and the area around the rocks on the south-west side are a favoured location.

Check the rocky areas for gangs of feeding Turnstones and you may just be lucky enough to find a Purple Sandpiper among them.

The open beach holds small numbers of Ringed Plovers sometimes accompanied by a few Dunlins and, with luck, a Sanderling.

Key points

- **Open access all year.**
- **Telescope desirable.**
- **Viewing possible from the car.**
- **Public toilets in car park may be locked in winter.**
- **Facilities in nearby village of Moelfre.**
- **Benllech has a good range of facilities, including fish and chip shop.**

147

Waders are often disturbed by dog walkers, so an early morning visit is best for birdwatching – very early to be absolutely sure of peace and quiet.

Low tide provides the best chance of getting good views of waders as a large area of beach is then available and flushed birds may land elsewhere in the bay.

Listen for the distinctive calls of Chough over the adjacent low cliffs and fields, as they are a regular feature here.

The surrounding farmland also holds a small population of Yellowhammers, no longer an easy bird to find in North Wales. You may also encounter introduced Red-legged Partridges from the nearby shooting estate.

At low tide, Atlantic grey seals may haul themselves out onto offshore rocks.

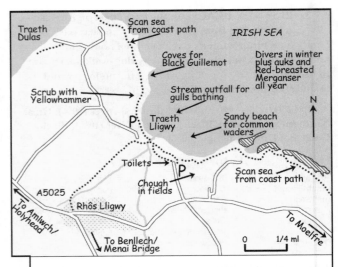

Traeth Dulas
Scan sea from coast path
IRISH SEA
Coves for Black Guillemot
Divers in winter plus auks and Red-breasted Merganser all year
Scrub with Yellowhammer
Stream outfall for gulls bathing
N
P
Traeth Lligwy
Sandy beach for common waders
Toilets
P
Scan sea from coast path
A5025
Chough in fields
To Amlwch/ Holyhead
Rhôs Lligwy
To Moelfre
To Benllech/ Menai Bridge
0   1/4 ml

Access details.

(Three miles N of Benllech).

Crossing the Menai Straits by Britannia Bridge on A55 North Wales Expressway, take second exit (after only a few hundred yards), signed for Amlwch. At top of slip road, turn right for Amlwch onto A5025.

Continue through village of Benllech for 1.5 miles, still on the A5025, to a roundabout. Go straight on here, onto a minor road running north. Follow this minor road,

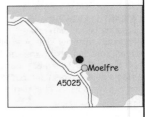

Moelfre
A5025

going straight on at the crossroads for just over one mile to reach Traeth Lligwy car park. View from the car park.

Other nearby sites

Point Lynas, Red Wharf Bay.

148

HOLY ISLAND'S Trearddur Bay should only be regarded as a winter birding site because it is too popular with tourists in the summer months. Apart from a few seaduck out to sea, Purple Sandpiper is the main attraction for birders.

Target Birds: *All year* – Goldeneye (100%), Purple Sandpiper (70%), Rock Pipit (80%).

Other possible bird species

Winter		
Fulmar	Redshank	Linnet
Cormorant	Turnstone	
Shag	Black-headed Gull	*Occasional*
Red-breasted Merganser	Common Gull	Surf Scoter (rare)
Peregrine	Herring Gull	Scaup
Oystercatcher	Great Black-backed Gull	Eider
Dunlin	Meadow Pipit	Long-tailed Duck
Ringed Plover	Pied Wagtail	Little Gull
Curlew	Stonechat	
	Raven	

A winter visit to Trearddur Bay is almost guaranteed to provide views of Purple Sandpipers.

Background information and birding tips

SITUATED just south of Holyhead, Trearddur Bay is a natural harbour with a gently sloping, sandy Blue Flag-winning beach, so it is a popular holiday destination for families in summer. Rock pools full of crabs, starfish and other sea creatures are a

natural attraction for children on holiday.

For birdwatchers, the site is worth visiting outside the main holiday season — particularly if you are keen to add Purple Sandpiper to your list.

Check out the high tide wader roost on the rocks just offshore from the car park, beside the slipway opposite the Trearddur Bay Hotel.

Look low down on the left-hand side of the rocks and you could see up to 30 Purple Sandpipers. Small numbers of Dunlins, Ringed Plovers and Turnstones also roost here.

Purple Sandpipers are well camouflaged and not easy to spot. They tend to roost close to the water's edge, so scan the splash zone carefully.

At low tide the Purple Sandpipers will be feeding, so a little more effort will be needed to locate them, though they still prefer to keep close to the breaking waves and are rarely seen more than a few feet away from the water's edge.

The bay is a favoured area for Rock Pipits and you should strike lucky if you put in a little effort to distinguish these dark grey-coloured birds from the surrounding rocks.

Check out any flying birds – Rock Pipits are highly mobile and you should be able to pick out one in flight between rocky outcrops.

It will also be worth checking the strand line in the bay if it is not too disturbed – Rock Pipits will also forage here.

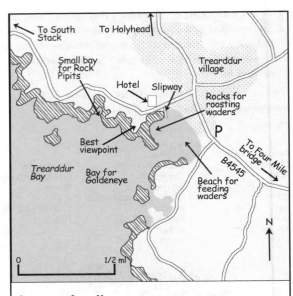

Access details

(Two miles S of Holyhead).

Leave A55 for Valley at junction 3. Turn left at the traffic lights onto B4545, continue for about two miles and park on the roadside on the west side of the bay, just before the Trearddur Bay Hotel.

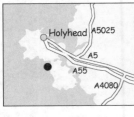

Out in the bay, a small flock of Goldeneyes are occasionally joined by the odd Scaup, Eider or Long-tailed Duck. A Surf Scoter recently spent a few weeks in the bay, so it is always worth giving birds at sea a second look. Red-throated and Great Northern Divers are scarce visitors.

Other nearby sites

Inland Sea, Holyhead Harbour and Soldiers Point, RSPB South Stack, RSPB Valley Reserve.

150

IF YOU ENJOY quiet contemplation of nature, head for this RSPB reserve, east of Holyhead, only at weekends. That's when jets from the nearby RAF base are grounded. The reserve comprises two major lakes, Llyn Penrhyn and Llyn Traffwll, plus a cluster of smaller waters that support a typical mix of wildfowl, and in recent years, a growing colony of Cetti's Warblers. Hopefully in years to come, Bittern and Marsh Harrier will also take advantage of the reedbeds.

Target birds: *All year* – Cetti's Warbler, hear (70%), see (10%). *Summer* – Grasshopper Warbler (50%).

Other possible bird species

All year		
Little Grebe	Pochard	Sedge Warbler
Great Crested Grebe	Tufted Duck	Reed Warbler
Cormorant	Ruddy Duck	Lesser Redpoll
Mute Swan	Coot	Reed Bunting
Greylag Goose	*Summer*	*Winter*
Canada Goose	Black-headed Gull	Goldeneye
Gadwall	Meadow Pipit	
Shoveler	Sky Lark	

Background information and birding tips

LLYN PENRHYN lies alongside the road at RAF Valley, south of Caergeiliog. There is a small car park at the southern end and from here you can walk along the edge of the reed-fringed lake.

Sedge and Reed Warblers will be singing throughout the summer months, along with Reed Buntings. Meadow Pipits and Sky Larks will be dancing in the sky above the grassy pasture on your left, while Grasshopper Warblers and Cuckoos will be noisy when they first arrive, but soon go quiet and are often difficult to see after the first few hours of daylight.

As you continue on this path alongside the railway line, it is worth stopping for a while as you should hear Cetti's Warbler (but very seldom see them)!

The path winds on past a couple of smaller pools and on to Llyn Dinan and its vast reedbed. Little and Great Crested Grebes, Tufted Ducks, Pochards, Mallards, Shovelers and Ruddy Ducks could all be breeding in any of the lakes, and ducklings will scurry or dive into cover as you pass. Three of the duck species – Pochard, Gadwall and Shoveler – breed in nationally important numbers, while in winter the flock of Shovelers exceeds 300 birds.

You will see Llyn Dinan in the distance on your left. If you climb one of the grassy hillocks, you will be able to overlook the reedbeds, but a telescope is required to see what is on the lake.

Bittern has been recorded regularly in the winter months, and the RSPB is doing everything it can in an attempt to get them to breed

Key points

- Open access at all times.
- Car parking available.
- No facilities on site. Café and shops in nearby Valley village
- Paths often muddy in places.
- Not a suitable site for wheelchair users, though Llyn Penrhyn can be viewed from roadside.
- Nearest public loo in village of Valley (SH 295 792).
- Very noisy during week with jets constantly flying, peaceful at weekends.

Contacts

01407 764 973
e-mail:south.stack@rspb.org.uk

Visit the website:
www.rspb.org.uk

here again. The same is true for Marsh Harrier: there have been regular sightings, but so far, no successful breeding attempts.

Llyn Traffwll is the other major lake in this complex. It is situated to the north-east of the RAF base and is accessed through the housing estate. There is a public footpath across an often-muddy field churned up by a herd of cattle, so the going is quite pot-holed.

Climb over the stile and make your way up onto the rocky outcrop overlooking the lake. From here – with a telescope – you can cover most of the area.

This is the only lake where the water will fall low enough to allow waders to drop in. Ruff, Common Sandpiper, Green Sandpiper, Black-tailed Godwit, Whimbrel and Little Stint are all species that could be found in the autumn and Red-necked Phalarope has occurred.

Black Terns used to be regular visitors, but are nowadays seen less often. Whiskered Terns and White-winged Black Terns have accompanied them in the past, along with occasional Little Gulls. Garganey, Green-winged Teal and Ring-necked Duck have also been found here.

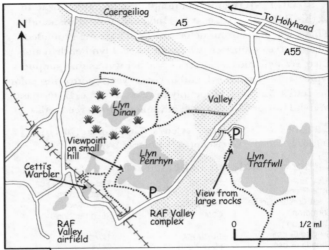

Access details.

(Eight miles east of Holyhead).

Leave A55 at junction 4, signposted Bodedern and Caereiliog. Turn left at roundabout, following signs to RAF Valley.

Look out for a chapel on your left. Turn left just past this onto the housing estate. After about 200m there is a turning down to Llyn Traffwll. Park carefully in estate and walk down this track to the footpath through the first field on

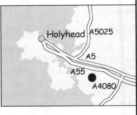

your right.

For the other lakes, continue on towards the airfield, passing Llyn Penrhyn on your right. The car park is on the right, at the end of the lake.

Other nearby sites

Beddmanarch Bay, Inland Sea.

BLACK GROUSE is the principal attraction of this fantastic area on the northern end of the Berwyn Mountains and a dawn visit in early spring will provide a truly memorable birding experience. World's End is an area of heather moorland bordered by conifer planting, unique in allowing easy vehicle access to superb upland birding. However, this is a sensitive site and all visiting birdwatchers should ensure that they do not disturb the scarce birds that breed here.

Key points

- **Birding on road from vehicle.**
- **Free access at all times.**
- **Telescope desirable.**
- **No facilities — nearest in Llangollen.**
- **Weather often poor in spring due to elevation.**
- **Road sometimes impassable due to snow and ice.**

Target birds   *Spring* – Hen Harrier (50%), Merlin (70%), Peregrine (70%), Goshawk (30%), Black Grouse (80%), Red Grouse (50%), Cuckoo (70%), Grey Wagtail (100%), Dipper (100%), Ring Ouzel (20%), Grasshopper Warbler (50%), Crossbill (70%).

Other possible bird species

Spring		
Buzzard	Tree Pipit	Redstart
Sparrowhawk	Wheatear	Pied Flycatcher
Kestrel	Whinchat	Wood Warbler
	Stonechat	

Background information and birding tips

TO VIEW Blackcock at their spectacular spring lek, it is essential to be in position at daybreak. On the south side of the moor there is a larch plantation and you should park on the roadside just north of this to look west across the small valley.

Do not leave your vehicle, as to do so will result only in brief views of the birds flying away. This is one of the few places remaining in the UK where lekking Black Grouse can be observed without causing disturbance, so all birders visiting the site should do everything possible to ensure its continued use by these special birds.

In the unlikely event that you do not meet success at this site, drive north a short distance to the brow of the hill and try again by looking left onto the moor. The Black

Grouse often lek among patches of juncus in the heather moorland.

Continue to drive north for just over half a mile to a footpath sign on the left-hand side of the road. Park off the road and scan for raptors. Hen Harrier, Merlin, Peregrine and Goshawk are all possible from this spot. Check any fence posts or exposed rocks for perched birds. Patience is the watchword as populations of raptors in these uplands are small.

This is also an excellent area to encounter Red Grouse, Whinchats and Grasshopper Warblers in spring and summer. Drive further along the road, stopping to scan the moors regularly for any missing species. Wheatears, Meadow Pipits and Stonechats will be easily seen.

Where the heather moorland meets the grassland on the north

side of the moor, stop to scan the stone walls and scattered hawthorns for Ring Ouzels and more Wheatears. Scan the distant heather moorland at the forest edge for more possible Black Grouse.

Retrace your route across the moor back to the larch plantation on the south side. Cross the cattle grid and park on the right beneath the larches.

Explore this area on foot, as it is an excellent site for Crossbills. Siskins and Cuckoos should be seen, and Tree Pipits and Lesser Redpolls may also be present.

It is worth walking a short distance down the road to the beech trees, an excellent spot to see and hear Wood Warblers. Return to your vehicle and drive downhill, stopping just beyond the ford and scan the stream for Dippers and Grey Wagtails.

Check the limestone cliffs above for Ring Ouzels. Keep a watchful eye for raptors overhead here, especially Goshawk.

Drive further down the hill, stopping frequently to check suitable stream areas for Dippers and Grey Wagtails. Roadside woodland should also provide Pied Flycatchers, Redstarts and Tree Pipits.

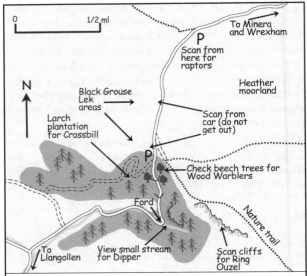

Access details

(Approx three miles N of Llangollen).

There are two entry points to the area: one from the north and one to the south.

From the North: **your starting point is Wrexham. Take A525 west to Coedpoeth and at far end of village, turn left at crossroads for Minera on B5426.**

Follow the twisting road through this small hamlet and take a sharp right turn that almost doubles back on itself, just over a mile from the A-road. Continue on this minor road onto moorland. The larch plantation lies approximately three miles from the start of the heather moorland.

From the South: **From Llangollen, take A542 N towards Ruthin. Pass the Valle Crucis Abbey remains on your right,**

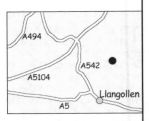

and then take the next right turn onto minor road.

Almost immediately, turn right again down a steep hill. Follow the narrow, twisting road to a 'T' junction by a church. Turn left and the road runs into a farmyard.

Keep right, signposted World's End. The road follows a stream through the valley, and then climbs up steeply through the larch plantation. Stop when you emerge from the trees.

The large industrial town of Wrexham has a surprising number of interesting bird sites close by, many of which feature kettle holes that were formed during the Ice Ages by blocks of ice separating from the main glacier. In some cases, the isolated blocks of ice then became partially or wholly buried in outwash. When the ice blocks eventually melted they left behind holes or depressions that filled with water. While none of these extra sites warrant their own chapter, a selection of the best are given below. We start with the best known site, Gresford Flash and proceed in a clockwork direction (see map overleaf).

Key points

- **Easy roadside viewing**
- **Telescope useful**
- **Disturbed by sailing on Sunday mornings**
- **No facilities at site.**
- **Public houses are at Pant-yr-Ochain and Gresford.**
- **All facilities available in Wrexham.**

① Gresford Flash

GULL WATCHERS have found this ten-acre natural lake north of Wrexham has yielded an impressive list of species that which use the site for bathing. In winter they are joined by a variety of common wildfowl species. There is a surrounding network of glacial kettle holes, many of which are not accessible to the general public, but which may hold a good variety of passing birds at any time.

Target birds

Winter – **Lesser Black-backed Gull (100%), Herring Gull (100%), Yellow-legged Gull (20%), Mediterranean Gull (15%), Glaucous Gull (15%), Iceland Gull (10%), Ring-billed Gull (rare), Caspian Gull (rare).**

Other possible bird species

Spring/summer	*Winter*	
Little Ringed Plover	Greylag Goose	Shoveler
Common Sandpiper	Canada Goose	Goosander

Background information and birding tips

GRESFORD FLASH has become an important site for bathing gulls. Large numbers of Lesser Black-backed and Herring Gulls may be seen here, and several scarcer species have been observed, including Iceland, Ring-billed, Caspian, Mediterranean and Glaucous Gulls. Yellow-legged Gulls are now fairly regular visitors each winter.

This is an easy roadside stop if passing en route to better known coastal sites and its track record of turning up scarce species for the dedicated local birders means it is always worth checking. You can simply view from the roadside but a telescope is recommended for the best views.

As always in such situations, park carefully with due regard to other road users. Early afternoon is the best time for observing the gulls, but for other species early morning visits are likely to be more productive.

Sunday mornings should be avoided altogether as the activities of the resident boating club cause disturbance to the birds.

Map and access details on page 157

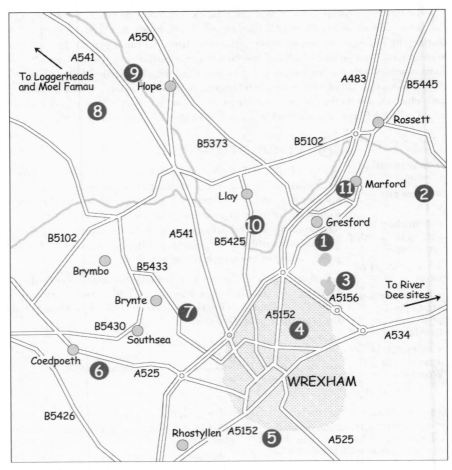

Key to sites

1. Gresford Flash
2. Cox Lane Wood
3. Borras Quarry and pools
4. Acton Park
5. Erdigg Country Park and Flash
6. Nant Mill
7. Moss Valley Country Park
8. Hope Mountain Country Park
9. Fagl Lane Quarry
10. Alyn Waters Country Park
11. Marford Quarry

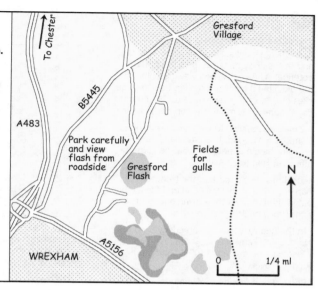

② Cox Lane Wood, Marford (SJ 370 555)

THE WOOD IS a 'hot-spot' for Lesser Spotted Woodpecker (60% chance) as well as Bullfinches (60%) and early Chiffchaffs/Willow Warblers each spring. Barn Owl and Buzzard

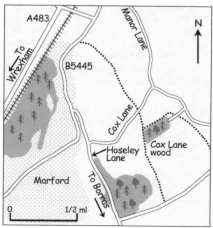

are resident. Curlew and Green Sandpipers on passage have also been seen in the fields around here.

Other target bird species include sizeable flocks of Lesser Redpoll (regular here – sometimes with Common Redpoll), Great Spotted (100%) and Green Woodpeckers (50%), Tree Pipit, Linnet and Marsh Tit.

Cox lane Wood can be reached from two directions. From the A483, leave via Rossett exit and turn right for Marford Hill. Turn left into Hosely Lane and the first left into Cox Lane. Park at gated entrance, taking the stile into the wood (Scout Camp).

Alternatively approach from the Wrexham bypass to the industrial estate (Borras exit). Follow Borras Road into Hosely Lane and then Cox Lane. Park near entrance to Trevalyn Hospital and search roadside trees, hedges and fields (it may be followed back to Hosely Lane via Park Lane to good effect). The hedges hold Tree Sparrows and Yellowhammers (50%).

③ Borras Quarry and Pools (SJ 354 530)

BORRAS QUARRY'S sand and gravel workings now seem to have petered out and this is likely to affect the site's birding potential. The established viewing point on the old airfield has been hidden behind huge piles of soil, so if you want to use it you must be prepared to climb to the top of the heap.

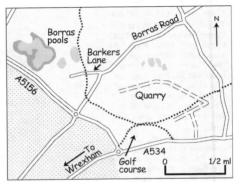

It may be possible to view the old workings from the main road, from the golf course or from the old airfield site, via the Tarmac offices at Holt Road site.

For Borras Pools, park at the truncated Barker's Lane off Borras Road and follow the public footpath, via the kissing gate on the right (not wheelchair accessible).

In the quarry, you'll find breeding Sand Martins and Lapwings (both 100%), plus Wheatears on passage (100%) and Little Ringed Plovers (80%).

Borras Pools feature wintering ducks and waders on passage, including Redshanks, Goldeneyes, Snipe and Teal. Breeding Mandarins, Little Grebes and Tufted Ducks may be present. Sand Martins can be seen in good numbers and Shelduck sometimes breed nearby. Bullfinches are an attractive resident species, while Wheatears can be seen on passage.

Hobbies are becoming more regular in the area and breeding Lesser Whitethroat may be encountered.

④ Acton Park (SJ 345 520)

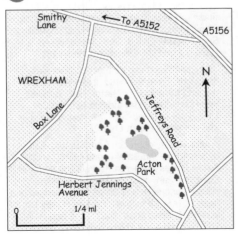

ALARGE LAKE and wetland area lie at the heart of this suburban multi-purpose park that originally formed part of the grounds of Acton Hall. It lies to the east of Chester Road, north of Wrexham town centre.

You can park in Herbert Jennings Avenue or behind the Cunliffe public house on Jeffrey's Road.

A wildflower meadow has also been created to encourage greater biodiversity at the site. A good variety of birds on passage have been seen here, including Wood Warbler and Water Rail.

Regular birds include Lesser Redpoll and Spotted Flycatcher and occasional sightings have included Mandarin Duck and Waxwing.

⑤ Erddig Country Park and Erddig Flash (SJ 327 482 and SJ 336 487)

THERE ARE a number of access points and car-parks for the National Trust property of Erdigg Hall, located two miles south of Wrexham and signposted from A525 Whitchurch road. Do not leave valuables in your parked car.

The Hall has rare fruit trees, a canal and pond and is open from mid-March to the end of October. Key bird species in the Country Park include Lesser Spotted Woodpecker (fairly regular but elusive), Green Woodpecker (formerly this area was a stronghold but the species has now declined drastically) and Greater Spotted Woodpecker (100%).

The Flash, which is not accessible to wheelchair users, lies just off the Sontley Road car park, just south of Coed-y-Glyn Wood. It has Snipe, Goosander and Teal regularly in winter and frequent Water Rails.

In the reeds, Reed Buntings and Sedge Warblers are regular and Reed Warbler occasional.

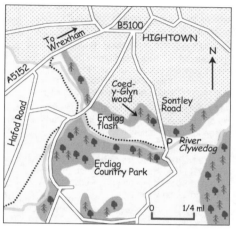

Breeding Grey Wagtail, Dipper and Kingfisher may be found along the river, especially near the weir. The woods hold a good selection of birds including Marsh Tit and Buzzard.

⑥ Nant Mill, Coedpoeth (SJ 288 504)

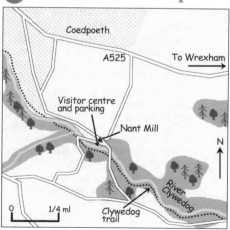

NANT MILL is situated on the Clywedog Trail, which stretches 6.5 miles from Minera through Plas Power woods to Erddig and covers a variety of habitats. Park at the Visitor Centre (signed from A483 and A525)

Target species: moorland birds at Minera include Wheatear, Peregrine, Red-legged Partridge and occasional Red Kite; woodland birds at Nant and Plas Power include summering Pied and Spotted Flycatchers, Wood Warbler, Dipper and Grey Wagtail.

Nearby sites include Nant-y-Ffrith Reservoir (SJ 245 530) and Pendinas Reservoir (SJ 245 530). This area can be good for a variety of birds including Black Grouse, Turtle Dove and scarce raptors, including regular passage Ospreys.

Moss Valley Country Park (SJ 312 523)

SITUATED three miles north of Wrexham between Brynteg and Gwersyllt, this site was reclaimed from coal mining spoil heaps in 1973.

Leave the A483 at the Mold turning. At the roundabout turn into Summerhill Road, and follow the yellow signs to Moss Valley Golf Course, then take the third left into Poolmouth Road. Park between the lakes.

The valley consists of two lakes, meadows, reedbeds, oak and beech woodlands. Park at the lakes and follow any footpaths for exploration.

More than 100 species of birds have been recorded here, including Kingfisher, Buzzard, Pied and Spotted Flycatchers, Redstart, Sky Lark and Wood Warbler.

The park is open all year round but there is no visitor centre.

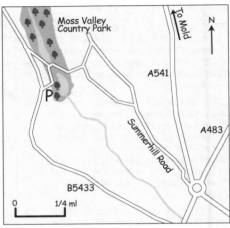

For more information contact the Community Ranger at: wx@groundwork.org.uk.

⑧ Hope Mountain Country Park (Waun y Llyn) (SJ 285 577)

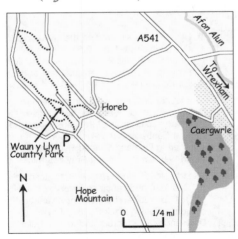

THIS quiet, attractive heather-covered park with extensive views of the Clwydian Hills to the west is ideal for short family walks, or as a start to longer routes.

However, because this is a hill-top site with steep slopes, wheelchair and pushchair use is not recommended. There are no toilet or refreshment facilities on-site.

From Wrexham follow A541 past Caergwrle. After road becomes dual carriageway, take small road on left signposted for Horeb. This takes you all the way up the mountain. Bear right at the white house built on the road junction, past the phone box and the car park is another 50 yards on right.

Bird species to look out for include Stonechat (all year), Wheatear (spring/ summer) and Snipe (winter).

⑨ Fagl Lane Quarry, Hope (SJ 301 588)

DESPITE owners Hanson announcing it was planning to close down this site in 2004, the gravel extraction has only just ceased. Now its future and ownership lie in the balance, though conservationists naturally hope the site can be protected and developed to benefit wildlife.

There is a large area of standing water. Access and viewing can be via Pigeonhouse Lane, Hope. A lay-by lies adjacent to a stile and public footpath.

Winter species include regular Pink-footed Geese, Goldeneye, Goosander and Wigeon. Highlights for summer include the Sand Martin colony, breeding Little Ringed Plover, Common Sandpiper, Garden Warbler, Green Woodpecker, Barn Owl, Kingfisher and Greylag Geese.

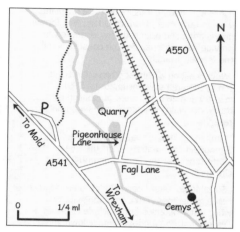

⑩ Alyn Waters Country Park and Llay Pool (SJ 332 553 and SJ 320 456)

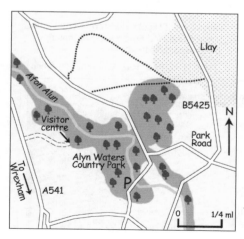

LOCATED in the beautiful Alyn Valley, this is the largest Country Park in the Wrexham area and offers visitors a choice of woodland, grassland and riverside walks.

Cycling is encouraged and the two mile cycleway and sculpture trail is suitable for wheelchair users. Disabled toilets are available at the visitor centre (10.30am-4.30pm each day) off Mold Road, Gwyrsyllt, along with a cafe, shop and a wildlife exhibition.

There are three sections to this CP and each can be accessed separately. The main areas for parking are at the visitor centre and at the car-park in Llay.

· Possible species include Sky Lark, Little Ringed Plover, Dipper, Green Woodpecker, Tree Pipit, Kingfisher, Lesser Whitethroat, plus breeding Buzzard.

⑪ Marford Quarry (SJ357 560)

KNOWN primarily as a good site for plants and butterflies, Marford Quarry is a former gravel and sand quarry that was created to provide raw materials for the construction of the Mersey Tunnel.

Now boasting a habitat of grassland and scrub, the area was designated a SSSI in 1989 and 26 acres were purchased by the North Wales Wildlife Trust as a nature reserve.

Limited parking is available near the Springfield Lane entrance, off the B5445 at Marford or near the Pant Lane entrance in Gresford.

Sizeable flocks of Lesser Redpolls are regular here (sometimes with Common Redpolls), while other notables birds include Green and Lesser Spotted Woodpeckers, Yellowhammer, Tree Pipit, Linnet and Marsh Tit.

In spring you can expect to see and hear a wide variety of migrant warblers.

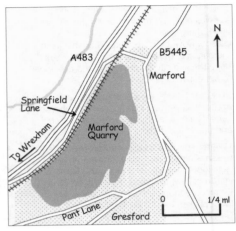

Loggerheads Country Park (SJ 205 627)

OCCUPYING around 80 acres of the Alyn Valley near Mold, this is a popular venue for families but if you are prepared to walk to quieter areas you are likely to be rewarded with views of Dipper, Redstart, Wood Warbler, Spotted and Pied Flycatchers, Nuthatch, Treecreeper and Kingfisher.

From Mold, head towards Ruthin on A494.

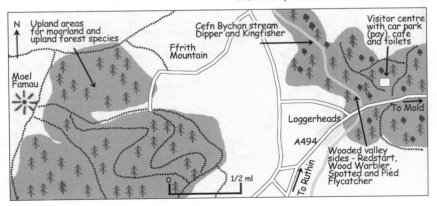

There is a car park (pay & display), café and toilets at the Visitor Centre (SJ 198 626).

Moel Famau (SJ 16 62)

At this adjoining site to Loggerheads Country Park, possible species are those birds associated with high moorland and afforested areas, such as Red and Black Grouse, Snow Buntings, Ravens, Short-eared and Long-eared Owls, Merlins, Red Kites and Crossbills.

Wheatears may also be seen around here as well as Linnets, Whinchats, Meadow Pipits, Redpolls, Common Sandpipers and Cuckoos.

The Dee Valley Borderlands

The River Dee and its floodplain is primarily an area of pastoral farming. The fields are subject to annual winter flooding and in some situations, roads may be impassable, so it is advisable to park on the main roads and access your chosen sites by public footpaths.

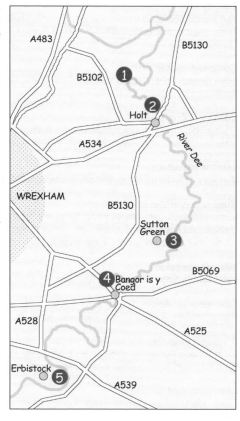

In winter, the Dee floods may bring in large numbers of swans, sometimes including Whoopers, plus wildfowl, especially Pintails and Wigeon.

In winter, Snipe may be present and large numbers of Fieldfares and Redwings. Small winter flocks of Yellowhammers and Tree Sparrows should be looked for.

Resident species include Barn Owl and Little Owl, Grey Partridge and Red-legged Partridge. Breeding Lapwings and Curlews can be found in the fields in summer together with breeding Sand Martins, Mandarins, Goosanders and Kingfishers along the river.

Suggested sites:

1. Almere Ferry & Trevalyn Meadows (SJ 39 55)

2. Holt Bridge (SJ 40 53)

3. Sutton Green (SJ 40 48)

4. Bangor on Dee (Bangor is y coed) (SJ 39 45)

5. Erbistock (SJ 358 415)

All sites are covered by Explorer Map No. 257.

163

DEFINITIONS OF BIRDGROUPS USED IN THIS BOOK

WHERE space allows, we have tried to provide comprehensive species lists for each site, but in some instances it has been necessary to group some of the most widespread species. Here is an explanation of some group terms we have used in the 'Target Birds' and 'Other Likely Species' sections:

Common woodland birds:
Woodpigeon, Tawny Owl, Great Spotted Woodpecker, Wren, Dunnock, Robin, Blackbird, Song Thrush, Mistle Thrush, migrant warblers, Goldcrest, Long-tailed Tit, Coal Tit, Blue Tit, Great Tit, Nuthatch, Treecreeper, Jackdaw, Rook, Crow, Chaffinch, Greenfinch, Goldfinch.

Common wildfowl:
Mute Swan, Greylag Goose, Canada Goose, Shelduck, Wigeon (usually in winter), Gadwall, Teal, Mallard, Shoveler, Pochard, Tufted Duck, Goldeneye (in winter), Red-breasted Merganser.

Common waterbirds:
Little Grebe, Great Crested Grebe, Cormorant, Grey Heron, common wildfowl, Moorhen, Coot.

Common finches:
House Sparrow (not strictly speaking a finch, of course), Chaffinch, Greenfinch, Goldfinch, Siskin, Linnet.

Winter thrushes:
Blackbird, Fieldfare, Song Thrush, Redwing, Mistle Thrush.

Summer warblers:
Lesser Whitethroat, Whitethroat, Garden Warbler, Blackcap, Chiffchaff, Willow Warbler. (Sedge and Reed Warblers are also summer visitors, but these are specifically mentioned in 'Other likely species' where they occur).

Winter raptors:
Hen Harrier, Sparrowhawk, Kestrel, Merlin, Peregrine, Barn Owl, Buzzard.

Common waders:
Oystercatcher, Ringed Plover, Lapwing, Knot, Dunlin, Snipe, Curlew, Redshank, Turnstone.

Passage waders:
Little Ringed Plover, Ringed Plover, Little Stint, Curlew, Sandpiper, Dunlin, Ruff, Whimbrel, Spotted Redshank, Greenshank, Green Sandpiper, Common Sandpiper.

Common gull species:
Black-headed Gull, Common Gull, Lesser Black-backed Gull, Herring Gull, Great Black-backed Gull.

DEFINITIONS OF BIRDGROUPS
USED IN THIS BOOK

Terns:
Sandwich Tern, Common Tern, Arctic Tern.

Seaducks and winter seabirds:
Red-throated Diver, Great Northern Diver, Great Crested Grebe, Slavonian Grebe, Wigeon, Eider, Long-tailed Duck, Common Scoter, Goldeneye, Red-breasted Merganser, Guillemot, Razorbill, Cormorant.

Hirundines:
Sand Martin, Swallow, House Martin, Swift (not a hirundine but included here to save space).

Passage migrants:
Hirundines, Tree Pipit, Whinchat, Wheatear, winter thrushes, Ring Ouzel, summer warblers, Goldcrest, Spotted Flycatcher, Pied Flycatcher, Brambling, and the chance of a rarity!

Common scrub birds:
Wren, Dunnock, Robin, Blackbird, Song Thrush, Mistle Thrush, summer warblers, Long-tailed Tit, Blue Tit, Great Tit, common finches.

USEFUL CONTACTS

BIRD & WILDLIFE GROUPS

British Trust for Ornithology
The Nunnery, Thetford,
Norfolk, IP24 2PU
01842 750050

Cambrian Ornithological Society
Pen-y-ffridd, Llangelnyw,
Abergele LL22 8RH
http://mysite.wanadoo-members.co.uk/
cambrianos/index.html

Countryside Council for Wales
Maes-y-Ffynnon, Penrhosgarnedd,
Bangor, Gwynedd LL57 2DW
08451 306 229

North Wales Wildlife Trust
376, High Street, Bangor, Gwynedd
LL57 1YE
01248 351 541
http://www.wildlifetrust.org.uk/northwales/

RSPB North Wales Office
Maes y Ffynnon, Penrhosgarnedd,
Bangor, Gwynedd
LL57 2DW
Tel: 01248 363 800

RSPB Wales Headquarters
Sutherland House, Castlebridge
Cowbridge Road East
Cardiff, CF11 9AB
Tel: 02920 353 000

OTHER USEFUL CONTACTS

Disabled Birders Association
Bo Boelens, 18 St Mildreds Road
Margate, Kent CT9 2LT
www.disabledbirdersassociation.org.uk

Disabled toilets leaflet
RADAR, 12 City Forum, 250 City Road,
London EC1V 8AF. 0207 125 03222

165

USEFUL CONTACTS

Forest Enterprise
Forestry Commission Wales
Victoria House, Victoria Terrace
Aberystwyth, Ceredigion SY23 2DQ
Tel: 0845 604 0845
www.forestry.gov.uk/wales

(The) National Trust
Wales Regional Office
Trinity Square, Llandudno LL30 2DE
01492 860 123

RSPCA
National contact number for all sick and
injured birds and animals – 08705 555 999

BIRD NEWS, RECORDS AND INFORMATION

County Recorders

ANGLESEY
Steve Cully
Mill House, Penmynydd Road
Menai Bridge, Anglesey LL59 5RT
01248 713 091
E-mail: SteCul10@aol.com

GWYNEDD
John Barnes
Fach Goch, Waunfawr, Caernarfon,
Gwynedd LL55 4YS
01286 650 362

CLWYD
Ian Spence
01352 750118
E-mail: ian.Spence@talktalk.net

Birdline Wales
09068 700 248 (premium rate number)
Phone news to 01492 544 588

OTHER CONTACTS

Council offices

Anglesey County Council
Anglesey Business Centre
Bryn Cefni Business Park, Llangefni,
Anglesey LL77 7XA
Tel: 01248 752 435 or 752 431
Fax: 01248 752 192
E-mail: tourism@anglesey.gov.uk
www.islandofchoice.com/tourism.asp

Conwy County Council
Bodlondeb, Conwy
North Wales LL32 8DU
Tel: 01492 574 000
Fax: 01492 592 114
E-mail: information@conwy.gov.uk.
www.conwy.gov.uk

Denbighshire County Council
County Hall, Wynnstay Road,
Ruthin LL15 1YN
Tel: 01824 706 000
E-mail: customerservicecentre@
denbighshire.gov.uk
http://www.denbighshire.gov.uk/

Flintshire County Council
County Hall, Mold, Flintshire CH7 6NB.
Tel: 01352 752 121
www.flintshire.gov.uk

Gwynedd County Council
Council Offices, Shirehall Street
Caernarfon, Gwynedd LL55 1SH
Tel: 01286 672 255
Fax: 01286 673 993
E-mail: enquiries@gwynedd.gov.uk
www.gwynedd.gov.uk

Tourist information offices

Directory of Tourist Information Offices in
North Wales:
www.information-britain.co.uk

Bala
Penllyn, Pensarn Road, Bala, LL23 7SR
Tel: 01678 521 021

Beddgelert
Yr Hen Gapel, Beddgelert, Caernarfon,
Gwynedd, LL55 4YD
Tel: 01766 890 615

Betws-y-Coed
Snowdonia National Park, Royal Oak Stables,
Betws-y-Coed, Conwy, LL24 0AH
Tel: 01690 710 426

Caernarfon
Oriel Pendeitsh, Castle Street, Caernarfon,
Gwynedd, LL55 2NA
Tel: 01286 672 232

Colwyn Bay
Station Square, Princes Drive, Colwyn Bay,
LL29 8LF
Tel: 01492 530 478

Conwy
Conwy Castle Visitor Centre, Conwy, LL32
8LD
Tel: 01492 592 248

Dolgellau
Ty Meirion, Eldon Square, Dolgellau, LL40
1PU
Tel: 01341 422 888

Harlech
Gwyddfor House, High Street, Harlech, LL46
2YA
Tel: 01766 780 658

Holyhead
Stena Line Terminal 1, Holyhead, Isle of
Anglesey, LL65 1DQ
Tel: 01407 762 622

Llanberis
41a High Street, Llanberis, Caernarfon,
Gwynedd, LL55 4EH
Tel: 01286 870 765

Llandudno
1-2 Chapel Street, Llandudno, LL30 2YU
Tel: 01492 876 413

Llanfairpg
Station Site, Llanfairpwllgwyngyll, LL61 5UJ
Tel: 01248 713 177

Llangollen
Town Hall, Castle Street, Llangollen,
Denbighshire, LL20 5PD
Tel: 01978 860 828

Porthmadog
Y Ganolfan, High Street, Porthmadog,
Gwynedd, LL49 9LP
Tel: 01766 512 981
Email: porthmadog.tic@gwynedd.gov.uk

Pwllheli
Min y Don, Station Square, Gwynedd, LL53
6HE
Tel: 01758 613 000

Rhos on Sea
The Promenade, Rhos on Sea, LL28 4EP
Tel: 01492 548 778

Rhyl
Childrenýs Village, The Promenade, Rhyl,
Denbighshire, LL18 1HZ
Tel: 01745 355 068

Ruthin
Ruthin Craft Centre, Park Road, Ruthin,
Denbighshire, LL15 1BB
Tel: 01824 703 992

Wrexham
Lambpit Street, PO Box 1291, Wrexham,
LL11 1WN
Tel: 01978 292 015
Email: tic@wrexham.gov.uk

Travel line Wales
For bus, coach and rail journey planning and
timetable information
www.traveline-cymru.org.uk/
Tel: 0871 200 22 33
(Calls from landlines cost 10p per minute).

LIKE ALL OTHER activities, birdwatching has generated a language of its own and in the *Best Birdwatching Sites* series of guides we have attempted to explain terms used in the birding world, which may not be familiar to less experienced birdwatchers.

BB RARITY: Rare bird of which a full description is required for the British Bird Rarities Committee, in order for a record to be officially accepted.

BIRDER: Someone who takes birdwatching seriously, (usually) his / (less frequently) her main passion.

BIRDLINE: Telephone information service with the latest update on birds' whereabouts. For Birdline Wales, call 09068 700 248.

BIRDRACE: A competition between groups of birders to see how many species of birds can be seen (and heard) in 24 hours.

BONXIE: Great Skua, Shetland name in common use.

BRITISH LIST: The official record of all bird species seen in the UK.

BTO: British Trust for Ornithology.

BOU: British Ornithologists' Union – the most senior bird organisation in Britain and keeper of the British List.

CATEGORY A: Species that have been recorded in an apparently natural state at least once since January 1, 1950.

CATEGORY B: Species that were recorded in an apparently natural state at least once between January 1, 1800 and December 31, 1949, but have not been recorded subsequently.

CATEGORY C: A category on the official British bird list containing species that have escaped from captivity in the past, but now have self-sustaining populations (e.g. Canada Goose).

COS: Cambrian Ornithological Society – meets at Pensychnant Centre.

DIP: To go on a 'twitch' and not see the bird you went for.

DIPPER: One who 'dips' – a person who 'twitches' but misses the target bird. Not good!!

DUDE: A person who has all the top birdwatching equipment, but lacks field skills (a bit like most politicians: style over content!).

DUFF GEN: Incorrect information about a bird or location.

ECLIPSE: The name given to the dowdy, female-type plumage adopted by male ducks when they moult out of breeding plumage in summer.

FALL: A mass grounding of migrating passerines, usually as a result of fog or heavy rain.

FIRST: First record of a species in the UK, a county, etc.

FENCE-HOPPER: A bird that has escaped from captivity.

FLUSH: To disturb a bird.

GRIP OFF: To see something that someone else has missed. Being 'gripped off' is particularly annoying if it happens to you on your 'local patch'.

JIZZ: The identification of a bird by its overall character, not by field marks.

LIFER: A bird species you have never seen before ("that Black Lark at South Stack was a lifer for us!").

LISTER: Someone who keeps a list of everything they see, everywhere they see it! Garden list, life list, world list, county list, year list, birds seen while gazing out of the office window, etc. Includes us!

LOCAL PATCH: An area regularly covered by a birdwatcher, usually close to home. The feeling when something new turns up on your patch, rare or not, is exciting, particularly to a 'lister'!

LOW LISTER: Someone who hasn't seen many species of bird.

LBJ: An affectionate short form for Little Brown Job, any bird which has dowdy plumage (Dunnock, pipits, Garden Warbler, etc).

LNR: Local Nature Reserve.

LRP: Shortened term for Little Ringed Plover.

MEGA: A very rare bird. This will cause extreme excitement when seen.

MIPIT: Slang for a Meadow Pipit.

MUCH ABOUT?: Traditional greeting from one birder to another.

NNR: National Nature Reserve.

NWWT: North Wales Wildlife Trust.

PAGER: Subscriber information service. Will usually bleep with a new message at the most inopportune moments!

PELAGIC: Trip out to sea by boat for seabirds.

PLASTIC: Can refer to an escaped cage bird, or a Category C species.

RAMSAR: A wetland site of international importance as defined at the convention in Ramsar, Iran.

RODING: The display flight of the Woodcock. Usually seen at dawn and dusk.

RSPB: Royal Society for the Protection of Birds

RSPCA: Royal Society for the Prevention

of Cruelty to Animals. The organisation to contact in the unfortunate event of finding an injured or sick bird.

SSSI: Site of Special Scientific Interest.

STRINGER: A person who misidentifies a bird and sticks to that identification, turning a common bird into a more exciting rarity. We have come across people 'stringing' a Common Scoter for a Black Scoter, a plastic bag for a Little Egret and a tree stump for an Osprey.

TICK: To see a bird. Probably derived from 'listers' seeing a bird, then ticking it off on one or more of their lists.

TRASH BIRDS: Gaudy, easy to identify species. Unfortunately more usually seen in exotic locations overseas than in North Wales.

TWITCH: Travel to see a specific bird (usually a rare species) as soon as news of it breaks. Can involve a journey of many miles, or can just be to your 'local patch' to see something you have never seen there before. Has gained a bad name with beginners and birdwatchers who don't 'twitch', but is usually well organised, friendly, and great fun (if you don't 'dip').

TWITCHER: Someone who goes on a twitch. Ardent 'twitchers' set off as soon as news breaks of a rare bird, anywhere in the country. Others go when they can, usually at the weekend, after the target bird has flown on the Friday night!

WWT: Wildfowl and Wetlands Trust.

YEAR LIST: A record of birds seen (in Britain) from January 1 to December 31.

YEAR LISTER: Someone who tries to see as many species of bird in a year as possible. This has sometimes involved people seeing a rare bird on December 31, and then travelling again to see it the next day to get it on two 'year lists'!

WELSH PRONUNCIATION GUIDE

At first sight, Welsh words may appear difficult to pronounce. You will need to remember that the Welsh alphabet is a little different to the English alphabet:

A B C Ch D Dd E F Ff G Ng H I L Ll M N O P Ph R Rh S T Th U W Y

As you can see, the Welsh alphabet has no letter J, K, Q, V, X or Z, although when Welsh uses English words, you will sometimes come across J, for example in garej (garage). W and Y are considered to be vowels.

Welsh vowels can be either short or long:

A	either as in 'cat' or as in 'card'
E	either as in 'men' or as in 'fair'
I	either as in 'ink' or as in 'mean'
O	either as in 'dog' or as in 'more'
U	either as in 'bin' or as in 'been'
W	either as in 'book' or as in 'moon'
Y	either as in 'bin' or as in 'been'

Unfortunately, there are no simple rules as to when a vowel sound is short or long, but if in doubt, use the short vowel sound.

Consonants, however, are always pronounced the same way with no exceptions or variations to pronunciation, unlike in English:

B	as in 'ball'
C	as in 'catch'
Ch	as in the Scottish word 'loch'
D	as in 'dog'
Dd	as in 'the' or 'smoothe'
F	as in 'have' like an English 'V'
Ff	as in 'face' like an English 'F'
G	as in 'good'
Ng	as in 'long'
H	as in 'hot'
L	as in 'lemon'
Ll	as an 'L' but you blow out air through your back teeth at the same time!

M	as in 'man'
N	as in 'nut'
P	as in 'pig'
Ph	as in 'face' like an English 'F'
R	as in 'round'
Rh	like an 'R' followed by a 'huh' sound
S	as in 'sea'
T	as in 'tea'
Th	as in 'think'

Mutations

It is not essential to your North Wales birding pleasure to understand the grammar of the Welsh language. However, it might help you to be aware that in Welsh, words that begin with certain consonants sometimes change their first letters to help with pronunciation, depending on the word that precedes it. For example, 'bach' may become 'fach' and 'caer' may become 'gaer'. Don't worry about the various rules, but being aware of mutations, may help you to spot words which have changed.

Place name glossary

In the Welsh language, many place names have meanings explaining the history or location of the places themselves. The glossary below may help you identify what's behind the names:

Cymraeg/ Welsh	Saesneg/ English	Cymraeg/ Welsh	Saesneg/ English
Afon	river	Cefn	ridge
Bach/Fach	little	Clogwyn	cliff
Bedd	grave	Coch/Goch	red
Bwlch	pass	Coed	wood
Bryn	hill	Copa	summit
Cae	field, enclosure	Cors/Gors	bog or marsh
Caer/Gaer	fort, camp	Craig/graig	rock
Canol	centre	Croes/groes	cross
Capel	chapel	Cwm	coombe
Carn, Carnedd	heap of stones	Dinas	city, fortress
Carreg	crag or stone	Ddu	black
Castell	castle or fortress	Dol/Ddol	meadow

Cymraeg/ Welsh	Saesneg/ English	Cymraeg/ Welsh	Saesneg/ English
Dŵr	water	Ogof	cave
Dyffryn	valley	Pant	hollow
Eglwys	church	Parc	park
Eryri	highland	Pen	head or point
Esgair	ridge	Penrhyn	promontory
Ffordd	road	Pentre	village
Ffynnon	well	Plas	mansion, house
Foel	bare hill	Pont/Bont	bridge
Galt	slope	Porth/Borth	port
Garth	enclosure	Pwll	pool
Glan	river bank	Rhaeadr	waterfall
Glas	blue	Rhiw	hill
Glyn	deep valley	Rhos	moorland
Gwyn	white	Rhyd	ford
Hafod	summer dwelling	Sarn	causeway
Hen	old	Tan	under
Hendre	winter dwelling	Traeth	beach, sandy shore
Isaf	lower	Tref/Dref	town
Llan	parish	Trwyn	peninsula
Llyn	lake	Twll	cave
Llys	hall or court	Twr	tower
Lon	lane	Twyni	sand dunes
Maen	stone	Tŷ	house
Maes/Faes	field or meadow	Tŷ bach	toilet
Mawr/Fawr	large	Tyddyn	farmstead
Melin/Felin	mill	Uchaf	upper
Moel	bare hill	Waun	moorland
Mor	sea	Wen	white
Morfa	flat seashore	Wern/Gwern	alder swamp
Mynydd/Fynydd	mountain	Y, Yr	the
Nant	stream	Yn	in
Newydd	new	Ynys	island

BIRD NAMES IN WELSH AND ENGLISH
Enwau Adar yn Gymraeg a Saesneg

Saesneg/ English	Cymraeg/ Welsh	Saesneg/ English	Cymraeg/ Welsh
American Wigeon	Chwiwell America	Chiffchaff	Siff Saff
Arctic Skua	Sgiwen y Gogledd	Chough	Bran Goesgoch
Arctic Tern	Morwennol y Gogledd	Coal Tit	Titw Penddu
Baird's Sandpiper	Pibydd Baird	Collared Dove	Turtur Dorchog
Balearic Shearwater	Aderyn-drycin Môr y Canoldir	Collared Flycatcher	Gwybedog Torchog
		Collared Pratincole	Cwtiadwennol Dorchog
Bar-tailed Godwit	Rhostog Gynffonfrith	Common Gull	Gwylan y Gweunydd
Barn Owl	Tylluan Wen	Common Sandpiper	Pibydd y Dorlan
Barnacle Goose	Gwydd Wyran	Common Scoter	Môr-hwyaden Ddu
Barred Warbler	Telor Rhesog	Common Tern	Morwennol Gyffredin
Bee-eater	Gwybedog y Gwenyn	Coot	Cwtiar
Bittern	Aderyn y Bwn	Cormorant	Mulfran
Black Grouse	Grugiar Ddu	Corn Bunting	Bras yr Yd
Black Guillemot	Gwylog Ddu	Corn Crake	Rhegen yr Yd
Black Kite	Barcud Du	Cory's Shearwater	Aderyn-drycin Cory
Black Redstart	Tingoch Ddu	Crane (Common)	Garan
Black Tern	Cors-wennol Ddu	Crossbill (Common)	Gylfin Groes
Black-headed Bunting	Bras Penddu	Cuckoo	Côg
Black-headed Gull	Gwylan Benddu	Curlew	Gylfinir
Black-necked Grebe	Gwyach Yddfddu	Curlew Sandpiper	Pibydd Cambig
Black-tailed Godwit	Rhostog Gynffonddu	Dipper	Bronwen y Dwr
Black-throated Diver	Trochydd Gyddfddu	Dotterel	Hutan y Mynydd
Black-winged Pratincole	Cwtiadwennol Ddu	Dunlin	Pibydd y Mawn
Blackbird	Mwyalchen	Dunnock	Llwyd y Gwrych
Blackcap	Telor Penddu	Eider	Hwyaden Fwythblu
Blue Tit	Titw Tomos Las	Feral Pigeon	Colomen y Graig
Bluethroat	Bronlas	Fieldfare	Socan Eira
Bonelli's Warbler	Telor Bonelli	Firecrest	Dryw Pennflamgoch
Brambling	Pinc y Mynydd	Forster's Tern	Morwennol Forster
Brent Goose	Gwydd Ddu	Fulmar	Aderyn-drycin y Graig
Bullfinch	Coch y Berllan	Gadwall	Hwyaden Lwyd
Buzzard (Common)	Bwncath	Gannet	Hugan
Canada Goose	Gwydd Canada	Garden Warbler	Telor yr Ardd
Carrion Crow	Bran Dyddyn	Garganey	Hwyaden Addrain
Cetti's Warbler	Telor Cetti	Glaucous Gull	Gwylan y Gogledd
Chaffinch	Ji-binc	Goldcrest	Dryw Eurben

Saesneg/English	Cymraeg/Welsh	Saesneg/English	Cymraeg/Welsh
Golden Eagle	Eryr Aur	Hoopoe	Copog
Golden Oriole	Euryn	House Martin	Gwennol y Bondo
Golden Plover	Cwtiad Aur	House Sparrow	Aderyn y To
Goldeneye	Hwyaden Lygad-aur	Iceland Gull	Gwylan yr Arctig
Goldfinch	Nico	Jack Snipe	Giach Fach
Goosander	Hwyaden Ddanheddog	Jackdaw	Jac y Do
Goshawk	Gwalch Marth	Jay	Ysgrech y Coed
Grasshopper Warbler	Troellwr Bach	Kestrel	Cudyll Coch
Great Crested Grebe	Gwyach Fawr Gopog	Kingfisher	Glas y Dorlan
Great Black-backed Gull	Gwylan Gefnddu Fwyaf	Kittiwake	Gwylan Goesddu
		Knot	Pibydd yr Aber
Great Grey Shrike	Cigydd Mawr	Lapland Bunting	Bras y Gogledd
Great Northern Diver	Trochydd Mawr	Lapwing	Cornchwiglen
Great Shearwater	Aderyn-drycin Mawr	Leach's Storm Petrel	Pedryn Cynffon Fforchog
Great Spotted Woodpecker	Cnocell Fraith Fwyaf	Lesser Black-backed Gull	Gwulan Gefnddu Leiaf
Great Skua	Sgiwen Fawr		
Great Tit	Titw Mawr	Lesser Spotted Woodpecker	Cnocell Fraith Leiaf
Great White Egret	Creyr Mawr Gwyn	Lesser Whitethroat	Llwydfron Bach
Green Sandpiper	Pibydd Gwyrdd	Linnet	Llinos
Green-winged Teal	Corhwyaden America	Little Auk	Carfil Bach
Green Woodpecker	Cnocell Werdd	Little Crake	Rhegen Fach
Greenfinch	Llinos Werdd	Little Egret	Creyr Bach
Greenshank	Pibydd Coeswerdd	Little Grebe	Gwyach Fach
Grey Heron	Creyr Glas	Little Gull	Gwylan Fechan
Grey Partridge	Petrisen	Little Ringed Plover	Cwtiad Torchog Bach
Grey Phalarope	Llydandroed Llwyd	Little Owl	Tylluan Fach
Grey Plover	Cwtiad Llwyd	Little Shearwater	Aderyn-drycin Bach
Grey Wagtail	Siglen Lwyd	Little Stint	Pibydd Bach
Greylag Goose	Gwydd Wyllt	Little Tern	Morwennol Fechan
Guillemot	Gwylog	Long-eared Owl	Tylluan Gorniog
Hawfinch	Gylfinbraff	Long-tailed Duck	Hwyaden Gynffon-hir
Hen Harrier	Bod Tinwen	Long-tailed Skua	Sgiwen Lostfain
Herring Gull	Gwylan y Penwaig	Long-tailed Tit	Titw Cynffon-hir
Hobby	Hebog yr Ehedydd	Magpie	Pioden
Honey Buzzard	Bod y Mel		

Saesneg/ English	Cymraeg/ Welsh	Saesneg/ English	Cymraeg/ Welsh
Mallard	Hwyaden Wyllt	Red-backed Shrike	Cigydd Cefngoch
Mandarin Duck	Hwyaden Gribog	Red-breasted Flycatcher	Gwybedog Brongoch
Manx Shearwater	Aderyn-drycin Manaw	Red-breasted Merganser	Hwyaden Frongoch
Marsh Harrier	Bod y Gwerni	Red-legged Partridge	Petrisen Goesgoch
Marsh Sandpiper	Pibydd y Gors	Red-necked Grebe	Gwyach Yddfgoch
Marsh Tit	Titw'r Wern	Red-necked Phalarope	Llydandroed
Meadow Pipit	Corhedydd y Waun	Red-throated Diver	Trochydd Gyddfgoch
Mediterranean Gull	Gwylan Môr y Canoldir	Red-throated Pipit	Corhedydd Gyddfgoch
Melodious Warbler	Telor Per	Redpoll (Lesser)	Llinos Bengoch
Merlin	Cudyll Bach	Redshank	Pibydd Coesgoch
Mistle Thrush	Brych y Coed	Redstart	Tingoch
Montagu's Harrier	Bod Montagu	Redwing	Coch Dan Adain
Moorhen	Iar Ddwr	Reed Bunting	Bras y Cyrs
Mute Swan	Alarch Dôf	Reed Warbler	Telor y Cyrs
Nightingale	Eos	Richard's Pipit	Corhedydd Richard
Nightjar	Troellwr Mawr	Ring Ouzel	Mwyalchen y Mynydd
Nuthatch	Delor y Cnau	Ring-billed Gull	Gwylan Fodrwybig
Osprey	Gwalch y Pysgod	Ringed Plover	Cwtiad Torchog
Oystercatcher	Pioden y Môr	Robin	Robin Goch
Pectoral Sandpiper	Pibydd Cain	Rock Dove	Colomen y Graig
Peregrine Falcon	Hebog Tramor	Rock Pipit	Corhedydd y Graig
Pheasant	Ffesant	Rook	Ydfran
Pied Flycatcher	Gwybedog Brith	Rose-coloured Starling	Drudwen Wridog
Pied Wagtail	Siglen Fraith	Roseate Tern	Morwennol Wridog
Pine Bunting	Bras y Pin	Rosefinch (Common)	Llinos Goch
Pink-footed Goose	Gwydd Droed-binc	Ruddy Duck	Hwyaden Goch
Pintail	Hwyaden Lostfain	Ruddy Shelduck	Hwyaden Goch yr Eithin
Pochard	Hwyaden Bengoch	Ruff	Pibydd Torchog
Pomarine Skua	Sgiwen Frech	Sabine's Gull	Gwylan Sabine
Puffin	Pâl	Sand Martin	Gwennol y Glennydd
Purple Sandpiper	Pibydd Du	Sanderling	Pibydd y Tywod
Quail	Sofliar	Sandwich Tern	Morwennol Bigddu
Raven	Cigfran	Savi's Warbler	Telor Savi
Razorbill	Llurs	Scaup	Hwyaden Benddu
Red Grouse	Grugiar	Sedge Warbler	Telor yr Hesg
Red Kite	Barcud		

Saesneg/ English	Cymraeg/ Welsh	Saesneg/ English	Cymraeg/ Welsh
Shag	Mulfran Werdd	Tufted Duck	Hwyaden Gopog
Shelduck	Hwyaden yr Eithin	Turnstone	Pibydd y Traeth
Shore Lark	Ehedydd y Traeth	Turtle Dove	Turtur
Short-eared Owl	Tylluan Glustiog	Twite	Llinos y Mynydd
Short-toed Lark	Ehedydd Llwyd	Velvet Scoter	Môr-hwyaden y Gogledd
Shoveler	Hwyaden Lydanbig	Water Pipit	Corhedydd y Dwr
Siskin	Pila Gwyrdd	Water Rail	Rhegen y Dwr
Sky Lark	Ehedydd	Waxwing	Cynffon Sidan
Slavonian Grebe	Gwyach Gorniog	Wheatear	Tinwen y Garn
Smew	Lleian Wen	Whimbrel	Coegylfinir
Snipe	Giach	Whinchat	Crec yr Eithin
Snow Bunting	Bras yr Eira	White Stork	Ciconia Gwyn
Snowy Owl	Tylluan yr Eira	White Wagtail	Siglen Wen
Song Thrush	Bronfraith	White-fronted Goose	Gwydd Dalcen-wen
Sooty Shearwater	Aderyn-drycin Du	Whitethroat (Common)	Llwydfron
Sparrowhawk	Gwalch Glas	Whooper Swan	Alarch y Gogledd
Spoonbill	Llwybig	Wigeon	Chwiwell
Spotted Flycatcher	Gwybedog Mannog	Willow Tit	Titw'r Helyg
Spotted Redshank	Pibydd Coesgoch Mannog	Willow Warbler	Telor yr Helyg
Starling	Drudwen	Wilson's Storm Petrel	Pedryn Wilson
Stock Dove	Colomen Wyllt	Wood Pigeon	Ysguthan
Stonechat	Clochdar y Cerrig	Wood Sandpiper	Pibydd y Graean
Storm Petrel	Pedryn Drycin	Wood Warbler	Telor y Coed
Subalpine Warbler	Telor Brongoch	Woodchat Shrike	Cigydd Pengoch
Surf Scoter	Môr-hwyaden yr Ewyn	Woodcock	Cyffylog
Swallow (Barn)	Gwennol	Wood Lark	Ehedydd y Coed
Swift	Gwennol Ddu	Wren	Dryw
Tawny Owl	Tylluan Frech	Wryneck	Pengam
Teal	Corhwyaden	Yellow Wagtail	Siglen Felen
Temminck's Stint	Pibydd Temminck	Yellow-browed Warbler	Telor Aelfelyn
Tree Pipit	Corhedydd y Coed	Yellow-legged Gull	Gwylan Goesfelen
Tree Sparrow	Golfan y Mynydd	Yellowhammer	Bras Melyn
Treecreeper	Dringwr Bach		

THIS IS a list of all the species of bird which have been seen in North Wales (presented in the order approved by the British Ornithologists' Union) with a brief note on their distribution. These notes are from our personal experiences of the birds, so some readers may disagree with our verdicts! Two tick boxes per species have been provided to assist your own record-keeping.

We have assigned all species to one of the following categories:

COMMON
Very easy to see, unlikely to be missed on a visit to the area.

WIDESPREAD
Present in small numbers throughout the area.

SCARCE
You would need to visit a specific site to look for these species. However, once found, birds could occur in reasonable numbers at that site.

RARE
Very small number of records, usually seen annually.

VERY RARE
Official British Bird Rarities which occur less than annually.

VAGRANT
Extreme rarities, once in a lifetime chance.

In an effort to standardise English-language bird names across the globe, many common British species acquired prefixes such as Common and Eurasian but these have not been widely adopted in the field. We have provided the full standardised names but those words which have not been absorbed into common usage among birdwatchers are shown in brackets.

		#	Name	Scientific name	Status
		1	**Mute Swan**	*Cygnus olor*	Common
		2	**Whooper Swan**	*Cygnus cygnus*	Scarce, winter
		3	**Bean Goose**	*Anser fabalis*	Very rare
		4	**Pink-footed Goose**	*Anser brachyrhynchus*	Scarce, winter
		5	**(Greater) White-fronted Goose**	*Anser albifrons*	Rare
		6	**Greylag Goose**	*Anser anser*	Widespread
		7	**(Greater) Canada Goose**	*Branta canadensis*	Common
		8	**Barnacle Goose**	*Branta leucopsis*	Rare
		9	**Brent Goose**	*Branta bernicla*	Scarce, winter
		10	**Egyptian Goose**	*Alopochen aegyptiaca*	Rare
		11	**Ruddy Shelduck**	*Tadorna ferruginea*	Rare
		12	**(Common) Shelduck**	*Tadorna tadorna*	Common
		13	**Mandarin Duck**	*Aix galericulata*	Rare

		14	**(Eurasian) Wigeon**	*Anas penelope*	Common, winter
		15	**American Wigeon**	*Anas americana*	Very rare
		16	**Gadwall**	*Anas strepera*	Scarce
		17	**(Eurasian) Teal**	*Anas crecca*	Common, winter
		18	**Green-winged Teal**	*Anas carolinensis*	Very rare
		19	**Mallard**	*Anas platyrhynchos*	Common
		20	**American Black Duck**	*Anas rubripes*	Vagrant
		21	**(Northern) Pintail**	*Anas acuta*	Scarce, winter
		22	**Garganey**	*Anas querquedula*	Rare
		23	**Blue-winged Teal**	*Anas discors*	Vagrant
		24	**(Northern) Shoveler**	*Anas clypeata*	Widespread
		25	**Red-crested Pochard**	*Netta rufina*	Rare
		26	**(Common) Pochard**	*Aythya ferina*	Widespread
		27	**Ring-necked Duck**	*Aythya collaris*	Very rare
		28	**Ferruginous Duck**	*Aythya nyroca*	Vagrant
		29	**Tufted Duck**	*Aythya fuligula*	Widespread
		30	**Greater Scaup**	*Aythya marila*	Scarce, winter
		31	**(Common) Eider**	*Somateria mollissima*	Scarce
		32	**King Eider**	*Somateria spectabilis*	Vagrant
		33	**Long-tailed Duck**	*Clangula hyemalis*	Scarce, winter
		34	**Common Scoter**	*Melanitta nigra*	Widespread, winter
		35	**Black Scoter**	*Melanitta americana*	Vagrant
		36	**Surf Scoter**	*Melanitta perspicillata*	Vagrant
		37	**Velvet Scoter**	*Melanitta fusca*	Rare
		38	**(Common) Goldeneye**	*Bucephala clangula*	Widespread, winter
		39	**Smew**	*Mergellus albellus*	Rare, winter
		40	**Red-breasted Merganser**	*Mergus serrator*	Widespread
		41	**Goosander**	*Mergus merganser*	Scarce
		42	**Ruddy Duck**	*Oxyura jamaicensis*	Scarce, declining
		43	**(Willow Ptarmigan) Red Grouse**	*Lagopus lagopus*	Scarce
		44	**Black Grouse**	*Tetrao tetrix*	Scarce
		45	**Red-legged Partridge**	*Alectoris rufa*	Scarce
		46	**Grey Partridge**	*Perdix perdix*	Scarce
		47	**(Common) Quail**	*Coturnix coturnix*	Rare, summer
		48	**(Common) Pheasant**	*Phasianus colchicus*	Common

			49	**Red-throated Diver**	*Gavia stellata*	Widespread, winter
			50	**Black-throated Diver**	*Gavia arctica*	Rare, winter
			51	**Great Northern Diver**	*Gavia immer*	Scarce, winter
			52	**Yellow-billed Diver**	*Gavia adamsii*	Vagrant
			53	**Little Grebe**	*Tachybaptus ruficollis*	Common
			54	**Great Crested Grebe**	*Podiceps cristatus*	Common
			55	**Red-necked Grebe**	*Podiceps grisegena*	Rare
			56	**Slavonian Grebe**	*Podiceps auritus*	Scarce, winter
			57	**Black-necked Grebe**	*Podiceps nigricollis*	Rare
			58	**Black-browed Albatross**	*Thalassarche melanophris*	Vagrant
			59	**(Northern) Fulmar**	*Fulmarus glacialis*	Common, coastal
			60	**Cory's Shearwater**	*Calonectris diomedea*	Very rare
			61	**Great Shearwater**	*Puffinus gravis*	Very rare
			62	**Sooty Shearwater**	*Puffinus griseus*	Rare
			63	**Manx Shearwater**	*Puffinus puffinus*	Scarce, coastal, summer
			64	**Balearic Shearwater**	*Puffinus mauretanicus*	Rare
			65	**European Storm-petrel**	*Hydrobates pelagicus*	Scarce, coastal, summer
			66	**Leach's Storm-petrel**	*Oceanodroma leucorhoa*	Rare
			67	**(Northern) Gannet**	*Morus bassanus*	Widespread, coastal
			68	**(Great) Cormorant**	*Phalacrocorax carbo*	Common
			69	**(European) Shag**	*Phalacrocorax aristotelis*	Scarce, coastal
			70	**(Great) Bittern**	*Botaurus stellaris*	Rare
			71	**Little Bittern**	*Ixobrychus minutus*	Vagrant
			72	**Black-crowned Night Heron**	*Nycticorax nycticorax*	Very rare
			73	**Green Heron**	*Butorides virescens*	Vagrant
			74	**Squacco Heron**	*Ardeola ralloides*	Vagrant
			75	**Cattle Egret**	*Bubulcus ibis*	Very rare
			76	**Little Egret**	*Egretta garzetta*	Scarce, increasing
			77	**Great Egret**	*Ardea alba*	Very rare
			78	**Grey Heron**	*Ardea cinerea*	Widespread
			79	**Purple Heron**	*Ardea purpurea*	Very rare
			80	**Black Stork**	*Ciconia nigra*	Vagrant
			81	**White Stork**	*Ciconia ciconia*	Very rare
			82	**Glossy Ibis**	*Plegadis falcinellus*	Vagrant
			83	**(Eurasian) Spoonbill**	*Platalea leucorodia*	Rare

			84	(European) Honey-buzzard	*Pernis apivorus*	Rare
			85	Black Kite	*Milvus migrans*	Vagrant
			86	Red Kite	*Milvus milvus*	Scarce
			87	White-tailed Eagle	*Haliaeetus albicilla*	Vagrant
			88	(Eurasian) Marsh Harrier	*Circus aeruginosus*	Rare
			89	Hen Harrier	*Circus cyaneus*	Scarce
			90	Montagu's Harrier	*Circus pygargus*	Very rare
			91	(Northern) Goshawk	*Accipiter gentilis*	Scarce
			92	(Eurasian) Sparrowhawk	*Accipiter nisus*	Widespread
			93	(Common) Buzzard	*Buteo buteo*	Common
			94	Rough-legged Buzzard	*Buteo lagopus*	Vagrant
			95	Osprey	*Pandion haliaetus*	Scarce, summer
			96	(Common) Kestrel	*Falco tinnunculus*	Widespread
			97	Red-footed Falcon	*Falco vespertinus*	Very rare
			98	Merlin	*Falco columbarius*	Scarce
			99	(Eurasian) Hobby	*Falco subbuteo*	Rare
			100	Gyr Falcon	*Falco rusticolus*	Vagrant
			101	Peregrine Falcon	*Falco peregrinus*	Scarce
			102	Water Rail	*Rallus aquaticus*	Scarce
			103	Spotted Crake	*Porzana porzana*	Very rare
			104	Sora	*Porzana carolina*	Vagrant
			105	Little Crake	*Porzana parva*	Vagrant
			106	Baillon's Crake	*Porzana pusilla*	Vagrant
			107	Corn Crake	*Crex crex*	Very rare
			108	(Common) Moorhen	*Gallinula chloropus*	Common
			109	(Common) Coot	*Fulica atra*	Common
			110	(Common) Crane	*Grus grus*	Very rare
			111	(Eurasian) Oystercatcher	*Haematopus ostralegus*	Common
			112	Black-winged Stilt	*Himantopus himantopus*	Very rare
			113	(Pied) Avocet	*Recurvirostra avosetta*	Rare
			114	Stone-curlew	*Burhinus oedicnemus*	Very rare
			115	Collared Pratincole	*Glareola pratincola*	Very rare
			116	Black-winged Pratincole	*Glareola nordmanni*	Vagrant
			117	Little (Ringed) Plover	*Charadrius dubius*	Scarce, summer
			118	Ringed Plover	*Charadrius hiaticula*	Widespread

			No.	Name	Scientific Name	Status
			119	**Killdeer**	*Charadrius vociferus*	Vagrant
			120	**Kentish Plover**	*Charadrius alexandrinus*	Very rare
			121	**(Eurasian) Dotterel**	*Charadrius morinellus*	Scarce, spring/autumn
			122	**American Golden Plover**	*Pluvialis dominica*	Very rare
			123	**(European) Golden Plover**	*Pluvialis apricaria*	Scarce
			124	**Grey Plover**	*Pluvialis squatarola*	Scarce
			125	**(Northern) Lapwing**	*Vanellus vanellus*	Widespread
			126	**(Red) Knot**	*Calidris canutus*	Scarce
			127	**Sanderling**	*Calidris alba*	Scarce
			128	**Little Stint**	*Calidris minuta*	Scarce, autumn
			129	**Temminck's Stint**	*Calidris temminckii*	Rare
			130	**White-rumped Sandpiper**	*Calidris fuscicollis*	Very rare
			131	**Baird's Sandpiper**	*Calidris bairdii*	Very rare
			132	**Pectoral Sandpiper**	*Calidris melanotos*	Rare
			133	**Sharp-tailed Sandpiper**	*Calidris acuminata*	Vagrant
			134	**Curlew Sandpiper**	*Calidris ferruginea*	Scarce, autumn
			135	**Stilt Sandpiper**	*Calidris himantopus*	Vagrant
			136	**Purple Sandpiper**	*Calidris maritima*	Scarce, coastal, not summer
			137	**Dunlin**	*Calidris alpina*	Widespread
			138	**Broad-billed Sandpiper**	*Limicola falcinellus*	Vagrant
			139	**Buff-breasted Sandpiper**	*Tryngites subruficollis A*	Vagrant
			140	**Ruff**	*Philomachus pugnax*	Scarce
			141	**Jack Snipe**	*Lymnocryptes minimus*	Scarce, winter
			142	**(Common) Snipe**	*Gallinago gallinago*	Widespread
			143	**Great Snipe**	*Gallinago media*	Vagrant
			144	**Long-billed Dowitcher**	*Limnodromus scolopaceus*	Very rare
			145	**(Eurasian) Woodcock**	*Scolopax rusticola*	Scarce
			146	**Black-tailed Godwit**	*Limosa limosa*	Widespread
			147	**Bar-tailed Godwit**	*Limosa lapponica*	Scarce
			148	**Whimbrel**	*Numenius phaeopus*	Scarce, coastal, not winter
			149	**(Eurasian) Curlew**	*Numenius arquata*	Widespread
			150	**Spotted Redshank**	*Tringa erythropus*	Scarce, not summer
			151	**(Common) Redshank**	*Tringa totanus*	Widespread
			152	**Marsh Sandpiper**	*Tringa stagnatilis*	Very rare
			153	**(Common) Greenshank**	*Tringa nebularia*	Scarce

			154	Greater Yellowlegs	*Tringa melanoleuca*	Vagrant, historical records only
			155	Lesser Yellowlegs	*Tringa flavipes*	Very rare
			156	Green Sandpiper	*Tringa ochropus*	Scarce
			157	Wood Sandpiper	*Tringa glareola*	Rare
			158	Terek Sandpiper	*Xenus cinereus*	Very rare
			159	Common Sandpiper	*Actitis hypoleucos*	Widespread, rare in winter
			160	Spotted Sandpiper	*Actitis macularius*	Vagrant
			161	Grey-tailed Tattler	*Heteroscelus brevipes*	Vagrant
			162	(Ruddy) Turnstone	*Arenaria interpres*	Widespread, coastal
			163	Wilson's Phalarope	*Phalaropus tricolor*	Very rare
			164	Red-necked Phalarope	*Phalaropus lobatus*	Rare
			165	Grey Phalarope	*Phalaropus fulicarius*	Rare
			166	Pomarine Skua	*Stercorarius pomarinus*	Rare
			167	Arctic Skua	*Stercorarius parasiticus*	Scarce, coastal, autumn
			168	Long-tailed Skua	*Stercorarius longicaudus*	Rare
			169	Great Skua	*Stercorarius skua*	Scarce, coastal, autumn
			170	Mediterranean Gull	*Larus melanocephalus*	Scarce
			171	Laughing Gull	*Larus atricilla*	Vagrant
			172	Franklin's Gull	*Larus pipixcan*	Vagrant
			173	Little Gull	*Larus minutus*	Scarce
			174	Sabine's Gull	*Larus sabini*	Scarce, coastal, autumn
			175	Bonaparte's Gull	*Larus philadelphia*	Very rare
			176	Black-headed Gull	*Larus ridibundus*	Common
			177	Ring-billed Gull	*Larus delawarensis*	Rare
			178	(Mew) Common Gull	*Larus canus*	Widespread
			179	Lesser Black-backed Gull	*Larus fuscus*	Common, summer
			180	Yellow-legged Gull	*Larus michahellis*	Rare
			181	Herring Gull	*Larus argentatus*	Common
			182	Iceland Gull	*Larus glaucoides*	Rare
			183	Glaucous Gull	*Larus hyperboreus*	Rare
			184	Great Black-backed Gull	*Larus marinus*	Widespread
			185	Ross's Gull	*Rhodostethia rosea*	Very rare
			186	(Black-legged) Kittiwake	*Rissa tridactyla*	Scarce, coastal
			187	Ivory Gull	*Pagophila eburnea*	Very rare
			188	Sooty Tern	*Onychoprion fuscata*	Vagrant

		189	**Bridled Tern**	*Onychoprion anaethetus*	Vagrant
		190	**Little Tern**	*Sternula albifrons*	Scarce, coastal, summer
		191	**Caspian Tern**	*Hydroprogne caspia*	Very rare
		192	**Whiskered Tern**	*Chlidonias hybrida*	Very rare
		193	**Black Tern**	*Chlidonias niger*	Scarce, spring/autumn
		194	**White-winged Tern**	*Chlidonias leucopterus*	Very rare
		195	**Sandwich Tern**	*Sterna sandvicensis*	Widespread, coastal, summer
		196	**Lesser Crested Tern**	*Sterna bengalensis*	Vagrant
		197	**Forster's Tern**	*Sterna forsteri*	Very rare
		198	**Common Tern**	*Sterna hirundo*	Widespread, coastal, summer
		199	**Roseate Tern**	*Sterna dougallii*	Rare
		200	**Arctic Tern**	*Sterna paradisaea*	Widespread, coastal, summer
		201	**(Common) Guillemot**	*Uria aalge*	Widespread, coastal, summer
		202	**Razorbill**	*Alca torda*	Widespread, coastal, summer
		203	**Black Guillemot**	*Cepphus grylle*	Scarce, coastal
		204	**Little Auk**	*Alle alle*	Very rare
		205	**(Atlantic) Puffin**	*Fratercula arctica*	Scarce, coastal, summer
		206	**Pallas's Sandgrouse**	*Syrrhaptes paradoxus*	Vagrant, historical records only
		207	**Stock Dove (Pigeon)**	*Columba oenas*	Scarce
		208	**(Common) Wood Pigeon**	*Columba palumbus*	Common
		209	**(Eurasian) Collared Dove**	*Streptopelia decaocto*	Common
		210	**(European) Turtle Dove**	*Streptopelia turtur*	Rare
		211	**Rose-ringed Parakeet**	*Psittacula krameri*	Very rare
		212	**Great Spotted Cuckoo**	*Clamator glandarius*	Vagrant, historical records only
		213	**(Common) Cuckoo**	*Cuculus canorus*	Scarce, summer
		214	**Yellow-billed Cuckoo**	*Coccyzus americanus*	Vagrant, historical records only
		215	**Barn Owl**	*Tyto alba*	Scarce
		216	**Snowy Owl**	*Bubo scandiaca*	Vagrant, historical records only
		217	**Little Owl**	*Athene noctua*	Scarce
		218	**Tawny Owl**	*Strix aluco*	Widespread
		219	**Long-eared Owl**	*Asio otus*	Rare
		220	**Short-eared Owl**	*Asio flammeus*	Scarce
		221	**(European) Nightjar**	*Caprimulgus europaeus*	Scarce, summer
		222	**Chimney Swift**	*Chaetura pelagica*	Vagrant
		223	**(Common) Swift**	*Apus apus*	Widespread, summer

183

			224	**Alpine Swift**	*Apus melba*	Very rare
			225	**(Common) Kingfisher**	*Alcedo atthis*	Scarce
			226	**European Bee-eater**	*Merops apiaster*	Very rare
			227	**Hoopoe**	*Upupa epops*	Rare
			228	**(Eurasian) Wryneck**	*Jynx torquilla*	Rare
			229	**Green Woodpecker**	*Picus viridis*	Scarce
			230	**Great Spotted Woodpecker**	*Dendrocopos major*	Widespread
			231	**Lesser Spotted Woodpecker**	*Dendrocopos minor*	Scarce
			232	**Black Lark**	*Melanocorypha yeltoniensis*	Vagrant
			233	**Greater Short-toed Lark**	*Calandrella brachydactyla*	Very rare
			234	**Crested Lark**	*Galerida cristata*	Vagrant
			235	**Wood Lark**	*Lullula arborea*	Rare
			236	**Sky Lark**	*Alauda arvensis*	Widespread
			237	**(Horned) Shore Lark**	*Eremophila alpestris*	Rare
			238	**Sand Martin**	*Riparia riparia*	Widespread, summer
			239	**(Eurasian) Crag Martin**	*Ptyonoprogne rupestris*	Vagrant
			240	**(Barn) Swallow**	*Hirundo rustica*	Common, summer
			241	**House Martin**	*Delichon urbicum*	Common, summer
			242	**Red-rumped Swallow**	*Cecropis daurica*	Very rare
			243	**Richard's Pipit**	*Anthus richardi*	Rare, autumn
			244	**Blyth's Pipit**	*Anthus godlewskii*	Vagrant
			245	**Tawny Pipit**	*Anthus campestris*	Very rare
			246	**Tree Pipit**	*Anthus trivialis*	Scarce, summer
			247	**Meadow Pipit**	*Anthus pratensis*	Common
			248	**Red-throated Pipit**	*Anthus cervinus*	Very rare
			249	**Rock Pipit**	*Anthus petrosus*	Scarce, coastal
			250	**Water Pipit**	*Anthus spinoletta*	Rare
			251	**Yellow Wagtail**	*Motacilla flava*	Scarce, summer
			252	**Grey Wagtail**	*Motacilla cinerea*	Scarce, present on most streams
			253	**White / Pied Wagtail**	*Motacilla alba*	Common
			254	**(Bohemian) Waxwing**	*Bombycilla garrulus*	Rare
			255	**(White-throated) Dipper**	*Cinclus cinclus*	Scarce
			256	**(Winter) Wren**	*Troglodytes troglodytes*	Common
			257	**Grey Catbird**	*Dumetella carolinensis*	Vagrant

		258	**(Hedge Accentor) Dunnock**	*Prunella modularis*	Common
		259	**Alpine Accentor**	*Prunella collaris*	Vagrant, historical record
		260	**(European) Robin**	*Erithacus rubecula*	Common
		261	**Thrush Nightingale**	*Luscinia luscinia*	Vagrant
		262	**(Common) Nightingale**	*Luscinia megarhynchos*	Very rare
		263	**Bluethroat**	*Luscinia svecica*	Very rare
		264	**Black Redstart**	*Phoenicurus ochruros*	Rare
		265	**(Common) Redstart**	*Phoenicurus phoenicurus*	Scarce, common in the right habitat, summer
		266	**Whinchat**	*Saxicola rubetra*	Scarce, common in the right habitat, summer
		267	**Stonechat**	*Saxicola torquata*	Widespread
		268	**Isabelline Wheatear**	*Oenanthe isabellina*	Very rare
		269	**(Northern) Wheatear**	*Oenanthe oenanthe*	Widespread, summer
		270	**Black-eared Wheatear**	*Oenanthe hispanica*	Very rare
		271	**Rufous-tailed Rock Thrush**	*Monticola saxatilis*	Vagrant
		272	**Blue Rock Thrush**	*Monticola solitarius*	Vagrant
		273	**Swainson's Thrush**	*Catharus ustulatus*	Vagrant
		274	**Grey-cheeked Thrush**	*Catharus minimus*	Vagrant
		275	**Ring Ouzel**	*Turdus torquatus*	Scarce, summer
		276	**(Common) Blackbird**	*Turdus merula*	Common
		277	**Eyebrowed Thrush**	*Turdus obscurus*	Vagrant
		278	**Fieldfare**	*Turdus pilaris*	Widespread, winter
		279	**Song Thrush**	*Turdus philomelos*	Common
		280	**Redwing**	*Turdus iliacus*	Widespread, winter
		281	**Mistle Thrush**	*Turdus viscivorus*	Common
		282	**American Robin**	*Turdus migratorius*	Vagrant
		283	**Cetti's Warbler**	*Cettia cetti*	Rare, small breeding population
		284	**Lanceolated Warbler**	*Locustella lanceolata*	Vagrant
		285	**(Common) Grasshopper Warbler**	*Locustella naevia*	Scarce, summer
		286	**River Warbler**	*Locustella fluviatilis*	Vagrant
		287	**Savi's Warbler**	*Locustella luscinioides*	Vagrant
		288	**Aquatic Warbler**	*Acrocephalus paludicola*	Vagrant
		289	**Sedge Warbler**	*Acrocephalus schoenobaenus*	Widespread, summer

185

			No.	Name	Scientific Name	Status
☐	☐		290	**Marsh Warbler**	*Acrocephalus palustris*	Very rare
☐	☐		291	**(Eurasian) Reed Warbler**	*Acrocephalus scirpaceus*	Widespread, summer
☐	☐		292	**Great Reed Warbler**	*Acrocephalus arundinaceus*	Very rare
☐	☐		293	**Booted Warbler**	*Hippolais caligata*	Vagrant
☐	☐		294	**Icterine Warbler**	*Hippolais icterina*	Very rare
☐	☐		295	**Melodious Warbler**	*Hippolais polyglotta*	Rare
☐	☐		296	**Blackcap**	*Sylvia atricapilla*	Widespread
☐	☐		297	**Garden Warbler**	*Sylvia borin*	Widespread, summer
☐	☐		298	**Barred Warbler**	*Sylvia nisoria*	Very rare
☐	☐		299	**Lesser Whitethroat**	*Sylvia curruca*	Widespread, summer
☐	☐		300	**(Common) Whitethroat**	*Sylvia communis*	Widespread, summer
☐	☐		301	**Dartford Warbler**	*Sylvia undata*	Very rare
☐	☐		302	**Rüppell's Warbler**	*Sylvia rueppelli*	Vagrant
☐	☐		303	**Subalpine Warbler**	*Sylvia cantillans*	Very rare
☐	☐		304	**Sardinian Warbler**	*Sylvia melanocephala*	Very rare
☐	☐		305	**Greenish Warbler**	*Phylloscopus trochiloides*	Very rare
☐	☐		306	**Arctic Warbler**	*Phylloscopus borealis*	Very rare
☐	☐		307	**Pallas's Leaf Warbler**	*Phylloscopus proregulus*	Very rare
☐	☐		308	**Yellow-browed Warbler**	*Phylloscopus inornatus*	Rare
☐	☐		309	**Hume's Leaf Warbler**	*Phylloscopus humei*	Vagrant
☐	☐		310	**Radde's Warbler**	*Phylloscopus schwarzi*	Very rare
☐	☐		311	**Dusky Warbler**	*Phylloscopus fuscatus*	Very rare
☐	☐		312	**Western Bonelli's Warbler**	*Phylloscopus bonelli*	Very rare
☐	☐		313	**Wood Warbler**	*Phylloscopus sibilatrix*	Scarce, summer
☐	☐		314	**(Common) Chiffchaff**	*Phylloscopus collybita*	Common
☐	☐		315	**Willow Warbler**	*Phylloscopus trochilus*	Common, summer
☐	☐		316	**Goldcrest**	*Regulus regulus*	Widespread
☐	☐		317	**Firecrest**	*Regulus ignicapilla*	Scarce, autumn/winter
☐	☐		318	**Spotted Flycatcher**	*Muscicapa striata*	Scarce, declining
☐	☐		319	**Red-breasted Flycatcher**	*Ficedula parva*	Rare
☐	☐		320	**Collared Flycatcher**	*Ficedula albicollis*	Vagrant
☐	☐		321	**Pied Flycatcher**	*Ficedula hypoleuca*	Scarce, common in the right habitat
☐	☐		322	**Bearded Tit (Reedling)**	*Panurus biarmicus*	Very rare
☐	☐		323	**Long-tailed Tit**	*Aegithalos caudatus*	Widespread

		324	**Blue Tit**	*Cyanistes caeruleus*	Common
		325	**Great Tit**	*Parus major*	Common
		326	**Coal Tit**	*Periparus ater*	Widespread
		327	**Willow Tit**	*Poecile montanus*	Rare
		328	**Marsh Tit**	*Poecile palustris*	Scarce
		329	**(Wood) Nuthatch**	*Sitta europaea*	Widespread
		330	**(Eurasian) Treecreeper**	*Certhia familiaris*	Widespread
		331	**(Eurasian) Penduline Tit**	*Remiz pendulinus*	Vagrant
		332	**(Eurasian) Golden Oriole**	*Oriolus oriolus*	Rare
		333	**Isabelline Shrike**	*Lanius isabellinus*	Vagrant
		334	**Red-backed Shrike**	*Lanius collurio*	Rare
		335	**Lesser Grey Shrike**	*Lanius minor*	Vagrant
		336	**Great Grey Shrike**	*Lanius excubitor*	Rare
		337	**Woodchat Shrike**	*Lanius senator*	Very rare
		338	**(Eurasian) Jay**	*Garrulus glandarius*	Widespread
		339	**(Black-billed) Magpie**	*Pica pica*	Common
		340	**(Red-billed) Chough**	*Pyrrhocorax pyrrhocorax*	Scarce
		341	**(Eurasian) Jackdaw**	*Corvus monedula*	Common
		342	**Rook**	*Corvus frugilegus*	Widespread
		343	**Carrion Crow**	*Corvus corone*	Common
		344	**Hooded Crow**	*Corvus cornix*	Rare
		345	**(Common) Raven**	*Corvus corax*	Widespread
		346	**(Common) Starling**	*Sturnus vulgaris*	Common
		347	**Rosy Starling**	*Sturnus roseus*	Very rare
		348	**House Sparrow**	*Passer domesticus*	Widespread
		349	**(Eurasian) Tree Sparrow**	*Passer montanus*	Scarce, declining
		350	**Red-eyed Vireo**	*Vireo olivaceus*	Vagrant
		351	**Chaffinch**	*Fringilla coelebs*	Common
		352	**Brambling**	*Fringilla montifringilla*	Scarce, winter
		353	**(European) Serin**	*Serinus serinus*	Very rare
		354	**(European) Greenfinch**	*Carduelis chloris*	Common
		355	**(European) Goldfinch**	*Carduelis carduelis*	Common
		356	**(Eurasian) Siskin**	*Carduelis spinus*	Widespread
		357	**(Common) Linnet**	*Carduelis cannabina*	Common
		358	**Twite**	*Carduelis flavirostris*	Scarce

		No.	Common Name	Scientific Name	Status
		359	**Common Redpoll**	*Carduelis flammea*	Very rare
		360	**Lesser Redpoll**	*Carduelis cabaret*	Scarce
		361	**Arctic Redpoll**	*Carduelis hornemanni*	Vagrant
		362	**Two-barred Crossbill**	*Loxia leucoptera*	Vagrant
		363	**(Common) Crossbill**	*Loxia curvirostra*	Scarce
		364	**Parrot Crossbill**	*Loxia pytyopsittacus*	Vagrant
		365	**Common Rosefinch**	*Carpodacus erythrinus*	Rare
		366	**(Common) Bullfinch**	*Pyrrhula pyrrhula*	Widespread
		367	**Hawfinch**	*Coccothraustes coccothraustes*	Scarce
		368	**Yellow Warbler**	*Dendroica petechia*	Vagrant
		369	**Blackpoll Warbler**	*Dendroica striata*	Vagrant
		370	**Common Yellowthroat**	*Geothlypis trichas*	Vagrant
		371	**Summer Tanager**	*Piranga rubra*	Vagrant
		372	**Song Sparrow**	*Melospiza melodia*	Vagrant
		373	**White-throated Sparrow**	*Zonotrichia albicollis*	Vagrant
		374	**Dark-eyed Junco**	*Junco hyemalis*	Vagrant
		375	**Lapland Longspur**	*Calcarius lapponicus*	Rare
		376	**Snow Bunting**	*Plectrophenax nivalis*	Scarce, autumn/winter
		377	**Yellowhammer**	*Emberiza citrinella*	Scarce
		378	**Rock Bunting**	*Emberiza cia*	Vagrant
		379	**Ortolan Bunting**	*Emberiza hortulana*	Very rare
		380	**Rustic Bunting**	*Emberiza rustica*	Very rare
		381	**Little Bunting**	*Emberiza pusilla*	Very rare
		382	**Reed Bunting**	*Emberiza schoeniclus*	Widespread
		383	**Black-headed Bunting**	*Emberiza melanocephala*	Very rare
		384	**Corn Bunting**	*Emberiza calandra*	Vagrant, historial records only
		385	**Rose-breasted Grosbeak**	*Pheucticus ludovicianus*	Vagrant

INDEX

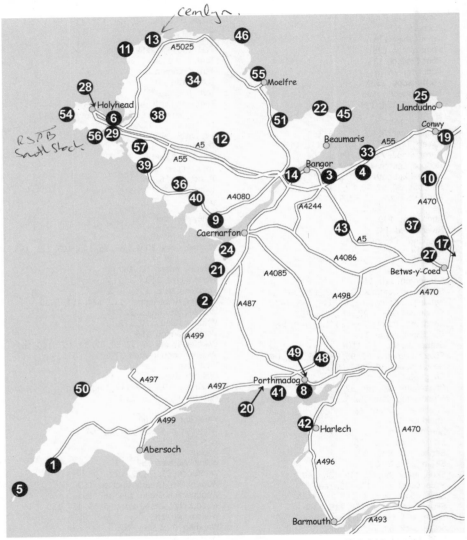

cemlyn.

RSPB South Stack